FRENCH AVIATION DURING THE FIRST WORLD WAR

"You can start a war when you like, but you can't end it in the same way."

Machiavelli

by Vital FERRY

*Iconographical researches by : Renaud Leblanc
Captions by : Dominique Breffort.
Profiles by : André Jouineau
Cover illustration : Claudio Fernandez
Translated from the French by : Alan McKay*

Note
The present book deals with the activities of the French air force engaged in the fighting over continental France and does not include anything else (e.g. Morocco, Suez, the Dardanelles, Italy, Romania or Siberia). It does not mention the Allied air forces – the British, Belgians or Americans – except where common operations are discussed, nor does it deal with the enemy's – German or Austrian. The same applies to the very important activities of the naval air arm and those, less significant, of airships although observation balloons do get a mention.

HISTOIRE & COLLECTIONS

LA GUERRE DE DEMAIN

From the Marne to the Somme

To begin with, it has to be said that the arrival of the combustion engine was not properly appreciated by European countries, except for the British who made sure that they got hold of the necessary resources from the Levant to keep the Royal Nay at sea properly. This shortcoming very quickly crippled the French Republic's finances.

GLOIRE À NOTRE FRANCE ÉTERNELLE!
GLOIRE À CEUX QUI VEILLENT SUR ELLE!

The mutual fear of aggression, revived by incidents like Agadir during which the French and the Germans confronted each other under the watchful gaze of the European community, and based largely on the frustrations engendered by the 1870-71 war, encouraged an arms race in France where politics had a large role to play. This last point was to affect the initial engagements in ways that made it very costly for the Republic's soldiers.

In aeronautics, Bleriot crossing the Channel successfully aroused the interest of the Military, who otherwise were prompt to consider aviation as a sport of little, or no, interest. The main preoccupation at the time was to develop a generation of airships, like on the other side of the Rhine. Moreover the twelve companies of air observation stations, created during the First Republic, were usually based at the four strongholds of Belfort, Épinal, Toul and Verdun. The stations' reduced mobility made them difficult to use. Therefore the possibility that this fragile machine called an aeroplane might be used for military purposes meant that the Army bought

French aviation

THE NEW MILITARY PILOT'S LICENCE

As of 1 April the pilots had to satisfy the following requirements: carry out a flight lasting at least one hour at an altitude of 1 000 metres, land the plane after a gliding approach, with the engine cut out over an airfield from an altitude of at least 500 metres. The landing was to be made less than 200 metres from a fixed point set up in advance without using the engine. Passing the theoretical exam meant carrying out three test trips of which one was a triangular trip of 200 km in less than 48 hours with two stopovers, one 150 km non-stop journey in a straight line and a 150 km trip in the same day and in a straight line along a route fixed in advance. A flight at 1 000 metres could be included in one of these flights, without a passenger.

five of them in September 1909 – two Wrights, two Farmans and one Bleriot – for testing. Bickering between the Artillery and the Engineers began at once as to how they should be used and caused a rift in the General Staff which prevaricated and then half-heartedly authorised a few officers to be trained in how to use them. "All that's just sport... aviation for the Army is zilch." (General Foch, summer 1910). The creation of an aeronautics department in June 1910 given to the Engineers settled the problem, at least temporarily, whilst the yearly manoeuvres found a rational use for these machines. The Permanent Military Aviation Inspectorate created immediately afterwards and headed by General Roques defined a doctrine which was published a short while later by a law voted in Parliament in March 1912.

An equipment programme for buying aircraft and engines was included in the Finance law. This programme, presented by General Hirshauer, Head of the Permanent Military Aviation Inspectorate, made provisions for purchasing 1,850 planes and spares, and 2,300 engines over a four-year period for a total cost of about fifty million gold francs. The planned deliveries were to include 343 machines in 1912, 400 in 1913, 500 in 1914 and the rest in 1915.

Putting the programme into practice ran foul of parliamentary debates which gradually reduced expenditure, and also of various manufacturers who were unable to mass-produce the aircraft, and who were more tempted to sell them to indifferent foreign customers at the asking price. Whilst 343 aircraft were duly acquired in 1912, only 200 were bought in 1913 and 279 written into the budget in 1914, which was only voted in July anyway. As at 1 August 1914, the Army owned 600 machines of which only 134 were in fighting units.

A decree of application dated 22 August established ten aeronautical sections shared out among three groups based at Versailles, Reims and Lyons, with

Right.
A Blériot XI, without its airscrew, perhaps in the manufacturer workshop.

during the First World War

Opposite.
Period postcard in favour of the National Subscription launched in 1911 to donate planes to the Army.

MR DUBUREAU'S FANCIES

The mobilisation bureaus favoured the infantry without checking out the recruit's qualifications. Thus a worker from Renault, a trained mechanic, might end up as a simple soldier. This was the case of a pilot, Alexis Maneyrol, with an FAI licence, n° 673 dated 10 November 1911, with a couple of hundred hours flying time on Blériots who found himself assigned to the 29th Infantry Regiment after having been put in the 19th Aviation Group on 27 August. He had to appeal to Members of Parliament to get him back to flying at the end of the year. Because he didn't have a military licence he had to go back to flying school. This was at Avord on 9 February 1915 and he obtained his licence on Morane M after 15 hours and 44 training flights. He started flying the Morane Parasol at the Réserve Générale d'Aviation on 21 April and was assigned to an escadrille, MS 49, at Belfort on 30 April where he flew 140 hours. He became a Sergeant in July, converted to Nieuport BBs and flew his first combat sortie on 28 August.

Right.
Capitaine Alfred Bordage, from Escadrille n°5 (future MF 5) in a Maurice Farman Model 1912.

the units officially receiving their flags at Longchamp earlier on 14 July from the hands of the President of the Republic. Little by little the planes were joined by others and in 1911, the Army organised an annual competition for military planes, together with a set of required performance criteria that a small number of builders could satisfy.

The first Escadrilles

It was decided to try out the equipment in five escadrilles made up in April 1912 with a strength of 6 planes, two flying Maurice Farmans (MF 2s at Buc and MF 5s at Saint-Cyr), one on Henry Farman (HF 1 at Chalons), one on Deperdussin (D4 at Saint-Cyr), and another on Blériot (BL 3 at Pau). Statutorily each had seven pilots (of which two were officers), nine NCOs and thirty soldiers for maintenance, plus a combat automobile train carrying equipment and tent shelters for the aircraft. An army park was also created for supplies and repairs.

The manoeuvres, particularly those carried out in the autumn of 1912, confirmed the results already obtained which revealed the machines' limitations, especially the frailty of certain types, but nonetheless also showing what could be got out of them. But making aviation and aircraft official did not prevent most staff officers from being reticent and sceptical about the possibilities of the new machine, called an "avion" (plane) in honour of Ader. The future immediately proved them to be wrong.

Interest was also shown in an armoured aircraft because the manoeuvres had shown that planes flying at an altitude of less than 3000 feet were vulnerable to gunfire. This idea was hardly compatible with the weak engines of the period and caused General Bernard, the

The letter of 4 August

During the weekly pilots' dinner, Jacques Mortane, the general secretary of the Group of Airmen, was given the task of writing the following letter to the Minister of War:

Dear Minister,

The pilots who make up this group, established by them, are pleased to inform you that they are putting themselves and their aircraft at your disposal. Because of their experience they think that they can render useful service to France, to which they would be happy to give even their lives if necessary. They ask to be granted the favour of being able to set up escadrilles which will serve for the greater glory of their country and continue the struggle together in war as they have done in peace.

Letter signed by Roland Garros, Marc Pourpre, Maurice Chevillard, Docteur Espanet, Eugène Guilbert, Gaubert.

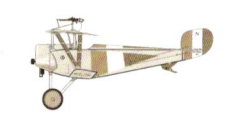

Opposite.
A crowd of curious has come to admire a Maurice Farman MF 7 which has landed in the middle of the countryside.

Below.
General Edouard-Auguste Hirschauer (1857-1943) commanded a balloon brigade in 1914 with the 5th and 8th Versailles Engineer Regiments before being appointed Chief of Staff of Paris and placed under the orders of General Gallieni.

Below.
Preparation for take-off of the Henri Farman HF 20 n°65.

boss of the Aéronautique, to suggest putting armour only on one side. The pilots liked that! The General Staff nonetheless ordered a small number of Dorand armoured planes. At the initiative of the newspaper le Temps, a permanent public subscription was set up from 1909 onwards throughout the country, to purchase planes for the Military Aviation. 208 planes had been purchased as at 1 January 1914.

When war was declared, the inventory comprised machines obtained by the Army, a certain number of machines ordered abroad and still in the builders' workshops, and the planes held by licensed civilian pilots who were mobilised with their planes. As a result French military aviation had a strength of some 130 operational machines – nine different types pooled in 21 escadrilles supported by 15 different kinds of airships and 150 reserve planes of which some were used for training.

These escadrilles were shared out into thirteen units (five with Maurice Farmans (MF 7 of 1912), four with Henri Farmans (HF 20 of 1912), two with Voisin Type 3s, one on Caudron G.2, and one on Breguet U-1s). There were also monoplane escadrilles, or five on Blériot XIU single or two-seaters, two on Deperdussins and one on REPs. The cavalry had its own two escadrilles (BLC 2, BLC 4) on three Blériots XIs.

In all, the military aviation assembled some 4 362 people, of which 200 were pilots. Each army disposed of the escadrilles which had gone to their operational assignments as follows: six in the 1st Army (BL 3, MF 5, BL 9, BL 10, BR 17, BL 18), four in the 2nd Army (HF 1, MF 8, HF 19, MF 20), four in the 3rd Army (MF 2, HF 7, HF, 13, MF 16). Meanwhile the twenty Morane-Saulnier LA types built for Turkey and the handful of Voisins for Russia had been requisitioned. They were put with ten or so so-called armoured Dorands, ordered by the Gene-

The crafty ones

In August 1914 during the Battle of Lorraine, the pilot Armengaud, attached to the 2nd Army under General de Castelnau, was called a "joker" in front of Colonel Duchêne's headquarters staff because he'd made a particularly precise report which, unfortunately, was not to the French troops' advantage.
At the beginning of the month near the fort at Manonvillier (in the Meurthe-et-Moselle department), Pilot-Sergeant Frantz from V 24 flying a Voisin, left Montmédy with an observer to carry out a reconnaissance flight over the Luxembourg border. They spotted long German convoys heading for Belgium. When he returned he landed at Mézières and reported what he had seen to a senior officer who answered: "That's impossible, it's defended!"

during the First World War

Right.
Offered by the Clermont-Ferrand arrondissement press committee, Blériot XI N° 216 was named "Clermont de l'Oise", as shown on the inscription under the training edge of the wing. *(DR)*

---

1. Including 1 200 Two-cylinders Renault.

Below.
A line-up of Blériot XIs at the very beginning of the war. The plane in the foreground, N° 217 was called "L'Indre", as it was presented by that department's committee. *(DR)*

Below. **In February 1914, at Villacoublay, demonstrating how to fire a machine gun mounted on an 80-hp Gnome engined Deperdussin type 1913 monoplane piloted par Maurice Prévost.**

tical industry's employers' federation). He planned a delivery schedule continuing up to 31 March 1915 for 1 200 planes and 1 500 engines to arm 50 escadrilles as at 1 April 1915.

Meanwhile the diversity of the machines, the low levels of stocks or even the lack of them, and the wear and tear of the equipment prompted the authorities to start standardising so as to have homogenous operational units. Three decisions were taken quickly. The first was to reduce the number of operational types in service, the surplus being put away as a reserve. The other two were less fortunate. With the perspective of a short war, the flying schools were closed and the instructors transferred to the escadrilles, all production was halted, and workers and management were sent to their assigned mobilisation units. The result was chaos, and the industrialists later had the greatest trouble recovering their qualified workers converted into infantry or other sorts of troops and lost in the huge mass.

Facing them, Germany had 41 escadrilles with a strength of 246 planes fitted with engines rated at 100 hp or more. Half of these machines was made up of single- or two-seater Taubes, the rest were Albatrosses or Aviatiks. This was not an end to the surprises for the air force since the German army had a larger proportion of automatic weapons (normal and heavy machine guns), and many more cannon of various calibres than the French forces had. Moreover, unlike France, they knew how to use them.

ral Staff, raising the number of escadrilles to 27, with 162 planes. British military aviation contributed some 65 machines which arrived higgledy-piggledy during August in support of the British Expeditionary Corps.

General Hirschauer was recalled on 8 October by President Poincaré who asked him to establish a construction programme in conjunction with the Chambre Syndicale des Industries Aéronautiques (the aeronau-

The first fighting

The French operational plan, called Plan XVII and based on a quick offensive to re-conquer the territory ceded in 1871, included an attack by the 1st Army (General Dubail) in the direction of Sarrebourg and by the 2nd Army (General de Castelnau) towards Château-Salins and Sarrebruck. The 7th Corps and the 8th Cavalry Division were to push towards Mulhouse. But the High Command, ignorant of the fact that the Germans possessed the French plans given to them by spies, neglected the warnings from the 2e Bureau (military intelligence) which warned of a massive German offensive through Belgium, a neutral country protected by international agreements, also signed by Germany.

This is exactly was happened on 2 August when the

Above.
Pilot Jacques Richard in front of his Blériot XI.

Opposite, from the top to the botton.
Henry Farman HF 20 in flight.

Voisin Type III carrying two passengers.

Breguet Model U15 from Escadrille Br 17 photographed in front of their sheds at Dijon-Longvic airfield.

Below.
Blériot XI at the camp at le Ruchard (near Chinon) during the 1912 manoeuvres. The inscription CB on the tail means "Chalais-Blériot".

German troops entered Belgium and Luxembourg. On the 3rd, Germany declared war on France and the next day on Great Britain, which was authorised by the House of Commons on the 5th to levy 500 000 volunteers.

On 7 August, Corporal-Pilot Joseph "Sadi" Lecointe from Escadrille BL 10 took off from Belfort on a reconnaissance flight for his passenger, Capitaine Langlois. They came under fire and when they returned they discovered that the observer had been wounded in the thigh. He was the first casualty of the war in the air. On 13 August, the fort at Liège was forced to surrender but the French offensive was under way towards Alsace and Lorraine as planned.

The weekly newspaper Le Miroir which published the General Headquarters' previous week's communiqués, wrote: "On 14 August, our airmen won a great advantage over their German counterparts who flee combat as much as possible." This was the first mention of flying. On 24 August, a plane from HF 7 flown by Lucien Finck with Capitaine Delavaux as his observer made a reconnaissance mission in the Sarrebrouk region. The plane suffered a structural failure and crashed killing the observer and seriously wounding the pilot who had to have a leg amputated in hospital, thereby losing his flying licence.

On 28 August the same weekly announced that Zeppelin LZ-VIII had been shot down by artillery near the fort at Manonviller (Meurthe-et-Moselle). This was the work of two 75-mm cannon aimed by Gondouin and

THE AIRMEN WERE THERE

On 3 September Lieutenant Charles Mendès, flying a Farman from HF 1 was shot down by German troops going round Paris. On the 5th, Pilot-Sergeant Georges Cohen, holder of licence N° 1620 dated 3 April 1914, accompanied by observer Lieutenant Ragot, was shot down by German gun fire as they were carrying out a reconnaissance mission over the Marne.

Above.
Planes from a Blériot escadrille being blessed on the front in 1914.

hundreds of times by fire from the soldiers in Reims and crashed at Courcy (Marne).

On 27 August, during the withdrawal, Escadrille HF 1 under Lieutenant Louis Mendès, landed on an airfield whose perimeter was already occupied by the enemy vanguard. Realising this, he made sure the other planes got off but just as he was about to leave with the last one, he was surrounded by German cavalry. Refusing to surrender he was gunned down on the spot.

To confront the columns coming down from Belgium, the 3rd Army started its move towards Arlon and the 4th Army had to do the same in the direction of Neufchâteau; all these movements were scouted out by the planes assigned to each army. The aeroplanes were not

Top.
Do-Huu-Vii is thought to be the first Indochinese airman. Assigned to North Africa after obtaining his licence, he fought in France from October 1914 and was seriously wounded in an accident the following year. Unable to fly because of his wounds, he fought in the Foreign Legion and was killed on the front in July 1916. *(DR)*

Above
The Etrich Taube (dove, because of the shape of its wings) was the first massed produced military aeroplane in Germany. It was used from 1910 to 1914 as a fighter, a bomber, and as an observation and training plane. *(DR)*

Opposite.
Preparations before take-off of a Blériot XI, perhaps from an aviation school.

Colibert under the orders of Lieutenant Quiquandon. These airships were the cause of mistakes for, as early as 11 August, the airship Fleurus was nearly attacked by Pelletier Doisy from HD 19 and Perrin de Brichambault from MF 8 who had scrambled from Toul with Pivolo's aircraft receiving a few hits from the airship's machine gun. Unfortunately Montgolfier, the French airship, was destroyed on 21 August by French bullets and on the 24th the airship Dupuy-de-Lôme was hit

French aviation

Opposite.
Blériot XI and Breguet U2 three-seater in front of Bessoneau hangars. These hangars were made of canvas and wood before the Great War and there were four different models, used in large numbers during and after the war not only by France, but also by other countries like Great Britain, Canada and Russia.

armed but they did carry a few light bombs to drop on troop gatherings. The crew had handguns to be used for setting fire to the plane if necessary. Communication with the ground was carried out, if necessary, by using weighted messages and the plane's toing and froing, cooperating with the artillery, would be noted by the enemy who then knew where to direct their own artillery.

However the rapidly manoeuvring German troops checked the French and forced them despite Joffre's orders to fall back on Grand-Couronné, before Nancy.

The fighting in Lorraine cost the French 40 000 killed, of which 27 000 on 22 August alone. Lanrezac's army opposing the German offensive at Charleroi and Mons on 21 and 23 August fell back fighting.

Faced with these retreats, Joffre was forced to cancel his orders, which had been carried out too timidly, and to recast his command: 162 generals and colonels were invited to transfer to an appointment in Limoges, a garrison town (the word "limogé", close in meaning to "being sent to Coventry", became very popular). The inexorable advance of the German columns towards Paris made the government bring General Galliéni back out of retirement and entrust him with defending Paris, with the Government and the Bank of France withdrawing to Bordeaux. The German advance made the isolated air raid on 13 August by the Taube flown by Lieutenant Frantz von Hindelson much easier. He dropped five bombs over the Paris region, killing a woman and wounding four people as the crowning achievement of his reconnaissance mission.

As a reprisal, the next day, 14 August, Lieutenant Cesari and Pilot-Corporal Roger Prudhommeau from Escadrille 16, leaving Verdun at the end of the afternoon, bombed the airship hangars at Metz-Frescati but in vain, carrying out the first French offensive of the war. This particular target was hit by Pilot-Sergeant Lucien Finck, from HF 7, returning from a mission over Sarrebrück: he dropped two 90-mm shells and some Aasen bombs on Frescati. But on 14 August the plane belonging to Adjudant-Pilot Didier and Sergeant-Gunner Martine from D4 was shot down during a reconnaissance over the German lines. The crew got back on the 15th after covering 62 miles on foot.

On the 15th it was the turn of a German plane to be shot down while flying over the 4th Cavalry Division. The pilot, wounded by ground fire, and his passenger were taken prisoner. On 23 August, Pilot Garaix, licence holder N° 940, dated 25 July 1912, went off on a Paul Schmitt from HF 13 to bomb an anti-aircraft gun in the Metz region but he was hit by a shell and crashed with his passenger Lieutenant de Saizieu.

On 31 August a communiqué from General Headquarters (GHQ) announced: "A second Taube flew over Paris and dropped two bombs which only caused minor damage." No mention was made of the first Taube.

During this period, observation planes brought back information for the HQ staffs that were often sceptical and did not transmit the intelligence gathered in this manner to higher authorities.

However thanks to the observations made by Lieutenant Roekel and Sergeant Châtelian from HF 7 in a

CAVALRY AGAINST PLANES

During this battle the last known charge by the French cavalry took place on 9 September by the 2nd Squadron of the 16th Dragoons (the squadron under Lieutenant Gaston de Gironde), from the 5th Cavalry Division, which had advanced beyond the Ourcq, towards Soissons. This platoon discovered a German airfield near Vivières (2), to the north of Villers-Cotterêts and during the night destroyed a flight of Aviatiks with their lances. The 27 survivors, including 8 wounded out of the hundred or so dragoons, managed to reach the French lines.

Centre.
Some Breguet U2s from the Champ d'Aviation at Longvic. This aviation centre near Dijon was inaugurated just before the war.

Above.
Blériot XI from an Escadrille BLC (for Blériot Cavalerie) at Vendôme in June 1914.

---

* *In recognition, a street in Vivières was given the name "Rue de l'Escadron de Gironde", and the main street in the hamlet of Vauberon was called "Rue de Gironde".*

THE SECOND CONFIRMED KILL

The pilot, Louis Gaubert, who obtained his licence in 1910 was flying with Capitaine Blaize as machine gunner when he ran into a German machine which he then attacked. After a brief exchange of shots, the enemy plane carrying an observer and a pilot crashed. They were removed from the debris seriously wounded. The observer survived but the pilot, Willy Finger, died in Sainte Menehould hospital on 9 October 1914.

ticular shape, christened "sausages" in France) which moved along in medium winds, which the French cylindrical observation balloons could not do. In bounds and leaps, the German columns got closer to Paris. Air units were recalled from the East including Escadrilles BL 3 and 10 from Belfort to take part in defending the capital which itself also armed an escadrille to protect the entrenched camp (Paris).

Victory has many fathers but defeat only one (General Joffre)

A map found on a German aviator however gave a first indication that the German penetration axis was not aiming at the capital but rather at tying the French armies engaged in the East up in a noose. Then Capitaine Lepic of the 15th Chasseurs à Cheval observed a German column at a crossroads taking the road to Compiègne. On 1 September 1914 at 23.55, General Manoury signalled headquarters that it was probable that the German 1st Army would slip towards the south-east. On the 2nd at around 18.00, a machine (a Breguet piloted by Sergeant Louis Breguet and his observer, Lieutenant-Balloonist Watteau) from the "Camp Retranché de Paris" (CRP), or the entrenched camp at Paris, signalled enemy columns near Creil and Mouy marching towards Paris. On the ground Capitaine La Metteraie and Lieutenant de Ponton d'Amécourt also observed large convoys heading for Château-Thierry.

Above.
A gathering of Blériot XIs from Escadrilles BL 3 and BL 10 on their airfield at Belfort at the beginning of 1914.

Opposite, right.
The Aviatik B.I was the standard reconnaissance model in the LSK, the German Military Aviation, at the beginning of the war.

Farman two-seater, the French artillery was able to destroy the German XVIth Army Corps' artillery – eleven batteries – caught by surprise, right in the middle of assembling in the Triaucourt (Meuse) region. On the whole, however, the high command was not convinced by intelligence furnished by the aviation.

The enemy advance, moving forward at the infantry pace, or 25 miles a day, was scouted for by their aircraft and their captive "Drachen" balloons (with their par-

Opposite.
Rail transport for Blériot XI. The machines had their wings removed and stacked alongside the fuselage.

INITIATIVE INVENTS A SYSTEM

The local system of resourcefulness found its uses. Thus Capitaine Raymond Yence, learning that the Dijon Park contained some unused Morane-Saulnier Type H single-seaters, took the initiative on 25 September to recover them and set up a half-flight (which became MS 31). Likewise it only took a handwritten message dated 6 August to set up a half flight of single-seat 1913 Caudron Type Fs powered by a Le Rhône 60 hp engine (Flight CM becoming C39), removed from the centre at Reims and used as mounts for three other pilots, all of them officer instructors. This four man unit (Gérard, Muiron, Vuillemin and Carrus) was proposed to General de Lanrezac who, not having any aviation, accepted them for his 5th Army, stationed them at Rethel and had them operate around Mézières. They were quickly reinforced by others from the Deperdussin flight whose equipment was completely worn out and replaced by Caudron Type Fs taken from the centres at Avord and Pau.

This was also the case of Capitaine André Faure, commanding Flight V 24 made up of six armoured Voisin LA 5 Type 31s powered by a 130 hp Canton-Unnè engine originally intended for the Russians but requisitioned. He asked Gabriel Voisin to install an infantry Hotchkiss machine gun, which the builder already had in his possession. This initiative raised protests from the commander of the 5th Army's aviation leading to an easily-imagined answer.

Above.
Capitaine Georges Bellenger, photographed aboard his Blériot XI-2, was given the task in 1912 of forming Escadrille N°3 (BL 3) which subsequently became the famous "Escadrille des Cigognes". (DR)

Left.
Among these three airmen from HF 19 posing proudly in front of the Henri Farman HF 20 is Georges Pelletier d'Oisy (right) nicknamed "Pivola", a WWI ace who distinguished himself in 1924 by succeeding in the Paris-Tokyo long distance flight. (DR)

In the afternoon of the 2nd, Corporal Touvet from the 6th Army (MF 16) reported that troops were coming up between Crépy-en-Valois and Villers-Cotterêts heading south-east.

In the morning Lieutenant Savary, accompanied by Capitaine Ménard from Escadrille D 4, reported the presence of a German vanguard division at Saint-Erme, near to Sissonne. In his report the observer noted: "An infantry battalion marching covers a distance of some 400 yards, a cavalry squadron 120 yards, a horse artillery battery 350 yards and a light ammunition column 360 yards. When an observer spots a column, he has to gather from its dimensions its strength and composition."

The following day Capitaine Bellenger, head of the 6th Army aviation, was waiting on the airfield at Tremblay-lès-Gonesses for the return of the machines sent on reconnaissance to the north and the northeast of Paris. He heard Lieutenant Prot, the pilot of a Mau-

during the First World War

Right.
Fanciful postcard showing the kill obtained on 2 September 1914 by Jules Védrine (pilot) and René Vicaire (gunner) aboard the armoured Blériot called "la Vache" over Struippes. The German Taube, damaged by several bullets from the machine gun which had been installed at the rear landed behind French lines. (DR)

Below.
The crew of a Voisin Type III. The rear-mounted engine on this two-seat bomber meant the firing field was uninterrupted for the single gun mounted on the front. (DR)

rice Farman announce that his observer, Lieutenant Hugel had spotted three columns about 3 ¾ to 5 miles long marching from Douy-la-Ramée, from Nanteuil-le-Haudouin and from Betz south-eastwards towards la Ferté-sous-Jarre and Château-Thierry. This information brought by Bellenger to the 6th Amy's HQ received the following comment from the head of the 2e Bureau (intelligence): "It's impossible. Your airmen can't see anything and because they can't see anything, they make something up!"

On the 3rd, three series of reconnaissance missions were launched, one at dawn, another between 11 AM and midday and the last, in the evening, carried out by the CRP at 16.45, was flown by Soldier Granet carrying Soldier Dufresne, an observer form REP 15; it was sent to the north of the Marne towards Meaux which confir-

DEATH OF A PIONEER

Marc Pourpe, a member of the Group of Airmen, volunteered with his plane at the outbreak of war. Assigned to MS 23 at Nancy where Roland Garros and Eugène Gilbert were also stationed, he carried out reconnaissance missions just like them. During one of these missions, his plane was hit by shell bursts and he returned to his airfield with part of his propeller missing. On 2 September, he left Treux (Somme) aboard his Morane which came out of a bend and went into a dive, crashing to the ground. He had chalked up 78 flying hours from 27 reconnaissance sorties.

med the earlier observations. Likewise in the evening, the observations made by the Royal Flying Corps airmen from the British army stationed to the south of the Coulommiers region confirmed the information of 3 September.

Joffre decided to stop the retreat and fortified his positions; troops were brought up by special trains from the Gare de l'Est and Galliéni exploited a fault in the German strategy on 3 September by pushing troops into a gap between the German armies (among which 5 000 men from the 62nd Division transported by a fleet of taxis, the famous "Taxis of the Marne" (1), to Nanteuil-le-Haudouin for a cost of 70 102 francs, paid to the taxi company).

On 4 September, aerial reconnaissance, including that by V 24, marked out the German advance accurately, the veering of von Kluk's 1st Army and the thrust towards Sézanne by von Bülow's 2nd Army.

The so-called Battle of the Marne which had started on 6 September ended with a victory on the 13th, but pursuing the retreating enemy dragged on slightly, the victorious troops being too tired and unable to keep up.

The exhausted French infantry was unable to exploit the breach created between the 1st and 2nd Armies and the German withdrawal ended on a prepared front line of resistance which started from Soissons, reached Reims then Verdun along the line of crests. The weather conditions (rain and very strong winds) put a damper on attempts to fly reconnaissance missions to determine the enemy's exact positions. In the night of the 13th-14th, a violent storm swept through the region, five planes from HF 7, two from MF 16 and three from V 24 were destroyed and the aviation park could not provide any replacements except worn-out machines.

On 14 September, French troops had settled on the Aisne. On the 15th, the weather was a little bit more clement for aerial reconnaissance and this went on during the following days. Another tactic definitely had to be found when confronting resolute enemy troops set up in strong positions. On the 17th, the Germans started bombarding Reims and on the 19th their shells set fire to the cathedral. The front line was well held by the German troops who tried to fix as many French

Opposite.
The crew of a Farman dressing for a recce mission in the company of a mechanic. All during the conflict, the plane crews had to wear warm clothes against the very low temperatures at high altitudes, restricting their movements in already cramped cockpits.

Opposite.
Anti-aircraft machine gun "against the Taubes" as the caption on this period photo.

THE FLAK AWARDS ITSELF A PLANE

On 6 December an Escadrille VB 1 Voisin was out on a recce mission on the Ypres-Ménin-Coutrai road when it came under fire from the German anti-aircraft artillery, the "Flugezugabwehrkanone" or "flak" for short. A shell burst hit a cylinder, the engine stopped and Pilot-Corporal Julien Serviès tried a crash landing. His observer, Sous-Lieutenant Barrès tried to set fire to the machine because the enemy was getting close. Serviès fired at the fuel tank with his rifle and the Germans hearing the shot riposted. The plane caught fire.

troops as possible. The relief of active German units started, replaced partly by units from the first reserve, well trained and armed. The relieved active troops started assembling with a view to the next offensive that the German High Command was preparing in order to obtain a decisive break-through. The main thrust was across the north of France in the hope of cutting off the English army from its supply sources.

From now on the war of movement ended and the infantryman became an earth-mover! Joffre learnt a lesson from the campaign which was costly in human terms, causing the death of 550 000 men – 299 000 Germans and about 250 000 Frenchmen and a little bit more than 11 000 British, not counting the civilian victims of the occupation troops.

He decided to surround himself with specialists and on 24 September sent for Commandant Barthès to replace Lieutenant-Colonel Voyer, a partisan of airships, at his headquarters.

General Bernard, the head of aeronautics, learning his lesson from his mismanagement in the circumstances, resigned and was replaced by General Hirschauer who took as his second-in-command General Bouttieaux, a change which appeared in a GHQ communiqué on 12 October. New rules were brought out concerning the whole of the aircraft sector: the schools were reopened (Avord in September, Pau in December) and their yield of pupils was increased later by the addition of civilian schools which were requisitioned (Chartres, Etampes, etc., in 1915). The equipment put at the disposal of the escadrilles was reviewed and the less efficient machines (the Dorand 01s, Paul Schmitts, two-seat Blériots and Deperdussins) were got rid of. Engine power was considered inadequate and the industrialists were encouraged as a first step to develop engines rated at 100 hp at least. A period of overall reorganisation started but not all the industrialists, except for Farman (aircraft) and Renault and Gnome-Rhône (engines) had the industrial means to fulfil the government's orders. Others preferred to supply their foreign customers and delay making planes under licence, like Blériot with the Caudron G-3. Others like Morane-Saulnier did not have any factories in which to build their machines, preventing the more promising machines from coming into service sooner. These difficulties encouraged the state to create its own production workshops.

From 20-23 September, some of the 2nd Army troops left the Lorraine theatre of operations to reinforce the Oise sector then, given that the German thrust was towards the sea, settled as a buffer in the Ham area. Its aircraft followed and took part actively while the infantry converted themselves into an excavation company.

Attempts at organisation

Commandant Barès' arrival on 25 September at the head of the Service de l'Aéronautique was marked by important decisions: getting the aviation to specialise

AVIATION MILITAIRE.

during the First World War

– observation planes, bombers and fighters – then rationalising the equipment, keeping the most effective. This was accompanied by an effort made by the industry: the builders were invited to set up in the country, to increase production rates and to build under licence. Thus Blériot built Caudron G.3s, likewise Esnault-Pelterie, Nieuport, Lioré and Olivier, Letord and Breguet built Voisins after creating workshops and building up stocks of material and equipment.

Under Commandant Barès' good influence, escadrille specialisation started by creating a bomber group (GB 1), particularly for reprisals, since Paris had been bombed on 13 and then 30 August (five bombs dropped from a Taube) and there had been four other air raids (Lunéville had been bombed as early as 3 August). The group was officially created on 29 November 1914 by the merging of three Voisin escadrilles (V 14, VB 3 and V 17) with the park, repair and supply workshops under Commandant Goÿs.

Both civilian and military schools, now open again,

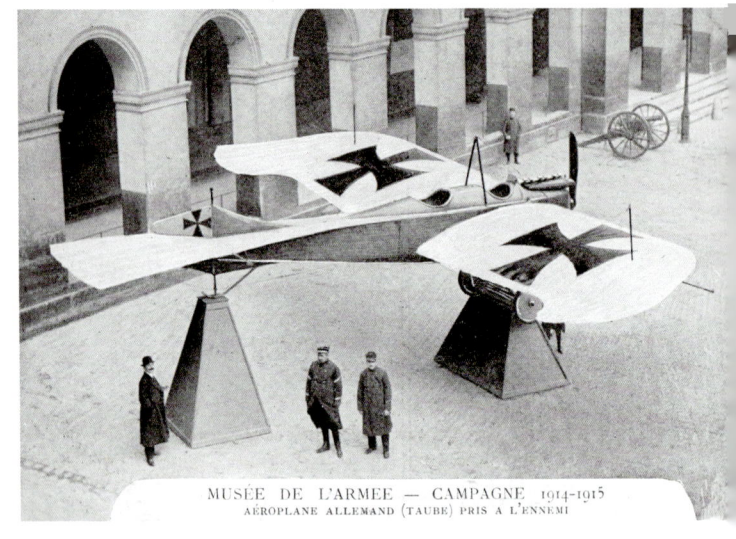

Above, right.
In the first weeks of the war, the Taubes were the German air threat par excellence for the French. One of them was captured intact and put on display in the main courtyard of the Musée de l'Armée in Paris during the winter of 1914-15. *(DR)*

were asked to make a considerable effort both in increasing the number of pupils and in reducing the number of accidents. The number of escadrilles was increased from 34 to 65, of which 16 escadrilles were or the various armies specialising as fighters which meant an order for 3 000 planes and 2 000 engines. The suppliers were a long way from meeting these needs because monthly plane production rose from 100 planes to only 137 in November and 192 in December.

Meanwhile there had been skirmishes between observation planes from both sides and one result appeared in a communiqué mentioning the first official "kill" against a Taube on 5 October, scored by Sergeant Joseph Frantz and his observer Quénault from Escadrille V 24 flying a Voisin fitted out with a light machine gun.

Others claimed to be the first to shoot down an enemy plane: Jules Védrine and his gunner René Vicaire brought down a Taube on 2 September over Suippes; there were three claims from English air force planes from N°2 Squadron, including Lieutenant Harvey-Kelly on B.E.2a against a German two-seater on 25 August. The kill by Joseph Frantz was not mentioned in the GHQ communiqué which, on the other hand, on 4 November, did mention "three Taubes have been destroyed by

On this page.
Fancy French, German and British postcards, illustrating air combat during the early years of the conflict.

during the First World War

Opposite.
Henri Farman HF 20 « returning from Verdun » on 17 October 1914.

our soldiers at Souain (Marne) between Reims and the Argonne" and also on 27 November, "a Taube has been captured near Saint-Omer".

Shortly afterwards the artillery aircraft had radio receivers to communicate with the batteries and aerial photography stopped being an invention reserved for a few amateurs. Naturally there were critics, including Major-General Berthelot, Joffre's advisor who, having expressed doubts about the information brought by Capitaine Bellenger to show him how the overall plans diverged from the aerial photographs, received the following reply: "General, I believed up till now that a camera recorded what was in front of it. You have just revealed to me that it records things that don't exist; I am grateful to you and I present my humble respects".

Then in October, between the 10th and the 17th, British forces deploying in Flanders at the same time as German troops flowing back after the Marne were involved in a race to the sea. The Kronprinz's VIth Army was trying to sever communications between Great Britain and its contingent fighting in France that was being reinforced. British troops supported by Belgian troops were trying to contain the German thrust that was successfully nibbling away territory. On 18 November, the air force innovated because the General Staff had to be informed about the size of the positions on which the Germans had halted and their resupply system and that meant having to send messengers behind enemy lines because there was no means of getting in touch with the occupied population. The experimental dropping of just such a envoy, with a supply of pigeons, was entrusted to Lieutenant Pinsard from MS 23 who, with his Morane-Saulnier L succeeded with his "Billard"-type mission (named after the creator of this system of transport). The success of this mission led to others.

The town of Ypres became the Germans' objective; the battle began on the 17th and stopped on 22 November because of the resistance put up by Belgian troops and French Fusiliers Marins (navy fusiliers) at Dixmude, with huge casualties – 148 000 men of which

Right.
At the beginning of the Battle of the Marne, one of the German observation Taubes was shot down by ground fire near May-en-Multien on 3 September 1914.

French aviation

67% were German. Nonetheless, the Kaiser's troops occupied a sizeable part of industrial Belgium and Northern France.

The first Battle of Vimy started in December to prevent the Germans from taking Arras. British aircraft suffered heavy losses despite support from French escadrilles brought up in a hurry. Two GB 1 escadrilles reached St-Pol-en-Ternoise (Pas-de-Calais) on 16 December and took part in the raging battle. On the 20th, a force of 20 planes from Escadrilles VB 1 and 2 bombed Givenchy-en-Gobelle, near Vimy (sixty-six 90-mm shells) and the station at Hénin-Liétard (12 shells), then the group returned to its unit at Verdun on 15 January with stopovers, where the 3rd Escadrille was waiting for them.

Individual bombing initiatives increased following that taken by Capitaine Happe from MF 29 who, taking off from Belfort if the weather was good, took to attacking German towns on the right hand bank of the Rhine and airfields in Alsace. So on the 4th and then the 19th, the station at Fribourg-en-Brisgau was bombed with six shells from an altitude of 2 500 feet despite very heavy fire from anti-aircraft guns.

Likewise MF 25, based in the Argonne, attacked bivouacs, stations, and trains in the occupied regions opposite the French 3rd Army.

At the end of the year, equipment reinforcements were still insufficient to allow for an increase in the number of escadrilles whereas recalling operational pilots and assigning them to training was only just made up for by the arrival of 134 new qualified pilots, trained since the beginning of war.

The first five months of the war were murderous for all the French armies, with 350 000 killed, 400 000 wounded and above all 150 000 prisoners, out of 4 million mobilised men. Big changes were in the pipeline to modify the infantry uniform, stop bayonet attacks and improve the resources in automatic weapons and in heavy artillery. What this meant was that there had to be an industrial organisation capable of adapting rapidly and producing in large numbers. For the air force, it was urgent to rationalise materiel and to renew training practices for flying crews, as well as increase the number of the ground personnel and train them how to maintain these machines.

Opposite.
It happened that airmen were sometimes confronted with the harsh realities of trench warfare, like the airman Marc Pourpe, photographed here at Albert, in the Somme, a few weeks before he died in aerial combat in December 1914.

Opposite.
The remains of a Morane Saulnier Type L belonging to Sergeant Marc Pourpe (pilot) and Lieutenant Eugène Vauglin (observer) from MS 23, on the airfield at Villers-Bretonneux after their accident on 2 December 1914, returning from a reconnaissance mission in very bad weather.

during the First World War

THE TRAINING SCHOOLS

After a few months' reflection as to what equipment to give the training centres and how long a pupil was to stay there, the study applied to the Maurice Farman (MF) planes showed that a pupil who had a machine could pass his military licence within a month, as follows: ten days before flying solo, another ten days before taking the civilian licence and ten days before taking the military licence. But the Minister had the training centres shut down at the beginning of the war. The ministerial dispatch 1649-12 dated 17 October authorised the training centres at Pau (training) and Avord (application) to open again. On around 15 November, Pau received a first contingent of 70-80 pupils in five divisions: MF, Voisin, Caudron, Morane-Saulnier and Blériot. Selected pupils from Pau went to Avord to take tests for the military licence; some who already had their civilian licence went to the Réserve Générale d'Aviation immediately when they left Pau.

In January the minister decided to create another training centre at Chartres for 50 then 90 pupils, and to make the schools specialise, Avord taking on training for the Farmans and Voisins with the other aircraft types remaining at Pau, except for the Blériot school which was suspended for the time being. With the need for pilots becoming more and more urgent, at the beginning of February 1915 the minister decided to militarise the civilian schools. The Farman School at Etampes took in its first pupils on 22 February, the Blériot School at Buc started to instruct them on Caudrons on 24 February and the Caudron School at Crotoy on 5 April. As this was still not enough, a new school opened at Dijon at the beginning of June 1915. Avord licensed 40 pupils in 1914 and 106 between 1 January and 1 June 1915.

---

* After the closure, pilots holding a civil licence obtained the army equivalent, 91 in August 1914, 24 in October and 390 during the first five months of 1915.

216 - CAMP D'AVIATION MILITAIRE, près DIJON — Escadrille de Biplans Bréguet

66 AVORD (Cher). — Centre Militaire d'Aviation. - Départ d'un Bi-Place

French aviation

German retreat on the Aisne and stabilisation of the front September/November 1914.

— Front in November 1914
--- German breakthrough
➡ Allied offensives
➡ German offensives
⬤ Battle of Verdun

Opposite and below.
The training centres used a variety of types of machines (fighters, bombers, etc.) like these Nieuports, seen here at Avord.

70 AVORD (Cher) – Centre Militaire d'Aviation – Ateliers de Réparations

72. AVORD (Cher)   Centre Militaire d'Aviation
Ligne de Départ – Division Nieuport

during the First World War

The year 1915

The General Staff no longer believed in a short war and became progressively aware that the offensives-based war of movement was too costly, that they had to get hold of larger calibre artillery than the rather ubiquitous 75, and supply automatic weapons to the infantry, who by force of circumstance had become earth-movers more than soldiers. However, the mobility that railway convoys provided was not enough and the troops had to be equipped with the more flexible means the automobile offered, as had been amply demonstrated at the Battle of the Marne.

Industrialists were encouraged to produce more trucks and engines even though this might delay the production of equipment for the aircraft units and the idea gradually sunk in that unless production was managed and the variety of types controlled all this would lead to an unmanageable situation as far as servicing and spare parts were concerned.

Like the other arms, the air force was completely reorganised; airships were the first victims, to the advantage of air observation balloons; and the number of different aircraft types put into the line was reduced. The 60 escadrilles totalled some 130 officers, 500 pilots, 250 observers and 5 000 men. During the summer, this became 91 escadrilles each equipped with eight or ten operational machines. The military aircraft competition in the so-called "powerful aircraft" (carrying 600 lb of bombs at a speed of 75 mph at 6 500 feet over 375 miles) category brought out two winners: Breguet and Schmitt. The latter had a lot of difficulty evolving from the prototype to the productions series machine and even to starting the production line in 1916. This was why the General Staff's choice went to the Breguet and Michelin-built aircraft.

The artillery had priority and took advantage of using observation balloons most, whilst at the same time improving this type of "machine" to make it as effective as the ones used by the enemy. Following on from the publicity given to Frantz's and Quenault's exploit, fighters were starting to become a speciality. Clashes on the ground were better prepared because aerial photography was used. Other armed planes started to protect these specialised observer crews, albeit tentatively. The arrival of the Morane Parasol LAs, then of the Nieuport 11 "Bébé", pioneered the use of fighter aircraft which began with individuals before specialised units were formed. The armour which the 1913

Below.
The Type M Balloon, or "Caquot" after its designer, was put into service in 1916. It could be distinguished by its tail made up of three identical lobes.

Above.
The French copy of the Drachen, the balloon Type H, had its baptism of fire in December 1914 and replaced the older models still in service which were much less effective.

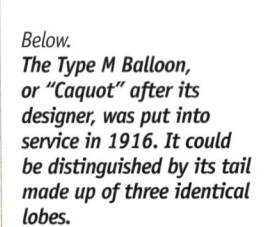

THE FIRST VICTORIES

On 10 September 1914, the 5th Train Squadron managed to shoot down one of the Taubes threatening the stations in the Verdun area. This machine, the first kill made by ground troops, was piloted by Capitaine Keisenberg with Lieutenant Dyckoff and crashed near Hill 340 between Erize-Saint-Dizier and Erize-la-Brulée. Escadrille Do 14 from Belfort was the first to have the shooting down of a Drachen confirmed, on 27 January 1915.

Above.
The German Drachen (dragon) was in service from the earliest days of the war whereas France had got rid of its balloon battalions.

Above.
The Type H balloon could be distinguished by the balance flaps located at the rear.

SHOOTING AT AVIATIKS

On 10 January 1915, Pilot-Sergeant Eugène Gilbert, returning from a mission near Chaulnes, spotted a German plane heading for Amiens. He chased it and his observer, Lieutenant de Puechredon succeeded in hitting the observer, Lieutenant von Falkenstein with his rifle. His third shot hit the pilot, Heller, and the fourth and last shot pierced the radiator. The German pilot landed the plane and surrendered. Gilbert already had two other kills, on 2 November with Observer-Capitaine de Vergnette and a short while later another, with his mechanic, Bayle, obtained between Albert and Bapaume. On the following 27 June, while taking part in the bombing of the Friedrichshafen Zeppelin hangars, his engine broke down on the way home and he was forced to crash land in Switzerland, at Rheinfelden. His later escape became famous.

Above.
The Aéronautique Militaire's second confirmed kill: on 10 January 1915, Sergent Gilbert (pilot) and Lieutenant de Puechredon, from Escadrille MS 23 managed to force an enemy plane (a Rumpler B.I) to land near Amiens after killing the observer, wounding the pilot and piercing the radiator with their rifle. On these photos, some dragoons are watching the body of the observer, removed from the plane which landed almost intact.

experts liked could not be made, hence the research into greater handling qualities and manoeuvrability and a faster rate of climb.

Observation units were reinforced, each army corps being associated with an escadrille which also did artillery spotting and ground photography. Moreover, each army had two or more reconnaissance escadrilles which could also go in for some bombing.

The creation of bomber groups

Bombing was regrouped into a unit made up of the three Voisin escadrilles under a specialist, Commandant Louis Mezeyrac de Goÿs. New Voisins coming off the production line enabled another group to be formed and also to prepare for a third one.

VICTIM OF THE WEATHER

Pilot-Corporal Granel from Escadrille Rep 27 was always volunteering to go reconnoitring, even in bad weather, thus showing his audacity and uncommon dexterity. On 11 January 1915, in stormy weather, he carried out a sortie during which his plane, made helpless by the gusts of wind, crashed to the ground.

during the First World War

Above, right.
Adolphe Pégoud photographed during an air show before the war.

THE DEATH OF PÉGOUD, SIX CONFIRMED KILLS

On 31 August while carrying out a reconnaissance mission in the Belfort region in a Nieuport 10 N°210 from MS 49, one of the first to be delivered to the front, Pégoud was shot down by Unteroffizier Walther Kandulski* flying an armoured Rumpler Taube whose Gunner-Lieutenant von Blitz managed to put a bullet in the Frenchman's aorta. He crashed near Petite-Croix, not far from Belfort. Two days later, the German crew dropped over the crash site a wreath bearing the inscription: "Dem in Kampfe für sein Vaterland gefallen Flieger Pégoud ehrt der Gegner." (to the pilot Pégoud who died in action for his country, a tribute from the victors).

Kandulski was in his turn shot down by Sergent Paul Ronserail on 18 June 1916.

Arriving in Lorraine at full strength, GB1 (Groupe de Bombardement 1 – Bomber Group 1) bombed Saint-Mihiel and its outskirts on 18 January then attacked any men or lorries that it found gathering at Chamley, Thiaucourt and Pagny, in order to disorganise the railway traffic. At the beginning of February it was the turn of Spincourt on the 4th, then Arnaville, Pagny and Château Salins. During a mission on 10 February, the crew of a Voisin shot down a German plane, of which one of the occupants was none other than Lieutenant Frantz von Hindelson, the first person to bomb Paris on 13 August. On 6 February, GB 1 moved to Chalons in or-

Above, left.
Remains of Pégoud's aircraft.

Above.
Funeral of Célestin Adolphe Pégoud at Belfort on 3 September 1915.

VICTIMS OF A NIGHT FLIGHT

*O*n 24 February 1915, Escadrille VB 1 tried flying by night using searchlights on the airfield at La Melette-l'Epine, near Châlons. The escadrille commander and pilot, Lieutenant René Mouchard, teamed up with his gunner, Sergeant Emile Maillard. During the night the Voisin crashed on the airfield. Both men were killed and were the unit's first casualties.

der to train for night flying, the first night flight being carried out by Lieutenant Mouchard, commanding VB 1, alone on board, on the 16th. The main activity was nonetheless supporting the troops on the ground in the Champagne area to block the Germans bringing up supplies by rail. On 7 March the bombers took part in the battle actively by destroying artillery batteries hidden in woods and sometimes despite the Albatrosses and Avaitiks, flew at low altitudes. On 21 March they moved to Malzéville via Toul.

The bombing escadrilles were numbered on 15 March to distinguish them. Those from GB 1: V 14 became VB 101, V17 VB 102 and VB 3 VB 103. In the meantime these escadrilles, including the ones being formed, started training together so that they would be more cohesive when manoeuvring. GB1 was ready to move to Malzéville in May, near Nancy. Meanwhile, GB 2 (Escadrilles VB, VB 5 and VB 6 – which had become VB 106), created on 16 January 1915, assembled at Saint-Pol-sur-Mer to carry out its activity over Flanders, especially the coastal stations at Bruges and Ostend (among the pilots of VB 106 was Adjudant Charles Nungesser, already well-known for his bravery). On 3 February, a plane flown by Lieutenant Armand Coutisson was caught in fog over the Yser, lost its way, and went and landed in Holland where the crew was interned. This pilot returned to France in August 1916.

GB 3 (Escadrilles VB 107, 108 and 109) appeared in March, followed a short time later by GB 4 (Escadrilles VB 110, 111 and 112 ex-29) which more or less adopted the tactics developed by GB 1 and ended up gathered together on the airfield at Malzéville, under the command of Commandant Roisin.

During the night of 20-21 March two zeppelins, LZ 29 and LZ 35 flew over Paris and under fire from anti-aircraft guns, started bombing, particularly the 18th Arrondissement, and then the northern suburbs. The alert was sounded.

All the CRP machines were brought out of the hangars. Pilot-Sergeant Jacques de Lesseps, accompanied by Lieutenant Galliot armed with a machine gun tried to take off but thick fog reduced visibility to forty yards and halted the attempt. The second monster, pierced by a multitude of shell bursts from the French anti-aircraft artillery and losing its oxygen, managed to reach the German lines and touch down near Saint-Quentin.

Getting rid of the Drachens, full of hydrogen, an inflammable gas, required an armament change, with incendiary bullets alternating with ordinary ones. Other new ideas were encouraged. In January, "Sergeant" Adolphe Pégoud, visiting MF 25, tried his luck by bombing a Drachen with his plane but only succeeded in making it fall to the ground quickly. His tally did not suffer because he obtained his first five kills (four confirmed) in MF 25 then in MS 37, adding a sixth on

Below.
On 18 May 1916 aboard his Caudron G.4 from C 34, Adjudant Roger Ronsérall was called "Pégoud's avenger" after shooting down the German pilot Otto Kandulski who himself had shot down Adolphe Pégoud a few months earlier. He is posing here after the war in front of a Nieuport used for aerobatics.

during the First World War

11 July when he was in MS 49, formed by Capitaine Zarapoff on 18 April.

Finally certain escadrilles were to be reserved for the needs of the Head of the Aeronautical Service whose job it was to keep the Army General Staff supplied with intelligence. In the long term, he was to have dedicated escadrilles for fighters, bombers and long-range reconnaissance. All these preparations had no effect on daily operations because the units had to be informed according to the principle "See but not be seen", in other words, get rid of all the enemy's means of observation and prevent him from flying over friendly lines. The chivalrous manner of the early months disappeared with the arrival of the machine gun and its server...

Other tactics saw the light of day thanks to determined individuals. Although the single seater gave the pilot a completely free rein, the machine with a pusher propeller, like in the RFC or with the two seat Voisin-Canon, was much less manoeuvrable. The pilot could not see to the rear where more and more attacks were coming from. On the single-seater, the gun was located on the top of the upper wing, firing outside the propeller arc. Changing ammunition drums, which still did not hold many rounds, meant the pilot in a single-seater had to let go of the controls. To solve the problem of weapons jamming, the crafty ones had a little mallet which they used to hit the weapon with. The best system was the one firing through the propeller arc.

Ground operations followed one after the other because Joffre had launched an offensive in Champagne on 16 February to reduce the Saint-Mihiel salient. A gain of about 800 yards near Vouziers caused disproportionately heavy casualties. The next day, the action spread to Eparges to the south east of Verdun and finished on 9 April only to flare up again on the 14th because of the Germans making a push in Flanders to unblock the situation at Ypres.

Below. **Fokker Eindecker (monoplane) captured at Chalons in 1916 and subsequently put on display in the courtyard of the Invalides, Paris.**

A RUINOUS GUST OF WIND

On 5 May towards 5 PM, the stormy weather became very threatening and a very strong gust blew through the ring of balloons deployed around Verdun by the 32nd, 34th and 53rd Balloon Companies and destroyed 24 of them. The balloon at Saint-Mihiel, ripped from its moorings, went off towards the enemy with its observers, that of the 53rd over Sartelles Fort, broke its cable and set off towards the enemy lines; its observer bailed out and landed on the barbed wire network; the one at Mort Homme was carried off by the wind and its occupant taken prisoner by the enemy. The 34th's got ripped by the force of the wind, its observer bailed out and landed a short distance away unscathed. On Hill 304, the balloon belonging to Sous-Lieutenant José Garcia Calderon*, a Peruvian volunteer from the 30th Balloon Company, broke its moorings in the last few yards and dragged its occupant across the ground over the bomb craters and onto barbed wire where he died.

---

* He was student at the École des Beaux-Arts and when he finished his studies, he didn't hesitate to join up when war was declared. He earned all his stripes, the Croix de Guerre with palm leaves and a host of citations. He was 26.

Gas in combat

During this offensive, for the first time on 22 April, and in spite of international agreements, a cloud of chlorine gas coming from a battery of cylindrical bottles and forming a 4 ½ mile-wide spread, preceded

BONNARD'S THEN GUYNEMER'S PLANE

Charles Bonnard, a civilian pilot before the war, started on Blériots then went on to Deperdussins. He did his military service in the air force at Reims then in the Escadrille Blériot 80 hp at Épinal. He was chosen by Lieutenant Brocard to be part of Escadrille MS 3 and was sent to Villacoublay to take over the Morane Parasols. Already among this escadrille's pilots were Védrines, Houssemant and Chainat and also the young Guynemer. When Bonnard moved to another escadrille, Guynemer took over his Nieuport 18M with the Rhône 80 hp powerplant. He had christened the plane "le Vieux Charles" and Guynemer out of respect for his senior kept the name.

Left.
Maréchal-des-Logis Georges Pelletier d'Oisy, aka "Pivolo", was an WWI ace (five kills) posing in front of his Nieuport when he was assigned to N 69 in 1917.

the German advance. In the trenches dug to link the craters made by the bombardments, were French soldiers from the 45th French Colonial Infantry Division, including the 3rd bis Zouave Regiment. 15 000 men were wounded and 5 000 killed in the attack. They had nothing to protect themselves except a simple handkerchief drenched in water or urine before the medical corps found a solution... The gas attack persisted until the 27th and each time the counterattack immobilised the attackers.

The antidote for this first attack arrived too late because the enemy chemists invented other, even more dangerous, products like phosgene and vesicant gases ("mustard" gas or "Yperite"). Shells loaded with yperite and then arsenic launched by the artillery quickly replaced these cylindrical bottles. Not to be outdone British and French scientists developed identical substances which if used incorrectly could turn this weapon against its senders if they hadn't made a proper note of the wind's direction.

Enormous blunders of this sort gave rise to an Army weather department on 15 August 1915, entrusted to Sous-Lieutenant David. He did the air force a huge favour by announcing the coming weather conditions, and also the General Staff, by preventing them from launching an offensive in the rain. But from the start the means the weather service was given were not sufficient to forecast sudden localised gusts of wind, like

Left.
Voisin Type IV, called the "Voisin Canon" because of its trainable 37-mm Hotchkiss canon in place of its usual machine gun. This weapon could also be pointed down almost vertically so it could shoot at targets on the ground.

Left.
Sergeant Henri Thouroude, aka de Losques (left), a painter and cartoonist for the big newspapers before the war before being assigned as a bomber-machine gunner to VB 110. He was lost in combat with his pilot on 9 August.

the one which hit Aerostation on 5 May 1916.

On 30 March the air force had 51 escadrilles at its disposal each with a strength of six to ten planes, plus nine reserve escadrilles supported by eleven parks for repairs and supplies. The strength engaged numbered some 500 pilots, 240 observers and 4 300-ground crews.

The creation of the fighter units

On 1 April Jean Navarre, Lieutenant Robert's pilot in MF 11, shot down an Aviatik armed with a machine gun. The same day, Roland Garros from MS 23 shot down a German machine thanks to a machine gun installed by his mechanic. The next day, Sous-Lieutenant Chambe, the observer aboard the Morane piloted by Aspirant Pelletier Doisy from MS 12, shot down

DEATH OF AN INCENDIARY

On 26 May 1915, the Morane Parasol flown by René Mesguich, licence N° 713 dated 12 January 1912, with Sous-Lieutenant Jacottet as observer attacked an Albatross over Cuiry-Housse (Aisne) near Soissons. The duel fought with rifles stared at 8 500 ft and ended with the enemy crashing. Both Germans, one of whom was von Bülow from Escadrille 13, were killed. Among the debris were found three incendiary bombs still intact. It was Mesguich's second kill the other one having been obtained on 28 April. Mesguisch, who was promoted to Lieutenant, disappeared over the sea at the beginning of October 1918.

an Albatros with a rifle. The crew was taken prisoner. In all the excitement, while landing near the victim, the plane nosed over, which caused the High Command to forbid this practice. Garros however had put his idea into practice, using his "Parasol" as a weapon by getting the machine gun fixed to the engine cowling to fire through the propeller arc. His mechanic had fitted him up with a system: a deflector made of steel fixed to the base of the blades which deflected the bullets, a method the builder approved of.

On 18 April, after three kills obtained in this way, Garros' engine broke down fording him land at Ingelmünster, to the north of Coutrai inside enemy territory, where he was taken prisoner before he could set fire to his machine. After the Germans examined it they were able to perfect the system installed on their Fokker E-1 mid-wing monoplane. This plane caused disarray among the Allied air forces until a captured German plane provided them with the solution. On each side enemy planes were carefully gone over and all technical solutions to various problems carefully noted or

Above.
Anti-aircraft 75-mm auto-canon mounted on a de Dion Bouton chassis, together with its mobile caisson.

Opposite.
"Atelier d'Aviation" (Aircraft workshop) on a de Dion Bouton EW chassis.

HUNGESSER AT NANCY

On 31 July, on duty on the Plateau at Malzéville, Hungesser, a pilot with VB 106, was bored. Five Albatrosses flew passed so he bounded over to a brand new Voisin which had arrived the day before, took off, caught up with the Germans and attacked them, succeeding in shooting down one of them, which earned him the Croix de Guerre for his courage, then a week in the guardhouse for indiscipline, and above all a transfer to a fighter unit. He was sent to the Morane School and returned to Nancy on 26 November this time to N 65 with which he shot down his first Taube on the 28th over Nomeny.

---

installed each time they represented a step forward.

The victories the communiqués praised gave rise to the creation of fighter units of which the first dedicated escadrille was MS 12, entrusted to Capitaine Raymond de Bernis. At the same time what was to become a deadly weapon was completing its trials: the single seat Nieuport X monoplane, and especially the XI, the so-called Bébé, started reaching the escadrilles during the summer.

Special Missions

On 20 April, Sergeant René Bodin from MS 12 dropped off André Borde and his pigeons who were to supply information to make bombing the German HQ easier at Mézières. Three weeks later, this passenger succeeded in getting into Holland. On his return to France, he asked for and was granted permission to become a pilot. Bodin did his job again on 12 May, this time dropping off Customs Officer Alphonse Hamiade who had to get information about the forces concentrating to the north of Signy-le-Petit. His work finished, once back in France he asked to go back.

On 16 May, Adjudant-Pilot William Hostein from C-6 took a customs man, Pierre Letannoux, aboard G-3 N° 181, to a spot near Charleville to obtain information during the Battle of Arras. He went back on the 31st to drop René Robert, another customs man, and pick up Letannoux again a bit further away.

Other similar missions were undertaken in June (two carried out by Jules Védrine from MS 3), in July (on the 19th carried out by Adjudant Jean Navarre, the brilliant MS 12 pilot), September (on the 8th by Sous-Lieutenant Richard from MS 3, on the 25th by Guynemer from MS 3, on 26th by Védrine again). Two other escadrilles flying Morane-Saulnier Ls carried out this type of operation (MS 38, 12, 23 and 37 with Adjudant Paolacci) and Caudron G.4s (25 September, flown by Billard (7) from C 4 who carried out 3 missions).

On 23 May Italy abandoned its policy of neutrality and joined the Entente so it could put forward its claims on the "unliberated" region then under Hapsburg domination. It mobilised slowly and carried out an offensive in June, the Isonzo Offensive, which was costly in human terms for little territorial gain.

During the first six months of the year, Zeppelin activity was in the news both in France and in Great Britain and a lot was done to try to get rid of them. One of these methods was successful thanks to Sub-Lieutenant R.A.J. Warneford, a Canadian pilot from N° 1 (Naval) Squadron on 6 June. He dropped six 20-lb bombs from his Morane-Saulnier Parasol from a height of 100 feet onto L 37 which caught fire and fell to the ground, onto the Grand Béguinage orphanage at Saint Élisabeth, near Ghent. Two nurses and two children were killed as well as all the Zeppelin crew. Warneford was not able to profit for long from his success since

Left.
A Renault Type EE anti-aircraft searchlight vehicle alongside some Farman biplanes.

Below.
90cm (3ft) Breguet searchlight on a De Dion-Bouton BY chassis.

A FOURTH WOUND

Pierre Perrin de Brichambauld, a civilian pilot from 3 May 1912, assigned to MF 8 carried out the war's first bombing operation on 4 August when reconnoitring towards Château-Salins. He was wounded in flight on 4 October 1914, then in the head on 30 July 1915, then on 22 February 1916 by shell bursts which went through his thigh. On 9 May 1916 during an artillery-spotting mission made difficult by clouds, he was shot in the thigh. He didn't say anything to his observer and carried on flying then returned to the airfield. Once the plane had halted, he could not get down and had to be helped and taken to his shelter. There he took out his medical kit and operated on himself, removed the bullet and refused to be evacuated. Two days later, he was back flying during which he chalked up a total of more than 1 000 flying hours over enemy territory.

Everyday women played an increasingly important role in the aircraft factories since most of the pre-war male workforce had left for the front.

CAPITAINE VUILLEMIN'S FIRST KILL

It was while flying a two-engined G.4 observation plane from Escadrille C 11 on 12 September 1915, that Pilot-Capitaine Jospeh Vuillemin, accompanied by Observer-Gunner Lieutenant Dumas, ran into three German planes during a barrage flight at 9 500 feet over Vigneulles. He headed for them and tried to split them up. Chasing one of them meant avoiding the other two. The fight went on for 30 minutes and dropped from 9 500 to 2 600 feet when the pursued plane went down in flames. One of the other two, bullet-ridden, was forced to land. As for the third, he got the message and skedaddled.

he was killed on 19 June during a demonstration flight in a Farman biplane at Villacoublay.

The May-September 1915 Champagne and Artois Offensive

Joffre launched a big offensive in Champagne and Artois, starting with a battle around Vimy from 9 May to 17 June resulting in a French advance of 3 000 yards for a cost of 95 000 dead.

Despite a heavy artillery concentration for which the forts at Verdun had been stripped of their heavy artillery, the attack marked time because the German entrenchments were so well defended and organised. The air forces also took part, the observation escadrilles often flying over at very low altitude just where the shells criss-crossed; the recently created fighter units were busy trying to destroy enemy balloons but their success was often limited by anti-aircraft guns installed round the balloon site.

The 18 aircraft-strong GB 1 carried out an air raid on 27 May 1915 against the Badische Anilin factories in Ludwigshafen as a reprisal for the German army using gas. On the outward trip, de Goÿs' plane broke down forcing him to make an emergency landing in enemy territory at Gainsheim, and set fire to his plane triggering off the shells he was carrying already primed for the raid.

The mission's success proved that an industrial site could be attacked, causing real damage for little loss. The High Command was persuaded and the group was mentioned in the order of the Army.

After an appetiser on 2 June (bombing the Frescati

MANEYROL'S LOGBOOK

Assigned to MS 49 as a sergeant, Alexis Maneyrol flew Morane LAs and then Nieuport "Bébés". His logbook shows:
"25 May 1915, yesterday morning I went off to reconnoitre. A Hun turned up and I had to turn back as I only had a carbine to defend myself with. I was furious for having to turn back. Fortunately in a few days we're going to have machine guns and then, all hell will be let loose. On 28 August, the day before yesterday I fought with a Hun in a fighter. But with my new Nieuport biplane, I easily caught up with him. Unfortunately, my machine gun jammed after the third belt. What a pity that was because a minute later I would have been able to shoot at him from 30 to 35 yards he would have been forced to go down or to say why he wouldn't…
(Extract from Alexis Maneyrol. "Le vol de l'aigle", Editions du Pays de Retz, 1983.)

Above.
Building of G.4 at the Caudron factory.

Top.
HD 1 production line in the Hanriot construction workshops. These were fighters destined to be used by the Belgians.

hangars by night), GB 1 joined Escadrille V 21 and on 15 June, they carried out a joint operation. At 3.30 AM, 23 planes dropped 121 90-mm shells and three 155-mm ones on the town of Karlsruhe to punish the Germans for bombing French towns, including Paris by Zeppelins and Verdun by the German heavy 420-mm artillery. On the homeward flight, the Voisins were attacked by enemy aircraft, which shot down one plane, and anti-aircraft fire damaged another forcing it to make an emergency landing at Schirmeck in the enemy zone. As a reprisal, five German planes came the same day to bomb Malzéville airfield without causing any damage.

Its lack of speed and its pusher engine blocking the rearward view made the Voisin an easy daylight prey for the German anti-aircraft fire and for the two-seat Albatrosses and Aviatiks armed with a machine gun served by the observer. So bombing changed from being a daytime activity to being a night-time one. As early as 25 June GB 2, at full strength joined GB 1, both commanded by Lieutenant de Vaisseau Cayla who made a point of introducing the precise navigation methods used in his original service, especially for calculating drift and for flying without landmarks. On 17 July, seventeen planes from GB 1 and thirteen from GB 2 bombed the station at Vigneulles-les-Hattonchâtel, a strategic point for the Germans, dropping 171 delayed-action 90-mm shells. On 19 July, GB 3 came up to reinforce the two others. On the 20th a joint operation against the station at Conflans-Jarny, with GB 3 supplying the Voisin-Canons for the escort, who had their hands full driving off obstinate Aviatiks which nonetheless caused two casualties in GB 1 with their explosive bullets. As a result, the canon-plane section was reinforced on 26 July and, so as to get rid of the Drachens, Escadrille V 113 was entirely equipped with Voisin-Canons.

On 9 August Escadrille V 110 bombed the station and installations at Sarrebrück and then had to fight off fighter attacks on the homeward trip. Voisin V 716 lagging behind the group became the object of an Aviatik's attentions, then it dived and crashed causing two deaths, the pilot Sous-Lieutenant Lemoine and the bomber Sergeant Thouroude, a famous illustrator better-known as Daniel de Losques. The Germans managed

during the First World War

THE FIRST NIGHT-FIGHTING VICTIM

Pilot-Corporal Jean Vialatoux, licence N° 2023 dated 14 June 1915, and his observer were the victims of a night-fighter on their way back from a bombing raid on 30 July 1915, without being able to respond because their machine gun had jammed. The engine caught fire but this was got under control. Then they ran out of petrol which meant a forced landing in the countryside near Lizingen. The pilot was trapped under the machine but was freed by the observer and both of them headed off to a POW camp where they were interned, in Strasbourg.

to get a message to the escadrille to say that the crew, which had defended itself courageously, had been buried with full military honours at Harbouey, near Blamont (Meurthe-et-Moselle). Sadly, that artist was not the only one to disappear. Thus André Bonnafont, aka Touraine, killed on 24 October 1916 on a Farman; Marcel Viallet, a pilot in N 67, shot down on 28 April 1916 and taken prisoner; Georges Villa, a pilot in F 50 forced for health reasons to leave the front; these are only a few of the names not to be forgotten.

It was also during the year that American volunteers, engaged earlier in the Foreign Legion (among whom William Thaw, a licensed pilot in the United States, who had come to France with his own plane), were enrolled in the flying schools. Norman Prince, a pilot since 1911, joined Escadrille VB 108 with his friend Elliott Cowdin immediately. On 23 September, the American pilot James J. Bach from MS 38 was captured by the Germans while carrying out a special mission.

In September, the number of escadrilles increased to 119 of which 24 for the Army (assembling 14 fighter and 10 reconnaissance escadrilles), 45 for the Army corps and 50 for bombing. The ground installations had done away with individual tents and replaced them with "Adrian" huts and "Bessonneau" hangars which could be taken apart. At distances varying from 3 to 4 ½ miles from the trenches, there was a line of captive balloons called "sausages", the French equivalent of the German Drachen.

Michelin's offer to supply a hundred or so planes materialised in the form of the creation of the Escadre

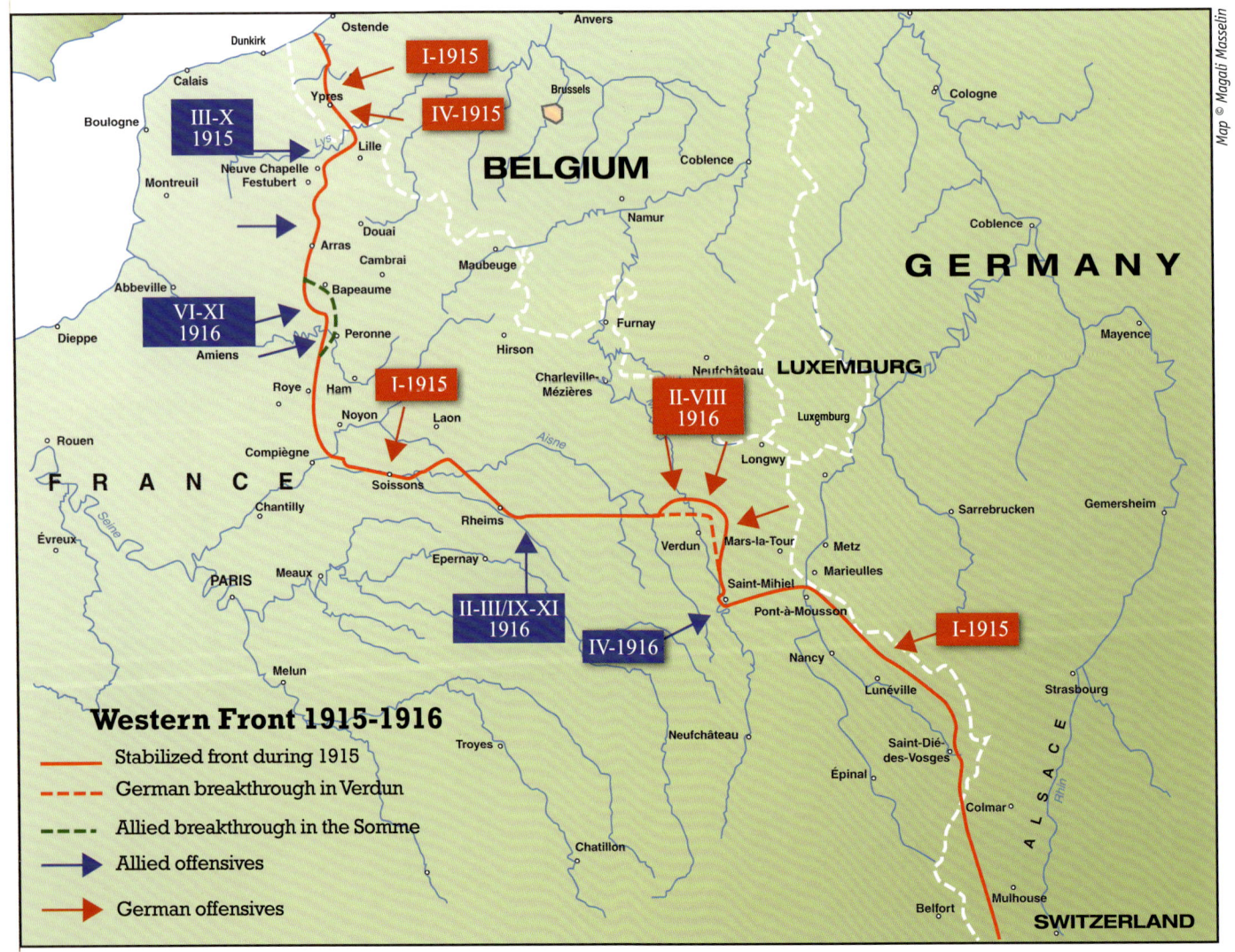

Western Front 1915-1916

- Stabilized front during 1915
- German breakthrough in Verdun
- Allied breakthrough in the Somme
- Allied offensives
- German offensives

Map © Magali Masselin

French aviation

Morane Saulnier Type N

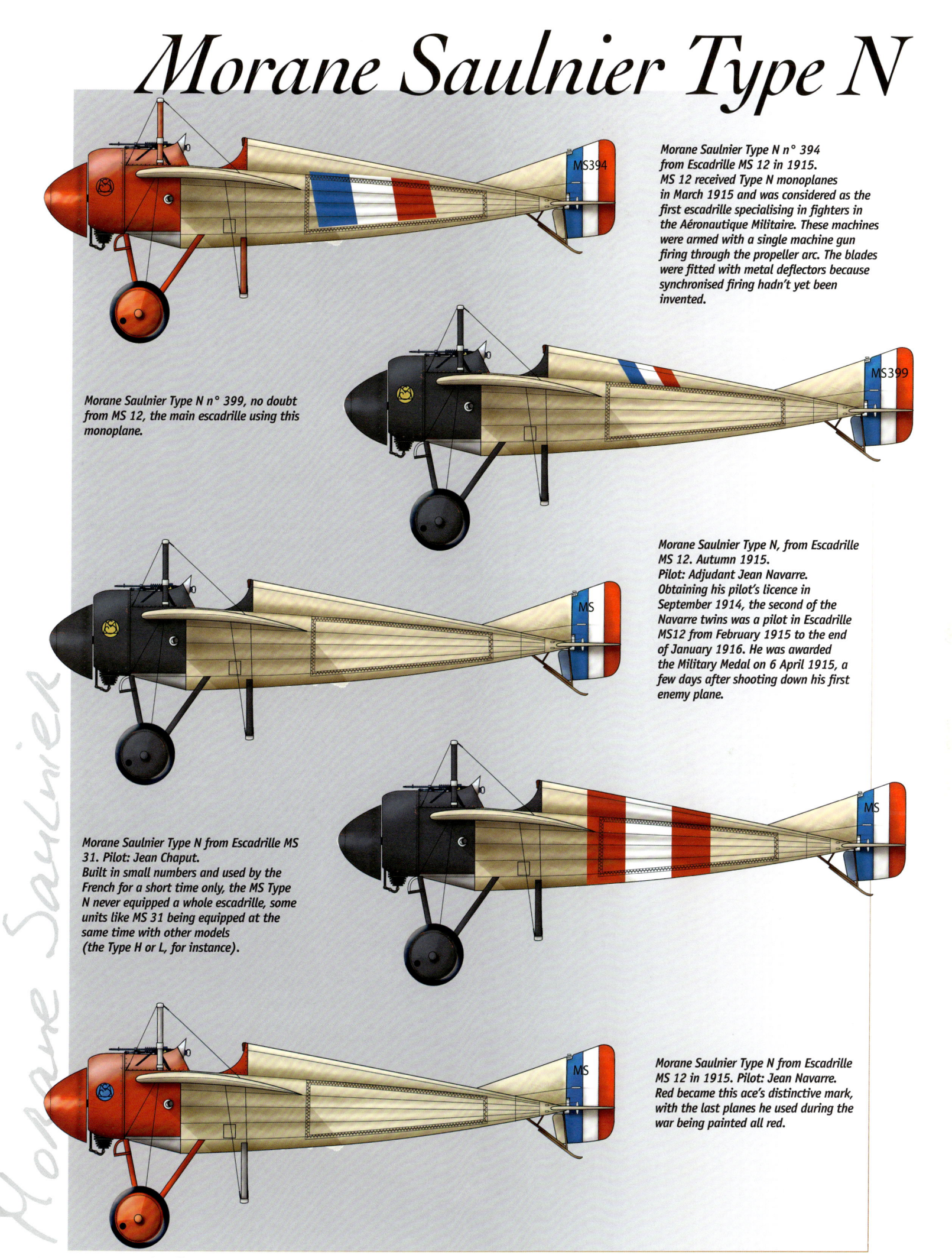

Morane Saulnier Type N n° 394 from Escadrille MS 12 in 1915. MS 12 received Type N monoplanes in March 1915 and was considered as the first escadrille specialising in fighters in the Aéronautique Militaire. These machines were armed with a single machine gun firing through the propeller arc. The blades were fitted with metal deflectors because synchronised firing hadn't yet been invented.

Morane Saulnier Type N n° 399, no doubt from MS 12, the main escadrille using this monoplane.

Morane Saulnier Type N, from Escadrille MS 12. Autumn 1915.
Pilot: Adjudant Jean Navarre.
Obtaining his pilot's licence in September 1914, the second of the Navarre twins was a pilot in Escadrille MS12 from February 1915 to the end of January 1916. He was awarded the Military Medal on 6 April 1915, a few days after shooting down his first enemy plane.

Morane Saulnier Type N from Escadrille MS 31. Pilot: Jean Chaput.
Built in small numbers and used by the French for a short time only, the MS Type N never equipped a whole escadrille, some units like MS 31 being equipped at the same time with other models (the Type H or L, for instance).

Morane Saulnier Type N from Escadrille MS 12 in 1915. Pilot: Jean Navarre. Red became this ace's distinctive mark, with the last planes he used during the war being painted all red.

during the First World War

Un des avions allemands, venus pour jeter des bombes sur Nancy, exposé dans cette ville après avoir été abattu dans la région de Nomeny.

(squadron) Breguet-Michelin (BM), in three thirty-plane sections, commanded by the Lieutenant de Vaisseau Dutertre. The first crews assembled at Avord to take on charge the new machines which were arriving in dribs and drabs. The squadron was supposed to be accompanied by a park train, a new maintenance unit and supplies. The first division under Capitaine Yence was the only one to be really set up; it was increased from three ten-plane escadrilles to four and then five escadrilles. The park, on a special train, was commanded by Capitaine Maillols. On 20 September, the squadron left Avord to move to the Champagne area with the escadrilles at half strength. The first engagement, involving two planes, took place on 30 September, but the Renault engines were often disappointing. The Escadre reached Lorraine on 1 December then became GB 5.

Administrative reorganisation

Decisions had to be taken about the various difficulties encountered supplying the front with the necessary materiel. The Aviation Directorate (Direction de l'Aeronautique) lost its decisional power to a political set-up, the Under-Secretariat of Aviation, appointed in September, then the Service Industriel de l'Aéronautique (Industrial Aviation Service) was created to ensure there was liaison between the various economic forecasting services and the Service des Fabrications specialising in mass-production. The Section Technique de l'Aéronautique (STAé) became especially important because it was given the task of checking the construction quality and of looking in particular for the most effective aircraft, whose production depended on its conclusions. This organisation was all the more important and necessary because GHQ wanted a strength of 100 combat escadrilles, to be reached by the end of the year. The programmes were specific: observation and spotting, fighters, reconnaissance, and bombers, for which specialist crews were trained for their capabilities.

Each specialisation meant determining the size, the range, the speed, bomb load and powerplants for each plane. The pilots themselves added to the list ease of handling and easy access to the aircraft, which had to be reliable. The technical department concentrated more especially on the engines whose power had to be increased whilst taking into account the increased fuel consumption and ensuring they were increasingly reliable. The rotary engine was replaced by a liquid-cooled inline or V-engine, but the engine makers

TRAINING WITH THREE ENGINES

On 1 September 1915, the pilot perfection school at Ambérieu-en-Bugey had to get hold of volunteers to make up an escadrille equipped with Capronis which were being built in the REP factories in Lyon. The first ones off the production line were handed over to Pilot-in-Chief Molla, who had the task of training the crews. As these three-engined planes (two 80-hp tractor engines and one 130 hp pusher engine) came off the assembly lines very slowly – fourteen in 1915, forty-one in 1916 and six in 1917, this training took a lot of time for a very insignificant result.

THE BOMBING OF NANCY

The target of a long-range canon was Nancy; it regularly shot off deadly shells. GB 2 escorted by Nieuports was given the task of identifying this monster and destroying it. It was discovered at Hampont, near Château Salins and immediately silenced. 24 machines from GB 1 protected by two fighter escadrilles carried out this operation on 21 January 1916 a short while before the Battle of Verdun, for the loss of one machine shot down by AA fire. Two Gothas flew over as a reprisal, and in return it was decided to pour a hail of fire onto the stations at Metz and Montigny.

ran into enormous difficulties trying to lighten their engines. Renault, Lorraine-Dietrich and Salmson were asked to find a solution or solutions. Furthermore old contracts between engine-makers and aircraft builders, like Renault with Farman, were one of the reasons why inefficient or uninteresting machines continued to be built.

The creation of bomber units in particular perpetuated the use of the Voisin, whose only improvement over the months was increased engine power. Another example was the Breguet-Michelin, which was produced against the will of the STAé and which was very late reaching the front. Other examples have been described in the descriptions below.

A final measure oiled the wheels in order to make the industrialists' lives easier: advances were subjected to a series of rules and regulations enabling them to be increased before the final delivery of the completed machines.

Back on the offensive

In September Joffre went back on the offensive in the Vimy region (Aisne), preceded by twelve special operations intended to sabotage the railways and to prevent the enemy re-supplying itself. But the infantry assault ran into very strong German resistance, even though the French did use combat gas on the 25th. The bombardment rained down on the lines supplying the German front, north of Arras. On the 23rd thirteen planes attacked Cambrai station and on 30 September, nineteen planes from GB 3 bombed Douai station, ten of them returning slightly damaged by the artillery.

An operation regrouping GB 1, 2 and 4 on 2 October, in all 62 machines, including the Nieuport escort, went to bomb Vouziers, an important HQ. They lost one GB 1 crew, shot down by a Fokker; GB 4 lost two machines. On 16 October during a bombing mission over Champagne, V 110 lost the crew made up of Sergeant Cadet and Corporal Vibert who were both killed.

When the French offensive resumed on 1 November, it was a failure and the positions remained the same, the results for Pétain's 2nd Army and Langle de Cary's 4th Army both engaged in this aimless fighting being the loss of 130 000 men against 25 000 German prisoners, 150 cannon taken and insignificant territorial gains. On 18 November GB 1 succeeded in intercepting a sortie made by 21 German bombers against Nancy and chasing them. It was the last daytime operation carried out by the Voisins. Meanwhile GB 2 slowly became a night bombing group and took over the pilots from GB 4 which had been disbanded. In December, this GB 2 had an escadrille of Nieuports, N 65 under Nungesser, which was attached to it to protect it. Escadrille C 66 flying Caudron G.4s was assigned to GB 1.

THE LOSS OF A PIONEER

Marie Marvingt remembers: "It was 6 September. With Nungesser, who shot down his first plane on 28 November, I used to give swimming lessons to airmen in case they came down in the sea. Suddenly Nungesser swam towards me and said: "Féquant has been shot down". Capitaine Albert Féquant, a good pilot and a comrade, had given the future President of the Republic, Albert Lebrun, his first ever flight. We rushed to the Plateau to learn the tragic news. He'd gone off as an observer to Sarrebrück in a V 102 plane flown by Niox, the son of the Governor of the Invalides. Standing in front of the pilot, Féquant tipped over the side of the fuselage, hit by a machine gun burst. Niox grabbed his leg and, still in this position, headed hell for leather to the airfield only to discover that he had brought back just a corpse."

The year 1916

Great offensives were made on both sides on the Western Front in the hope of ending it all, because the war of attrition had been going on now since 1915 and there seemed to be no opportunity to end it. These huge blows were struck in order to break down the defences and force the other side to come to a negotiated peace.

As far as the French air force was concerned, Parliament had just authorised a plan for 1 400 operational planes, 300 of which were fighters and more than 300 bombers. They were assembled in 150 combat escadrilles of which 31 were for bombers, 45 for the Army corps and 54 artillery sections. This was slightly more than the programme Barès proposed the previous November but a long way off what people at the front wanted.

The new materiel was being distributed to the escadrilles.

- The observation units gradually had two seat Caudron G.4s, light two-engined escort planes and the single-engined two-seat Farman 40 at their disposal. The escadrilles already had a small number of Morane-Saulniers and Nieuports armed with machine guns to ensure close quarters protection during operations. The observation units had the greatest numbers of planes, some four fifths of the total fleet, or more than 800 planes of which 271 MF 11s, replaced by Farman 40s. Fortunately, the better-armed two-engined, three-seat Caudron R.4 reached the frontline on 15 June 1916, after Capitaine Vuillemin and Moulines his mechanic from C 11 had tested it at le Plessis-Belleville between 16 and 26 May.

- The fighter units replaced their Nieuport 10s with a little marvel, the Nieuport "Bébé", and the Morane Saulnier which could fly faster than 100 mph at 6 500 feet with a good rate of climb.

The Champagne offensive in September-October 1915 showed the importance of obtaining and keeping air superiority over the lines and of being able to accompany observation planes and bombers to protect them, hence the new missions given over to the fighter units. The planes were given sectors in order to make the most of the planes' ranges. However in the end Commandant Barès' had three choices: avoid all specialisation and let the planes' defensive armament do the work, or have the fighters protect the observation planes or, finally, organise large formations of planes as for the bombing, whose job was to clear the sky. The last option was chosen at the Battle of Verdun

- Bombing was divided into two sections: on the one hand the planes covering the battlefield and operating against railway lines and the front line, and on the other, strategic bombing. On this last point, Barès did not have any long-range multi-engined bombers at his disposal in spite of all the prototypes presented by the builders. This was because there wasn't a reliable engine rated at more than 150 hp. The available fleet was made up of only the single-engined Breguet-Michelins and Voisins which were the most numerous. The only three-engined plane built under licence, the Caproni-REP did not live up to expectations. The standard projectile (the 90- or 155-mm shell) was being replaced by the Gros-Andreau bomb fitted with directional winglets available in three calibres: 22 lb of which 13 were explosive, 55 lb and 110 lb, and 22 lb incendiary bombs. Special sights were also developed for the Breguet-Michelins. As of 1 February, the bomber units went over to the army groups who were asked to provide them with a bombing schedule.

The enemy had put a single-engined Fokker fighter into the line which became a serious threat to daytime bombing. This threat was warded off six months later, but the enemy's great superiority was due to its building powerful and reliable engines. Besides, their machines were used following procedures which were better than those used in France in that they favoured group rather than individual action. On 10 January 1916, a group of Voisin-Canons was attacked by Fokker monoplanes near Dixmude. The Voisin flown by the crew François Padieu (pilot) and François Fahler (gunner) shot down one.

Winter reduced the possibilities of large-scale ground offensives but did offer periods during which aircraft could operate. Thus Paris was bombed during the night of 29-30 January by Hauptmann Viktor Gaissert's Zeppelin LZ 79 which dropped forty eight 132-lb and 220-lb spherical bombs and 16 incendiary cordons killing 23 people and wounding 31. LZ 77 was part of the mission but had to give up because of an engine breakdown. The fighter protection intervened and fired 300 rounds without result. LZ 79 was hit by fire from a group of 26 planes among which was Farman N° 1187 belonging to Sergeant Denneboude, carrying Gunner-Corporal Louis Vallin, and the Voisin 130 hp belonging to Sous-Lieutenant Jacques de Lesseps and observer-gunner Lieutenant Galliot. The Voisin succeeded in approaching and shooting at the monster which accelerated and climbed gradually. Above Rouen, the Voisin turned back and the LZ continued on its way, heading north and leaking gas. It collapsed on the roof of a farm at Mainvault, near Ath (Belgium).

Verdun

From mid-January French observation planes found it very difficult to get near the enemy lines since fighter activity and AA fire had made flying there hazardous. These missions had to be carried out by two planes, one of them a G-4 watching the sky and protecting the other, a G-3. On 24 January then on 17 and 20 February, photos showed that new battery emplacements or earth-moving work had been carried out, leaving tracks in the snow. On 20 February C 11, taking advantage of the weather clearing up, was able to photograph the whole line of Saint-Mihiel batteries at Montmédy, information which was at once transmitted to GHQ with a request for reinforcements. On 5 February Sergeant Guynemer fought his fifteenth dogfight against an enemy aircraft in the Frise sector and shot it down between Asseville and Herbecourt. He thus obtained his fifth kill, after those won on 5, 8, 11 and 14 December 1915.

On 7 February 28 pilots were listed on the aces' (five or more kills) roll of honour including those who had disappeared like Maxime Lenoir (11 kills), Hughes de Rochefort (eight), André Delorme (five), Joannès Sauvage (seven) and the gunners Jean Loste (six), Léon Vitalis (five) and Martin (five).

On 21 February the sky around Verdun was ablaze. The moving 1 200-cannon artillery barrage preceded the German attack developing on two fronts, from the 21st onwards along the right bank of the Meuse, and after 6 March along the left bank. Both these merged on 9 April and continued until the middle of the summer. Nearly 270 German planes had been assembled along the Meuse including forty or so single-seat fighters, 96 reconnaissance planes and 144 other machines, all grouped into four combat units, facing 70 French planes. As all the heavy French guns had been removed from the forts to supply the battle in Artois and Champagne, the defence rested almost solely on the infantry and their light weapons, buried in a discontinuous system of trenches. The German cannon poured hellish fire onto the front line before hordes of troops rushed to attack the fortified sector of Verdun forming a salient. On 25 February a German unit managed to get into the Fort at Douaumont. On 21 March the infantry introduced a new weapon, the "Flammenwerfer" (flame-throwers) in the Avocourt-Malancourt sector, near Varenne-en-Argonne.

More than a hundred and fifty German aircraft were engaged on a narrow front and from the very first day had complete control of the air space. The aircraft whose job it was to defend Verdun started assembling when the attack started. They comprised two fighter escadrilles (N 23 and N 67), four from the army corps (MF 63, MF 72 C 11 and C 18) of which only two were present on 20 February. From morning to evening, groups of ten aircraft with "black crosses" flew over the battlefield and took on the French "Meufeus" (MFs) and observation balloons. In just Escadrille C 11, the plane belonging to Lieutenant Barthe was attacked by an LVG and returned to the airfield with his observer, Lieutenant Picard killed by a bullet straight through the heart. The G-3 belonging to Sergent-Chef Maillet was shot down by AA fire during a fight against some Fokkers near Douaumont, with Capitaine de Beauchêne, the observer, seriously wounded. Within a few days, the French air force was in a desperate situation and N 67's Navarre, although the first official double ace, could not solve the problem all by himself. He was already flying ten hours a day with his tricolour-fuselaged (so he could be recognised from far off) Bébé.

On the 28th Pétain was promoted to command the 2nd Army defending Verdun; he called in Commandant Tricornot de Rose from MS 12 of whose qualities he was aware. The order Tricornot was given was simple: "Just clear the skies for me!" Together with the pilots from MS 12 who had changed to Nieuport XIs, all of whom were volunteers under the command of Capitaine de Bernis including Navarre, Pelletier Doisy and Boyau, de Rose gathered together all the available Moranes and the Nieuports, together with the best pilots, those from MS 3 including Brocard, Heurtaux, Chaput, Boillot, Chainat, Nungesser, Deulin, Lenoir or Flachaire to make up a first fighter group with a simple instruction: one flight = one kill.

In record time, five escadrilles, N 15, 37, 57, 65 and 69 were assembled near Bar-le-Duc and spread out over summarily prepared airfields.

Out of the 200 pilots called to Verdun at the beginning of the battle, 70 had been killed by the end of the first month. Among the greatest three, Navarre and Chaput were wounded and quickly but briefly out of action, Boillot was shot down on 19 May. Individual sorties often turned out to be very dangerous so that little by little sorties were carried out in pairs, one theoretically ensuring the protection of the other.

From March onwards the daily GHQ communiqué started mentioning the dogfights more and more frequently, saying where the enemy pilots had been shot down (on 30 March, five planes over Verdun, on 2 April, six planes, etc.), also mentioning how the English air force (4 April) or AA fire (2 April) contributed and mentioning balloons for the first time on 2 April. On 4 March in the morning over Verdun Sergeant Guynemer was wounded twice in the arm by bullets and in his face by splinters from his windscreen after attacking four planes.

Above.
The end of a Caudron, after a ground loop.

Below.
21 May 1916. Some German soldiers pose in front of a Caudron G.4 from C 43, forced to land near Noyon after being chased by enemy planes. The pilot, Sergent Olivier Schneider was captured but his observer, Sous-Lieutenant Félix-André Danne, killed most likely by ground fire.

Right.
A Nieuport Type XI, known more by its nickname "Bébé".

WHY THE NAME "BÉBÉ"?

At the time of the first standardisation, when designating its spare parts, the Type XI was given the designation "B = XI", indicating that this was a biplane. The 1916 aircraft building programme introduced a new category, the single-seaters called "light combat aircraft type B", and the builder's response was exactly like the type "B = XI" which thus became "BB = XI" hence the phonetic use of the word "Bébé". Another explanation could be that this little 140 ft² fighter was a homothetic reduction of the previous plane with a wing surface of 194 ft², making it its "Bébé" (baby).

During this battle Commandant de Rose managed to perfect his doctrine on how to use fighters. An all-out attack had to prevent the adversary from flying over the French sector and above all from attacking their lines. To get this result, pilots had to make massed attacks not individual ones.

Hence a standby system whereby, thanks to escadrille rotas, the sky was constantly occupied by an offensive patrol subjected to strict flight discipline, though this did not preclude individual exploits by solitary patrollers concealed high up in the clouds and attacking in the best conditions. This meant that the ultimate conclusion was that an autonomous fleet of combat planes had to be formed and be at GHQ's disposal to take on any offensive action GHQ wanted.

The pilots gave all they had, Jean Navarre in particular since he was called the "Verdun Sentinel". Adjudant Charles Nungesser, recently assigned to N 65 and still in hospital, hearing of the attack, fled to le Bourget on his crutches and succeeded in reaching his unit at Béhonne on 29 March. He flew the next day and obtained his third kill on 2 April against a Drachen at Sesparges, followed by four others in April (two on the 4th and one on both the 25th and 27th). As a result of the intensity of the fighting GHQ decided to publish the names of any pilots who had shot down five or more enemy planes in its daily communiqués.

As usual there were always problems and the Head of the Aeronautical office in Verdun decided to disband the group of planes at Bar-le-Duc on 17 March and to share out the escadrilles between the various air sectors. As the remedy was worse than the illness, the combat group was reformed on 21 March under the command of Capitaine Le Révérend. The German pilots were then only able to operate in pairs and refused as often as possible to give battle. On 30 March a Farman 40 from MF 44 piloted by Adjudant

Opposite.
Nieuports from Escadrille N 12 at Lemmes airfield (Verdun area), in June 1916.

during the First World War

Nieuport 11 « Bébé »

Nieuport 11 from Escadrille N 48 in 1916.
Pilot: Lieutenant Armand Galliot de Turenne. A descendant of the famous Maréchal de France, this ace scored fifteen kills and joined N 48 in June 1916 a few months after obtaining his pilot's licence. He used several Ni 11s including this one, decorated with a tricolour pennant on three sides of the fuselage.

Nieuport 11 n°1313 from Escadrille Br 11 in 1916.
This plane was the only machine of its type in this escadrille, equipped at the time with Caudron G.3s and G.5s. This was the personal mount of Capitaine Joseph Vuillemin, an ace with seven kills during the Great War, who was the Armée de l'Air's Commander-in-Chief in 1939-40.

Nieuport 11 n°557 from Escadrille N 12.
According to a common practice in this unit, the pilot's personal insignia was painted on the fuselage behind the escadrille's pennant.

Nieuport 11 n° 1135 from Escadrille N 26.
Flown by Capitaine Jean de Sieyes de Veynes, this machine landed behind enemy lines on 3 July 1916 after shooting down a Drachen and was captured by the Germans. The hand holding a torch was one of the escadrille's insignias used by the Nieuport 11s and 16s from Spring 1916 onwards, the motif being black and red on the aluminium-coloured planes and white on the camouflaged ones.

Nieuport 11 n°576 from Escadrille N 67 during the winter of 1915-16. Pilot: Sergent Jean Navarre.
This ace with 12 confirmed kills (plus 9 probables) served in N 67 from 24 February to 17 June 1916 and used this fighter, proudly sporting the national colours.

Nieuport 11 from Escadrille N 67.
The brown and orange ("nègre" and "tango") on the pennant were from the racing stables belonging to the unit CO, Capitaine de St-Sauveur, at the time it was created, at the beginning of 1916. The original bird of prey was replaced by a stork when Escadrille 67 was attached to Combat Group 12.

38

French aviation

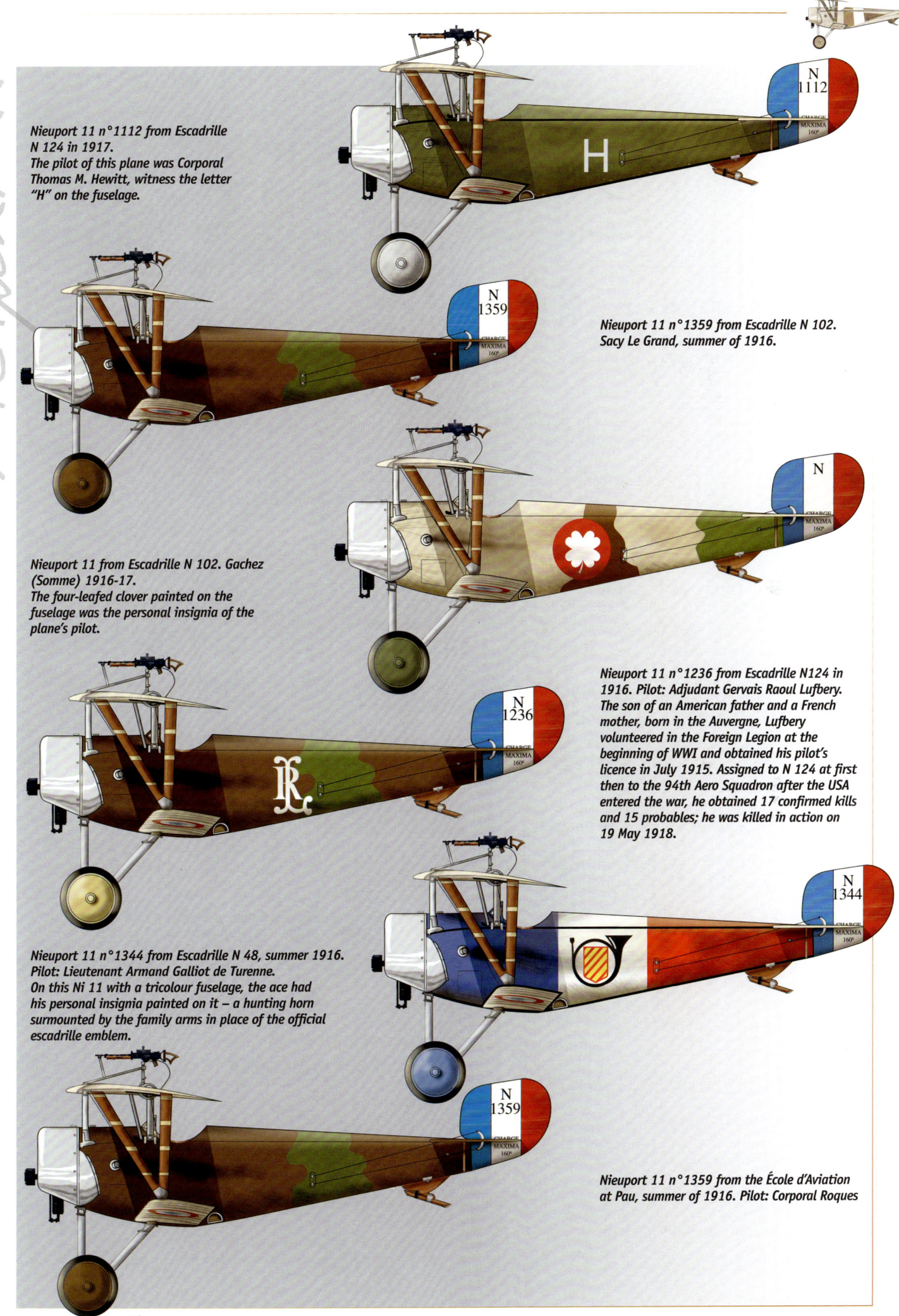

Nieuport 11

Nieuport 11 n°1112 from Escadrille N 124 in 1917. The pilot of this plane was Corporal Thomas M. Hewitt, witness the letter "H" on the fuselage.

Nieuport 11 n°1359 from Escadrille N 102. Sacy Le Grand, summer of 1916.

Nieuport 11 from Escadrille N 102. Gachez (Somme) 1916-17. The four-leafed clover painted on the fuselage was the personal insignia of the plane's pilot.

Nieuport 11 n°1236 from Escadrille N124 in 1916. Pilot: Adjudant Gervais Raoul Lufbery. The son of an American father and a French mother, born in the Auvergne, Lufbery volunteered in the Foreign Legion at the beginning of WWI and obtained his pilot's licence in July 1915. Assigned to N 124 at first then to the 94th Aero Squadron after the USA entered the war, he obtained 17 confirmed kills and 15 probables; he was killed in action on 19 May 1918.

Nieuport 11 n°1344 from Escadrille N 48, summer 1916. Pilot: Lieutenant Armand Galliot de Turenne. On this Ni 11 with a tricolour fuselage, the ace had his personal insignia painted on it – a hunting horn surmounted by the family arms in place of the official escadrille emblem.

Nieuport 11 n°1359 from the École d'Aviation at Pau, summer of 1916. Pilot: Corporal Roques

during the First World War

39

Opposite.
Pelletier d'Oisy from the N12 at Verdun in June 1916.

Below.
L'adjudant Gaston Guignand de la N 67 à bord de son Nieuport. (DR)

Below, right.
Jean Navarre, nicknamed 'The Sentinel of Verdun', was seriously injured in an air combat on 17 June, 1916 and never return to the front afterwards.

Chanaron, assisted by Sergeant Hypolite were protecting another F-40 on a photo mission over Montsec at Pannes (Meurther-et-Moselle) when they were attacked by a Fokker. The protection F-40 was hit by five bullets but both of them got back to their base at Toul.

The artillery spotters could carry on with their missions without too much difficulty, most of which came from the ground. To get rid of the Drachens, the Nieuports were equipped with eight rocket launchers thought up by Lieutenant de Vaisseau le Prieur, who had four of them fitted on either side on the inter-plane struts; they were triggered electrically. On 22 May, very early in the morning eight Nieuports including those of Nungesser and Chaput, shot down eight Drachens in only a few minutes using their incendiary rockets between Etain and Sevry-sur-Meuse. In May, the problem of synchronised firing was solved by using the Vickers machine gun on a Nieuport XII powered by a 110-hp engined entrusted to Lieutenant Chaput. He was delighted with it, but the system was not put into common practice until 1917. On 15 June, the communiqué published the names of several aviators who had broken the rule about remaining discreet. It was Capitaine Happe, who had made a successful bombing mission, followed by five fighter pilots according to the number of kills in decreasing order down from 12 to five: Navarre, Guynemer, Nungesser, Chaput and Chainat.

On the ground the German advance carried on slowly. Vaux Fort capitulated on 7 June and Souville Fort came under a very heavy gas attack on 20 June. Two days later Nungesser obtained two more kills of which only one was confirmed but because he was wounded again in the fight he returned to hospital.

On the other hand, air observers had detected the excavation work for setting up German batteries around

HOW TO LEARN ON THE JOB

Maurice Nogués from Escadrille VB 107 suggested to his observer, Lieutenant Le Barazec, that he become a pilot. He gave him a few lessons on an old machine with twin controls, then on their unit's plane and then taught him how to turn. One of them would slip between the seat and the fuselage to let the other pass. He made him do several landings then let him go off by himself. All he had to do afterwards was obtain his licence; this was all the harder to obtain because the group CO, Commandant Faure, wanted to hang on to his most experienced observers. Nogués had him take the tests – the two triangles and the hour flying at 6 500 feet in a straight line – on the quiet. When Le Barazec decided to obtain his homologation he had to hand over the results to the CO who took them coolly but eventually granted him his licence on 31 May 1916, with the number 2 484.

Opposite.
Marcel Brindejonc des Moulinais was known internationally before the war as a record man. He quickly became an officer in the Aéronautique Militaire, and specialised in "special missions", behind enemy lines; he perished tragically near Verdun on 8 August 1916, shot down by two French Nieuports who mistook his camouflaged Nieuport for an enemy plane…

Opposite.
Brindejonc des Moulinais near his machine before going off on a mission in 1914. On the ground, the five bombs to be loaded into the plane and the musketoon carried for its own defence.

Below.
Lighting with searchlights for the night landing of a Farman

during the First World War

Opposite.
The Zeppelin LZ-66 in flight.

A PILOT SHOOTS DOWN A ZEPPELIN

Lieutenant Maurice Mandinaud was probably the only French pilot to have a night-time escapade running into a Zeppelin, LZ 97, on 26 April 1916 off the Belgian coast, and shooting it down to the east of Bruges after attacking it seventeen times with his Maurice Farman, with Lieutenant Deramond as gunner. Having pursued it for such a long time he was forced to land his damaged plane in Holland. He returned to France in the autumn of 1916, as a Capitaine he himself was then shot down on 10 March 1917 over Belfort during a dogfight with two enemy fighters. He fell in no man's land and his plane was machine gunned by his victors.

A CAMOUFLAGE OPERATION

The Château of Frétoy (Oise) was used during the summer of 1916 as a residence and HQ for Prince Eitel-Frederick, commanding the 1st Division of the Guard. Because of its large moat and the avenue leading to it, it was easy to make out from the air and was a target for the French night bomber force. To prevent this, the moat was covered with wire netting on which fir tree branches were placed. At dusk, other branches were laid out on the avenue. The pilots often returned but were unable to find this important target.

Above.
The remains of Zeppelin LZ-77 shot down at Revigny-sur-Ornain (near Verdun, in the Meuse), on 21 February 1916, by French armoured cars.

French aviation

THE ESCADRILLES AT THE PARIS CRP (CAMP RETRANCHÉ DE PARIS)

Abow.
Main entrance of Le Bourget airfield (here in 1922), one of the bases used by the CRP during World War One.

At Saint-Cyr, Capitaine Désiré Lucca, second in command of Escadrille MF 16 based in the Argonne, was ordered to assemble units urgently on 29 August 1914 in order to form an escadrille for the Army of Paris. Using Maurice Farmans, they went to the airfield at Issy-les-Moulineaux where they joined another escadrille flying the same type of machine commanded by Capitaine Bordage. After the Battle of the Marne, the air units in the entrenched camp were disbanded. On 24 September General Galliéni decided to make up a unit to protect Paris in the air whose initial job was finding themselves an aerodrome. Capitaine Lucca with his Farman powered by a de Dion Bouton engine flew around on 9 October 1914 and came across some land near le Bourget where he landed to requisition it.

They practised night flying there because intercepting Zeppelins was daily business. From March 1915 onwards, permanent escadrilles replaced the temporary 1914 ones, numbered at first 93 to 97 then finally 461 to 469. 461, 462 and 463 used Nieuport 11s then Spad fighters, then other planes from the G-3 and the Voisin to the Breguet XIIs, Letords and Dorands because their job also included testing various new aircraft, projectiles and marking systems. They scored in all six kills, one went to 464, including a Drachen.
This group of escadrilles was disbanded on 12 September 1918, with the different combat groups taking charge of defending the capital, depending on the circumstances.

Verdun: they contrasted too much with the snow-covered ground. Likewise reconnaissance carried out on 6, 7 and 20 February detected large troop movements and intense activity on the railways lines in the Meuse region.

Bombers also took part, even though the only unit on the spot was MF 25, based at Vadelaincourt. It was quickly reinforced by GB 5 and elements from GB 2, C 66, V 110 and V 101, which attacked the communication lines along the Meuse valley. On 14 March, five Breguet-Michelins from GB 5 escorted by a BM fighter and fifteen Nieuports or G-4s dropped 100 bombs on Brieulles station. On the 18th elements of GB 2 again attacked Brieulles Station then the one at Dun-sur-Meuse. In April, two new Farman escadrilles (MF 43s and 44s) took part in the night bombing. In May, MF 63, 218 and 14, the reinforcements were in place. Night-time raids carried out by selected crews attacked targets which were further away like for instance the one during the night of 20-21 May led by Capitaine Laurens, the VB 101 CO, against the marshalling yards at Lumes (Ardennes) to the south of Mézières which caused a huge fire.

On 1 June, five machines from MF 5 escorted by some Nieuports from N 31 succeeded in dropping 28

PLANE ARMAMENT

At the beginning the only weapon carried aboard a plane was an ordnance revolver or a carbine so the crew could set fire to the plane if they made a forced landing. Individual initiative led to using the weapon to stop the enemy from getting information about friendly positions. The machine gun appeared in 1914 and it was up to the observer how he was to use it and installing the guns meant no doubt some decisions that were difficult to take.

The weapon could be fitted on the front spar of the upper wing surface on a two-seater where the observer was in front and could therefore fire rearwards; or on the rear spar to fire forwards. Voisin also built a mounting to enable the observer in front to fire above the head of the pilot. These d.i.y. jobs led to the study of a mounting enabling the gunner to fire in all directions, hence the tripod on which one of the legs could be lengthened or shortened, a solution the Farman observation planes incorporated. A 37-mm canon installed in front of the observer in the front seat was also fitted to the Voisin bombers (the "Voisin-Canon") or the protection three-seaters.

For the single-seaters, the weapon with a drum containing at least 50 rounds was placed on the upper surface and operated by the pilot standing then by a bungee cord, the weapon being tilted for reloading or un-jamming. Roland Garros put forward the idea of having the plane considered as the mounting for a gun firing through the propeller arc, by protecting the blades with steel – an armoured deflector, ejecting the bullet away from the foot of the blade. This armoured propeller was the work of Garros together with Mr Panhard and Mr Chauvière. On 1 April his Morane-Saulnier was equipped in this way but a breakdown forcing him to land behind enemy lines interrupted a series of three kills. His plane did not burn entirely and provided the Germans with the solution they were looking for; they were able to perfect the idea and to put it into operation in the form of the Fokker E.III. The fleet of pusher-engined observer planes (offering the observers a grandstand view) was devastated by this plane during the six months that it took to find the effective remedy: replacing pusher engines by tractor engines, putting the observer at the rear on two-seaters and adopting a synchronising system firing through the propeller arc.

Synchronised firing was adopted in France in 1916 although General Bernard had rejected Raymond Saulnier's 5 May 1914 proposal for the same type of system, which freed the pilot from all the acrobatics needed for rearming the weapon fitted on the upper wing surface. Besides at the beginning of the war, there was only one type of machine gun in France, mounted on a Farman with a rear pusher engine. Capitaine Mailfert and Sergeant Darbos tried one out at Mourmelon and using this Hotchkiss machine gun encouraged them to prefer the British Lewis gun, or others.

The armament consisting of two machine guns shooting along the centerline appeared in France 1917, complemented by a 37-mm canon shooting through the propeller boss at the Guynemer's request. Le Prieuré rockets were also installed on the braces of the Nieuport biplanes so they could attack balloons, but these missiles' rather erratic trajectory precluded any accuracy except when fired at almost point blank range, often to the detriment of the plane firing them. Later this armament increased regularly, either by doubling the synchronised machine guns, or by multiplying the machine gun positions in the case of the multi-engined protection aircraft.

Above.
Lewis machine gun installed on the upper wing of a Nieuport 11.

Above.
7,65 mm Colt machine gun 1895 model mounted on a Maurice Farman MF 11. This weapon, designed by the famous John Browning, was fed by 250-round canvas belts.

Opposite.
Twin Lewis machine-gun used by the observer in a Breguet XIV.

1914-15... La Pluie de Fléchettes : Servants d'une batterie allemande décimés par nos avions

1914-15 A Shower of arrows. Gunners of a German battery decimated by our aeros

MISSILES ON BOARD

As Capitaine Féquant wrote: "We thought of throwing projectiles during a reconnaissance mission, if we were flying over an important or vulnerable target." At the beginning the stocks coming from the peace-making operations in Morocco were used: Aasen bombs – 3 in x 2 ½ in white metal cylinders containing lead pellets stuck inside a melinite mixture, fitted with a parachute to prevent them from digging themselves into the ground without exploding. Boxes of 500 little Bon steel darts were also carried, attached to the fuselage sides or to its bottom where a cover could be removed prior to launching. Then there were 90-mm tail-less shells, transported loose in the cabin or on the observer's knees, and thrown overboard after priming.

Thus, from the beginning of 1915, the Voisin de Bombardement (the Voisin bomber) carried a typical load of twelve 90-mm shells which had been "wafered" to obtain a maximum of shrapnel. They were housed in bomb launchers on fittings improvised by the mechanics and held in place by string which they just cut to launch them (Capitaine Césari put in for a patent for an installation of this type made up by his mechanic Vaubourgeix). Under the cabin a cradle held a 120-mm, then 150-mm then 220-mm shell, shaped and fixed by wire, which had only to be pulled for it to drop. The detonator was screwed into the tip at the very last moment. In October 1914, the first Claude bombs made up of liquid oxygen and pulverulent coal were put at the disposal of the crews but when they remarked on how complicated they were to use, the bombs disappeared quickly. Subsequently a systematic study of bomb characteristics led to finned 150-mm and 220-mm shells and the designing of sights based on the Michelin brothers' experiments.

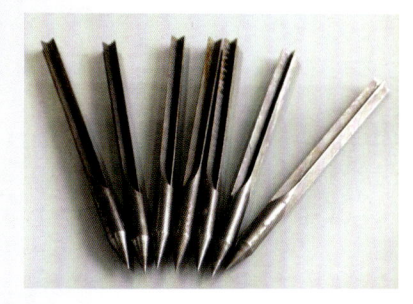

Top and above.
Types of dart bombs dropped by plane and the damage they caused the enemy, after an illustrated period postcard.

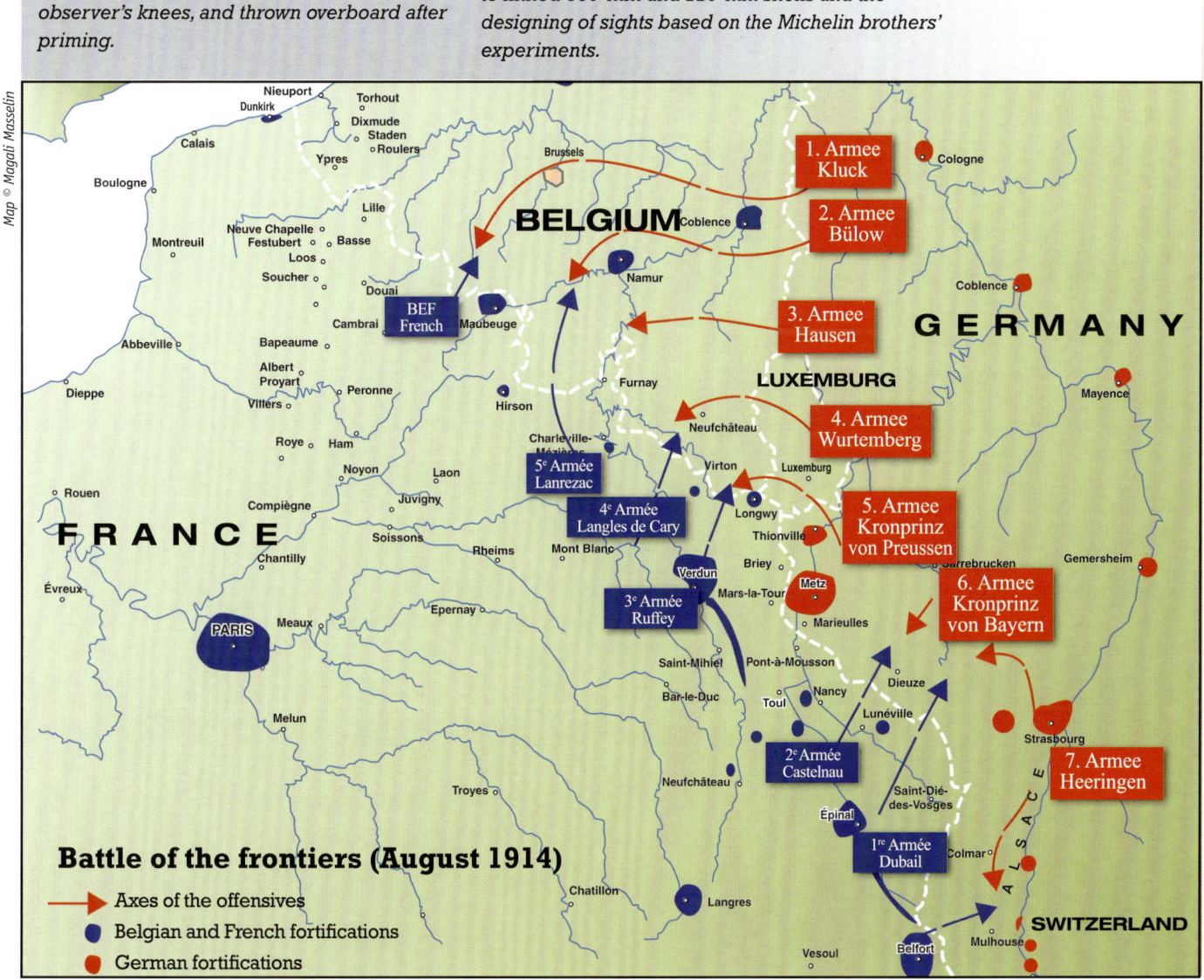

Battle of the frontiers (August 1914)

→ Axes of the offensives
● Belgian and French fortifications
● German fortifications

during the First World War

PILOT TRAINING

Above.
A Blériot XI and student pilots in a hangar of the military centre of Avord.

The civilian pilot's licence issued by the Aéroclub de France existed since 1 January 1910; the military licence comprising more comprehensive tests appeared in 1912 (out of the 52 military licences before 1912, about thirty pilots held this new licence). The first five licensed were the horse riders Jean-Baptiste Tricornot de Rose and Marie de Malherbe, the gunner George Bellenger, the sapper Victor Ménard and the sailor Jean-Louis Conneau, aka André de Beaumont. After war was declared, 657 military pilots had been trained though some of them fell quickly because of their inexperience or their temerity. Acrobatics were not being taught when Pégoud discovered the roll in 1913. Here are a few examples of changes made in the training: Pierre Perrin de Brichambaut, a medical intern, decided to learn to fly during his holidays at Easter 1912. He turned up at Maurice Farman's and told him he had at least eight days. Six days later he left Buc with his licence (N° 861 dated 3 May 1912) in his pocket. During his military service he obtained his military licence (N° 324, dated 1 August 1913) and was assigned to MF 8 on 3 August 1914 where his status as a doctor was at odds with that of combatant. Guynemer's first kill was obtained on a two-seater in MS 3 on 9 July 1915 against an Aviatik piloted by Lieutenant Werner Johannes over the village of Septmonts, to the south of Soissons. In his logbook he noted he had flown 40 hours 35 minutes. Soldier Armand Viguier, engaged in the 10th Dragoons on 12 March 1913 asked at the beginning of 1915 to transfer into the Air Force as a pupil pilot. He was sent to the aircraft mechanics school at Dijon on 16 March 1915 and obtained his mechanics licence. He was then directed to the pilot preparation school still in Dijon for the theoretical lessons until 3 June. He was in Etampes on 6 June. At the time there were three divisions according to the type of plane:
- Farman where the boxer Georges Carpentier, the jockey René Dauval, the soldiers Gondre, Lafaille, Poréaux and the Sergeants Chemin and Lenfant were pupils.
- Morane with the students Guynemer, Barne, Sanglier and Lemaître.
- REP, which had two planes and where Viguier was assigned to and from where he was released on 9 June to obtain his civilian licence, after eight days' schooling and 1 ½ hours solo flying (licence N° 21234 dated 6 July). The Military licence dated 19 July was acquired when he totalled fourteen flying hours, 43 days after his request was accepted. On 12 June he was assigned to the Voisin specialisation school at Abérieu with his comrades Poréaux, Gondrer and Lafaille. From 1 to 15 August he attended classes and went to le Bourget while waiting to be assigned to an operational unit, which happened when he was sent to GB 3 with Bousquet and Bentejac on 14 September. He then joined VB 107 under Capitaine Glaize in which he served until July 1917 then transferred to the fighters.
Lieutenant Albert Roper of the 3rd Cavalry Division in 1914 was transferred to the 3rd Cyclist Group. His request to be transferred to the Air Force was accepted on 10 November 1916 and he went to Avord. He was handed over to the instructor Sénéchal and after theory and taxiing sessions, he was released for solo flight on 6 January 1917 with 46 circuits on dual control planes. He obtained his military licence on 27 January, or in 32 winter days, which earned him the right to be selected for the fighter units. Six weeks of improvement on Blériots, Moranes and Nieuports opened the way to the Air Acrobatics School at Pau. There was such a need for pilots that attending the Gunnery School at Cazaux was now out of the question. Instead three weeks at Pau where the bad weather limited the work to three half-days on the Nieuport Bébé and five minute flights on a 140-hp Spad, earned him a licence; three weeks in the Air Force general reserve at le Plessis-Belleville and then he was assigned to Escadrille N°68 where he arrived on 26 April 1917 (Roper was the inspired instigator of the Convention on Air Navigation Regulations of 13 October 1919 attached to the Peace Treaties).
Pupil Pilot Joseph Zacharie Heu, incorporated on 2 August 1912 and in action as early as August 1914, asked to be transferred to the Air Force in 1918. He was directed to the Dijon Preparation School on 11 March 1918. On 12 April he was a pupil pilot at Voives (in the Eure-et-Loir Department) from which he was released on 14 May after 3 h 32 min of dual control flying and 35 landings. He reached Vineuil (in the Indre Department) on 5 June to take the official tests between 3 and 5 July. Obtaining his licence on 6 July after 29 h 32 min of solo flight, he was sent to Avord for improvement; he then changed to Nieuports then went to Pau from 5 to 12 September then ended up at the Gunnery School at Biscarosse from 25 to 27 September. He converted to the Morane-Saulnier AI fighter from 30 September to 15 October then to Spads for the acrobatics school and group flying. When he joined his operational unit he had totalled 95 h 31 min flying time.

Below.
Loading of bombs in a Caudron G.4.

120-mm shells onto a German HQ in daytime at the Château of Saint-Benoit-en-Woëvre.

During the Battle of Verdun, the 3rd Staff Bureau published Note N° 14548 dated 21 May which contained the new organigram of the Army Aeronautics (Aéronautique à l'Armée) consecrating once and for all aviation as a force and Lieutenant-Colonel Barès as the Head of Aeronautics at GHQ. The commander of Army Aeronautics, General Galliéni, who was ill, was replaced as Minister of War on 16 March by General Roques.

Among the confusion of all the bits of news, often bad, coming one after another there were some rather noteworthy ones like Capitaine Brocard's decision to adopt a stork insignia (Cigogne) for his escadrille, N 3, then that of the Minister of War to award the Médaille Militaire on 20 April to Elliot Cowdin, the first American pilot to receive this distinction. The most surprising was the announcement of the operation carried out by Sous-Lieutenant Anselme Marchal on 20 June in an 80-hp Nieuport XVI single-seat biplane. Taking off from Nancy-Malzéville, he flew over Frankfurt, Gotha and Berlin successively early in the morning to drop 5 000 tracts as proof of his passing. He was forced to land out of petrol at Chelm, 62 miles from the Russian border, after flying 862 miles (breaking the record by almost 250 miles!). However the best announcement was that the synchronised firing problem had been solved in May thanks to the use of the Vickers, or Lewis, machine guns with a 97-round magazine with which the Nieuport 17 and other fighters going through their trials were going to be equipped.

On 4 May Mr Poincaré, the President of the Republic, visited the installations of the escadrille protecting the entrenched camp (CRP - Camp Retranché de Paris) at Paris and was presented to the pilot officers.

On 25 May, the Council of Ministers (the Cabinet), fed up with the German air raids on the French towns of Dunkirk, Épinal, Nancy, Lunéville, Belfort and others decided to lift the ban on bombing German towns, a decision taken in the vain hope of preventing Paris from being bombed. A punitive expedition commanded by Capitaine Adrien de Kérillis was therefore launched by C 66 against Karlsruhe as a reprisal for the German bombings of Bar-le-Duc and other towns in the east that had killed 32 people and wounded 77 others. Nine G-4s took off from Malzéville in daylight and dropped thirty-eight 120-mm Gros-Andreau anilite bombs on the target. On the homeward trip, C 66 ran into a pack of fighters and lost a third of its strength: the plane belonging to Maréchal-des-Logis-pilot Bousquet was shot down, two others were forced to land with their tanks holed, and the crews taken prisoner. This attack provoked considerable emotion in Germany; there was talk of 110 killed and 1 232 wounded among the civilian population and German planes stopped attacking French towns for six months. Moreover German GHQ forbade observation planes from dropping bombs during their operations.

The results of the ground operations at Verdun were very bad for the French troops. GHQ summed up the losses as at 25 May and since the beginning of February at Verdun: 600 officers and 22 743 soldiers killed; 1 944 officers and 73 000 men wounded; 1 000 officers and 53 000 men missing, of which some had been taken prisoner. At the end of the fighting the official French statistics revealed the loss of 221 000 killed and 216 000 wounded as against 270 000 Germans killed.

The air force lost a hundred or so crews of which 51 were killed or missing, especially for the period from 19 to 24 May when 25% of the strength engaged was put out of action. Among the killed there were Boilot (from N 65, on 19 May), Réservat (N 65, 22 May), Perretti (MS 3, 28 April) and Quillien (N 37, 3 April). To be added to those were Tricornot de Rose on 11 May at the controls of his Nieuport and the pioneer Marcel Brindejonc de Moulinais from MS 23 who disappeared in the sky on 18 May over Vadelaincourt while he was returning from a reconnaissance mission over the Verdun front. On the other hand, Navarre added 8 kills to his tally, like Nungesser and Chaput; Chainat five, Guynemer (wounded) and Jaillier four, Deullin, Lenoir, Pelletier-Doisy and Auger, three; Viuallet Dorme, Federoff, Bloch, Pulpe and Revol-Tissot two; Heurtaux, Cassalle, Ortoli, Royer-Massent, Flachaire, de Rochefort, Sayaret, Vitalis, Vuillemin, du Bois d'Aiche (gunner), Coudouret, Delorme, Gastin, de Gaillardde la Valdene, Guzerrier, Guiuet, Malaviale, Rodde, and Vuillemin one (from C 11, on 26 February) and no doubt many others who did not have the honour of being mentioned in the communiqué. The assaults were slackening off at Verdun because the British allies had just launched an attack on the Somme on 1 July where the French armies joined the British ones. The Germans rapidly moved up their reserves towards this new, more active front.

A LATVIAN AT THE FRONT

The aviator Edwards Pulpe was born in Riga, Latvia – then part of the Russian Empire. He obtained his pilot's licence N° 1571 on 19 December 1913 on Deperdussin and his military licence N° 602. He volunteered and was a Pilot-Sergeant in MS 23. In June 1916, with a score of four confirmed kills, as a Sous-Lieutenant he was member of the French Aviation Mission sent to the Russian Front. He was killed in action on 22 July 1916 after having shot down one of his five adversaries.

LIEUTENANT ANGOT'S ODYSSEY

In C 11, the crew consisting of Pilot-Lieutenant Ciccoli and Lieutenant-Observer Angot was attacked by a German plane on 3 July 1916. The two Frenchmen, wounded by enemy fire were forced to land behind enemy lines where they went to a POW camp after a stay in hospital. When he was better, Angot was interned at Wülzburg-bei-Weissenburg from which he tried to escape five times. On 3 September 1918 his efforts were at last successful and the following day he took the train at Nuremberg and reached Frankfurt in the night of 5-6 September. On the 7th, during the night, he crossed the Dutch border near Maastricht whence he reached England, then France. On 3 November 1918 he was back with his unit and then took part in the air raids carried out done by Escadre 12.

Caudron G.4

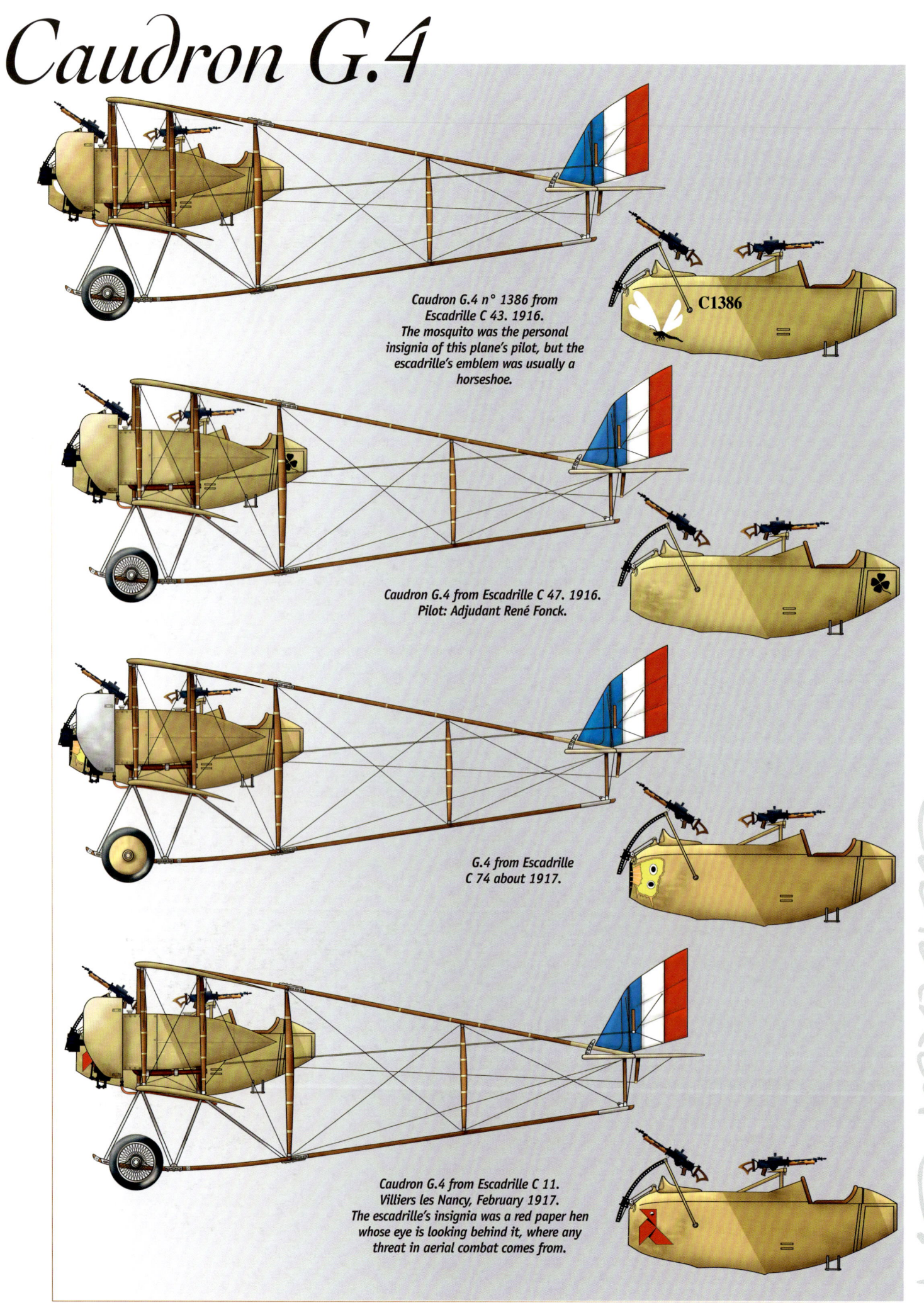

Caudron G.4 n° 1386 from Escadrille C 43. 1916.
The mosquito was the personal insignia of this plane's pilot, but the escadrille's emblem was usually a horseshoe.

Caudron G.4 from Escadrille C 47. 1916.
Pilot: Adjudant René Fonck.

G.4 from Escadrille C 74 about 1917.

Caudron G.4 from Escadrille C 11. Villiers les Nancy, February 1917.
The escadrille's insignia was a red paper hen whose eye is looking behind it, where any threat in aerial combat comes from.

French aviation

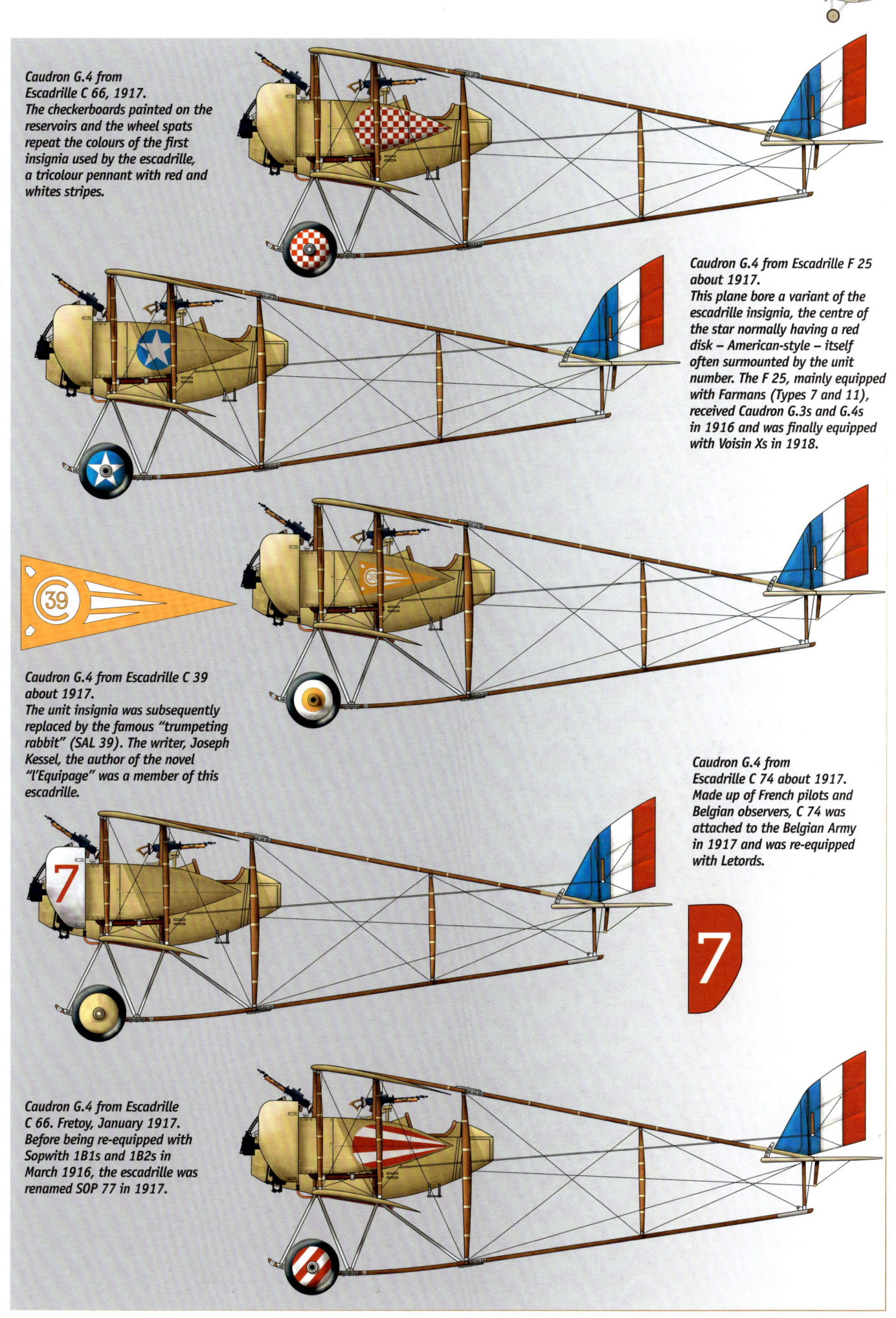

Caudron G.4 from Escadrille C 66, 1917.
The checkerboards painted on the reservoirs and the wheel spats repeat the colours of the first insignia used by the escadrille, a tricolour pennant with red and whites stripes.

Caudron G.4 from Escadrille F 25 about 1917.
This plane bore a variant of the escadrille insignia, the centre of the star normally having a red disk – American-style – itself often surmounted by the unit number. The F 25, mainly equipped with Farmans (Types 7 and 11), received Caudron G.3s and G.4s in 1916 and was finally equipped with Voisin Xs in 1918.

Caudron G.4 from Escadrille C 39 about 1917.
The unit insignia was subsequently replaced by the famous "trumpeting rabbit" (SAL 39). The writer, Joseph Kessel, the author of the novel "l'Equipage" was a member of this escadrille.

Caudron G.4 from Escadrille C 74 about 1917.
Made up of French pilots and Belgian observers, C 74 was attached to the Belgian Army in 1917 and was re-equipped with Letords.

Caudron G.4 from Escadrille C 66. Fretoy, January 1917.
Before being re-equipped with Sopwith 1B1s and 1B2s in March 1916, the escadrille was renamed SOP 77 in 1917.

during the First World War

Bleriot FRENCH AIRCRAFT

Védrines starts with his monoplan "The Cow"

The armoured Blériot XXXIX two-seater with a 160-hp Gnome engine was used by the fanciful Jules Védrine who called it "la Vache", much to the military authorities' displeasure.

The plane equipping the front line escadrilles at the beginning of the war came from the Blériot XI which had flown over the Channel. On 30 June 1912 the Army agreed to buy some Blériot XIs and on 1 September 25 single seaters were delivered to the Cavalry, and two-seaters to the Artillery. In all a hundred or so of these machines were used, including the planes which were built through Public Subscription and were given a name including N° 155, 156, 157, 158, 160, 161, 163, 165, 203, 206, 207, 208, 216 and 228; or even from private sources, like Garros' N° 108, l'Illustration's N° 124, the Lycée Condorcet's N°159, the City of Rouen's N° 175, Belfort's N° 177 and 178, the Department of l'Indre's N°217, or the Department of the Seine Inférieure's N° 231.

Type XI

The single-seat version used a 50-hp Gnome engine and the two-seat version used an 80-hp Gnome engine. With its warpable wings cut out near the fuselage so the crew could see the ground, and its undercarriage with two steerable wheels – a source of more or less serious accidents – this machine was quite out of date. The two-seat version was underpowered which made flying it difficult. Structural defects had been reported and partly rectified (reinforcing the fuselage-wing junction, replacing the upper surface cables by firmer ones). Which is why the builder was strongly encouraged to build Caudron G 3s.

Technical Specifications
Wingspan: 31 ft 10 in
Total Length: 25 ft 6 in
Wing surface: 193.680 sq ft
Maximum take off weight: 913 lb
Payload: 506 lb
Max. Speed: 59 mph with a passenger, 62 1/2 mph as a single seater
Flying Time: 3 hours
The two-seat Type Génie was different as follows:
Total length: 27 ft 3 in
Maximum take off weight: 1 210 lb
Max. Speed: 75 mph

A high-wing two-seat monoplane version with all-round vision appeared in February 1914, called the "Blériot-Gouin"; twenty examples were ordered though their careers in Escadrilles BL 2, 4 and 5 were not very long.

Technical Specifications
Wingspan: 30 ft
Total Length: 25 ft 6 in
Wing surface: 193.680 sq ft
Maximum take off weight: 924 lb
Max. Speed: 68 ¾ mph with a 60 or 80-hp Gnome engine
About 700 examples were built in France in various versions of which 180 were delivered to the French Army. It was built under licence in Great Britain, Russia and Italy.

TYPE XXXIX

A two-seat armoured plane used by Védrines who nicknamed it "la Vache" (the cow). It was a monocoque with a 160 hp Gnome engine, armed with a Hotchkiss machine gun fitted on the left hand side, with the armour being made of special steel. The plane was based at Buc in July 1914 and it was aboard this machine that the gunner René Vicaire shot down a Taube over Suippes on 2 September 1914.

Military Blériot Type XI.

1914-16 Caudron

Caudron Type G.3

This was a two-seat biplane equipped with an 80-hp Rhône rotary tractor engine designed by the engineer Paul Deville and derived from the 1912 G 2. The first one (N°127) appeared on 4 September 1914, the last (N° 5639) on 15 September 1924. For the pilots there were only advantages with this plane since it was easy to fly, could land almost anywhere and manoeuvred correctly. The observer was situated between the two wings – not an ergonomic position – and this was later changed: the pilot and his passenger exchanged places. In August 1915 there were already 128 Caudron G.3s in the fighting units, used for observation and artillery spotting.

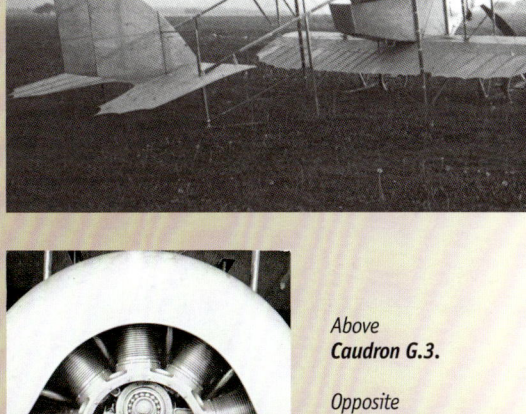

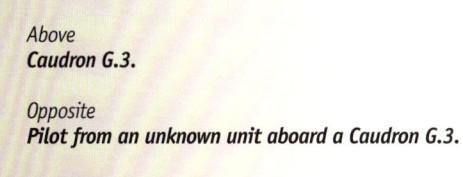

Above
Caudron G.3.

Opposite
Pilot from an unknown unit aboard a Caudron G.3.

Opposite.
80-hp nine-cylinder le Rhône rotary engine installed on the Caudron G.3.

Below.
On the Caudron G.3, the observer was uncomfortably seated in front of the pilot under the wing.

Technical Specifications

Wingspan: 43 ft 11 ½ in (upper wing), 32 ft 11 in (lower wing)
Total Length: 21 ft
Wing surface: 290.520 sq ft
Height: 7 ft 4 in
Maximum take off weight: 1 386 lb with the le Rhône engine.
Payload: 385 lb
Max. Speed: 84 ½ mph
Rate of climb: 6 560 ft in 20 minutes
Flying Time: 4 hours.
Several versions were given a fixed 100-hp Anzani engine. More than 2 540 examples were built by Caudron, and under licence by builders like Blériot and Deperdussin. This plane had flexible wings and had ailerons fitted after the war. When the plane was withdrawn from the fighting units, it was at first used by the training centres then sold to private individuals who used it until WWII.

during the First World War

*Note that on 25 April 1914, Poulet broke the world record for the longest flight, 16 hours and 29 minutes in a modified G.2 foreshadowing the G.3.
À signaler que le 25 avril 1914, Poulet a battu le record de durée de vol avec 16 heures et 29 minutes sur un G.2 modifié préfigurant le G.3.*

Caudron Type G.4

A two-engined biplane derived from the G.3 but with a greater wingspan, with the wing surface increasing to 398.120 ft², whilst the two 80 hp Gnome engines were positioned between the two wings. To make flying easier with one engine stopped, the rudders were doubled.

Technical Specifications
Wingspan: 23 ft 11 in
Height: 8 ft 9 in
Maximum take off weight: 1 100 lb including fuel
Max. Speed: 81 ¼ mph
Rate of climb: 6 560 ft in 14 min
Flying Time: 5 hours
This biplane could be powered by a 100-hp Clerget or Anzani engine. The observer sitting in front of the wings had one Lewis machine gun, fixed on the upper wing so it could be fired to the rear, and a Colt machine gun towards the front. Some machines were armoured for ground attacks and also used for bombing.

*Above.
A Caudron G.3 captured intact by the Germans near Nesles (Pas-de-Calais).*

*Below.
A line-up of Caudron G.3s on the airfield at la Cheppe (Marne) in September 1915.*

*Below.
Caudron G.3 n°6656. (DR).*

Opposite.
Caudron Type G.4.

Opposite.
A Caudron Type G.4 seen from the front showing the position of the fuselage and the engine nacelles.

Below, left.
Caudron G.4 N° 2412 from C 89S with its left hand engine damaged by shell bursts.

Above.
A Caudron G.3 in flight.

Opposite.
This view of a G.3 after a ground loop gives a clear view of the curvature of its wing.

Above.
On 12 August 1915 the Caudron G.4 belonging to Sergent François Drouhet (pilot) and Lieutenant Pierre Guillemin (observer) was seriously damaged by an AA shell during an observation mission. Two cylinders on the right hand engine and the propeller were seriously damaged. The pilot managed to bring his machine back to the French lines, but his observer, whose arm had been torn off died from his wounds.

Opposite.
A Caudron G.4 from Escadrille C 89S (S for Serbia, this unit being part of the Army of the Orient) on 2 April 1916, most likely in the airfield at Topsin in Greece.

Opposite.
Accident of a G.4 from an unknown unit.

Opposite.
Caudron G.4 N° 2179 armed with a Colt machine gun, large numbers of which were bought to make up for the lack of Hotchkisses.

Below, left.
The pilot of this G.4, Sous-lieutenant Robert de Toulouse-Lautrec, from Escadrille C 47 had had his cockpit modified by adding some armour plating at the back and by fitting a Lewis machine gun on the upper wing, a weapon he could use himself, like the observer in front of him.

Above.
A shot of the cockpit of a Caudron G 4. The upper wing is cut out to improve vision.

Opposite.
A line up of Caudron G.4s from an unknown unit.

during the First World War

Breguet-Michelin Bombers

Above.
Breguet Michelin BM 5.

Above, right and opposite.
This Breguet Michelin BM 4 N° 229 from BM 120, nicknamed "Le Voilà/Le Foudroyant" was captured, undamaged, by the Germans after landing behind their lines after an air-to-air combat, on 12 October 1916.

Below.
Breguet-Michelin BM 4 N° 187.

With patriotic fervour, the Michelin brothers at first offered to build a 100 airframes then added a further 200; the only restriction they imposed was for the payload to be limited to 400 kg (882 lb) for a 400 km (216 nm) return flight. GHQ was free to choose any aircraft selected from the military aircraft competition in 1915.

Breguet proposed a version of the Voisin with a pusher engine and a four-wheel undercarriage. The first BM prototype was fitted with a 200-hp Canton Unné engine which was compared to an identical airframe fitted with the 200-hp Renault engine, called the BLM; both machines were able to carry a payload of 980 lb. The BLM won the competition, because it could bomb the town of Essen, and on the condition that it be transformed into a Breguet SN 5, Essen being conveniently found phonetically in the designation "SN"! Breguet finally proposed the BM IV which was accepted by Michelin, but its payload was only 830 lb which meant it was overweight when loaded with the forty 17 ½-lb bombs installed in a launcher, hence the aircraft's reputation for being sluggardly.

With its 716.616 ft² wing surface, it flew at 81.25 mph at 6 560 ft, which it reached after a 22-minute climb. With five hours of flying time and a service ceiling of 9 840 ft, it was already out of date when it reached the units, where seven escadrilles used it from September 1915 onwards.

French aviation

The Farman brothers' aircraft

Above..
A Maurice Farman MF 7 from the school at Etampes in 1917.

Maurice Farman Type 7

This plane appeared in 1913 and called the "birdcage", distinguishable by its tail units made up of two horizontal surfaces giving a bit of lift, and rudders placed between the two surfaces. At the rear of the upper tail surface was the elevator flap which operated at the same time as the one at the front, called the "bread board". The sled-like landing gear comprised two large skids which extended forwards up to the front elevator flap, and to which were attached two wheels with rubber shock absorbers. The nacelle housing the two-man crew was placed on the lower wing. The aircraft was powered by a 70-hp air-cooled V-8 Renault pusher engine. It was easy to fly and was supplied to the reconnaissance escadrilles but as it was so vulnerable it was quickly replaced by the MF 11.
Calling them the "Long Horns", the English used a certain number of them particularly in the training centres. In all 350 examples were built, not counting those built under licence. The MF 11 was issued to MF 2, 5, 8, 16 and 20.

Opposite.
A pilot getting ready to get into a Maurice Farman MF Type 11 in 1915. The fur clothing was not a luxury when flying at heights where the temperature was way below zero in unheated cockpits and in the open air.

during the First World War

Opposite.
An MF 11 from Escadrille MF 14 in August 1915, no doubt on the airfield at Saint-Léonard (Vosges)

Technical Specifications
Wingspan: 50 ft 9 in
Total Length: 39 ft 4 in
Height: 11 ft 4 in
Wing surface: 645.600 sq ft
Maximum take off weight: 1 881 lb
Max. Speed: 59 ½ mph
Service ceiling: 13 120 ft
Flying Time: 3 ¼ hrs

Maurice Farman Type 11

This biplane appeared in 1914 and was an improved version of the previous model. The forward rudder was removed, the skids shortened, the fuselage lifted up further and the tail reduced to one surface. The power plant was still a 80-hp Renault pusher engine, but the nacelle was bigger giving total all-round vision for the observer; in 1915 a machine gun turret was installed (11-bis version). The machine was supplied to the observation escadrilles and used until June 1918.

Technical Specifications
Wingspan: 53 ft
Total Length: 31 ft 1 ½ in
Height: 12 ft 9 in
Wing surface: 613.320 sq ft
Maximum take off weight: 1 848 lb
Payload: eighteen 17 ½ lb bombs plus armament comprising a machine gun and sometimes something with a bigger calibre
Max. Speed: 72 mph at sea level
Rate of climb: 6 560 ft in 20 min
Flying Time: 4 hrs
At least 40 observation escadrilles flew this type which was most active in 1915.
A variant called "Happe" could carry extra weight, increasing the payload from 370 lb to 480 lb for a flight lasting 7 hours at the maximum

Opposite.
Maurice Farman Type 11 N° 8.

speed of 72½ mph; it took 30 minutes to reach 6 560 ft. In the struggle against the Zeppelins, the MF 11s were equipped with a searchlight mounted in front of the observer who was supposed to use it together with three landing lights. A version with a 130-hp engine gave a speed of 80 mph and a climb to 6 560 ft in 13 minutes, but although the payload rose to 517 lb, it could only fly for 3 hours.

Type 40

Under pressure from GHQ to reduce the number of machine types and speed up the number of machines built, the Farman Brothers made the same type of aircraft, combining HF 22 and MF 11 elements with a 130-hp, then a 160-hp and even a 200-hp Renault pusher engine. If necessary, other motors could be used, including the 140-hp de Dion Bouton and the 170 hp Lorraine. The English who also made and used them, called them "Horace".

It served in 55 escadrilles from 1916 onwards and several versions were built including one armed with le Prieur rockets, then there was the F-41 variant with a roomier nacelle, the F-56 with a 190-hp Renault engine, the F-51 with the airframe of an F-41, wings with a simple curvature and a 190-hp engine. The Type 40 was withdrawn from operational units 1917 and replaced by planes with tractor engines.

Technical Specifications
Wingspan: 57 ft 9 in
Total Length: 30 ft 4 in
Height: 12 ft 9 in
Wing surface: 559.520 sq ft
Payload: Varying according to the version of the power plant from 462 lb to 539 lb, 500 lb being the payload for 130-hp Renault powered F-40, the most common variant
Max. Speed: 80 mph (at 6 560 ft)
Rate of climb: 6 560 ft in 18 min
Flying Time: 3 hrs

Above, left.
Maurice Farman Type 11 N° 994 from MF 88bis during the winter of 1915-16.

Above, right.
Lieutenant Louis Paulhan, an aviation pioneer, aboard MF 11 N° 193 from Escadrille MF 995 fighting in Serbia where he scored two kills.

Below.
Farman F 40 N° 2265 from the 4th Escadrille of the Belgian Air Force.

Morane Saulnier planes
(Types L, LA and P)

Opposite.
Morane-Saulnier Type L with damaged propeller and undercarriage

Below.
The military Maurane-Saulnier P MoS 26A2 with a wide frontal engine cowling ring without a propeller spinner.

Below.
Morane-Saulnier L, nicknamed "Parasol". The wing is widely cut out in the cockpit section in order to maximize the pilot's field of vision.

Type L

Derived from the 1912 Type G with new strutted parasol wings this single-engined two-seater appeared in 1914. Initially 50 were ordered by Turkey but they were requisitioned by the French government. It was powered by an 80-hp Gnome or le Rhône rotary engine with three fuel tanks (two in the nose and one in the fuselage, totalling 31 gallons) which gave it three hours flying time. More than 600 were built. It was Roland Garros' favourite mount, as a single-seater, and he used it to try out shooting through the propeller arc. It was with this machine that he was forced to land behind the enemy lines where the armament was examined at length by German experts who managed to perfect the system, enabling them to regain air superiority for the next six months.

Technical Specifications
Wingspan: 36 ft 9 in
Total Length: 22 ft 6 in
Height: 9 ft 11 ½ in
Wing surface: 196.908 sq ft
Maximum take off weight: 1 441 lb
Max. Speed: 78 mph
Rate of climb: 6 560 ft in 18 ½ min
Flying Time: 2 hrs

Type LA

This was a variant of the previous model but with a lot of modifications, the most important of which being the wing tightening system and the fitting of ailerons. It had the same engine and the observer in the rear cockpit could train his weapon over a larger sector. Compared with Type L, the wingspan was reduced to 35 ft 9 in, the length increased to 23 ft 2 in and height 12 ft 8 in. Its speed rose to 84.37 mph and it climbed to 6 560 ft in 15 minutes 25 seconds. It had a short career because it was quickly replaced by the Nieuport 10 which performed better.

Type N

With an-80-hp le Rhône rotary engine, this plane used the monocoque formula derived from the Deperdussin planes and was called "Bullet" by the English. The first ten were delivered at the beginning of June 1915 and were assigned to escorting the more vulnerable Types L and LA. It equipped Escadrilles 12, 23, and 49 then 3, 37 and 48 when deliveries permitted. At the request of Roland Garros, a variant was fitted with a 120-hp le Rhône engine.

Technical Specifications (normal version)
Wingspan: 26 ft 8 in
Total Length: 19 ft 1 in
Height: 7 ft 5 in
Wing surface: 118.36 sq ft
Maximum take off weight: 977 lb
Max. Speed: 90 ½ mph
There were two versions but not many were made. Type I with a 110-hp le Rhône rotary engine whose wingspan was increased to 27 ft and its height to 8 ft 2 in, and Type V with an 28 ft 7 in wingspan and increased flying time at the cost of fairing in the front part of the fuselage to house an extra fuel tank.

Type P

This parasol variant of Type LA was quite an improvement and the two-seat prototype started its trials at the end of March 1916. 565 were ordered at first but in the end more than 1 200 were built. The standard machine was powered by a 110-hp le Rhône rotary engine. It was armed with one machine gun firing above the propeller arc and another for the observer in the rear position. A single seat version was also built and was also armed with the machine gun firing forwards, but only two examples were made.

Technical Specifications
Wingspan: 36 ft 7 in
Total Length: 23 ft 6 in
Wing surface: 193.680 sq ft
Maximum take off weight: 1 606 lb

Above.
A military Morane-Saulnier P type MoS 21A2 with a thin engine ring and a spinner on the propeller.

Opposite.
Morane-Saulnier Type P two-seater armed with two machine guns, one over the wing to avoid the propeller arc.

Below.
Morane Saulnier N. It is especially within the RFC, the British military aviation, that this monoplane will know the success, the British nicknaming it "Bullet" according to the shape of its fuselage

Nieuport fighters

Opposite.
A period postcard showing a Nieuport 12 from the Avord military pilots' school. It has in fact been touched up, the rear of the plane resting on a trestle which has been rubbed out.

Sous-Lieutenant Georges Guynemer from Escadrille N 3 aboard his Nieuport 108 N° 328, the "Vieux Charles III" at the beginning of the summer of 1916. This biplane which has not yet been painted with either the famous insignia of the "Cigognes" or an individual number, has been improved by the fitting of a 110-hp le Rhône engine, a windshield, a mirror and a headrest.

Below.
The Nieuport 12 Prototype.

This was a single-engined biplane derived from the Type X which was not built because of the war, with unequal length wings or not, or staggered wings or not, designed by the engineer Gustave Delage whose combat types also gave rise to training versions with less powerful engines, numbered from 80 onwards. The combat types were often referred to in airmen's memoirs by their wing areas, so it was often the Nieuport 18 metres or the 23 metres, etc.

Type 10 (also called Type XB)

This fighter biplane was made in two versions depending on the position of the observer, AV for in front of the pilot or AR for behind him. The rear place was often chosen by the observer who had a machine gun. The plane was powered by an 80-hp Clerget radial engine or a Gnome or le Rhône 80-hp rotary engine which gave it a top speed of 87 ½ mph and a ceiling of 12 460 ft. It was widely used by the French, British, Belgian and Russian air forces until 1916 when its lack of power meant it often had to be used as a single-seater.
A new power plant, this time a 110-hp then a 130-hp Clerget rotary engine, made it into a Type 12 with larger wings.

Technical Specifications
Wingspan: 25 ft 10 in
Total Length: 22 ft 11 ½ in
Height: 9 ft 4 in
Wing surface: 200.136 sq ft
Maximum take off weight: 1 452 lb
Rate of climb: 6 560 ft in 17 min

Type 11

Also called "BB" (pronounced "Bébé"), this biplane was France's answer to the German Fokker E.111 when it appeared. It was powered by an 80-hp Gnome or le Rhône engine. This biplane was very effective and manoeuvrable, appearing at the end of the summer of 1915, and immediately conquering the

French aviation

hearts of the pilots despite the fact that a 7.7 mm Hotchkiss then a Lewis machine gun was fitted on the top wing without enough ammunition.

It was Guynemer's favourite plane and aboard it he scored fourteen kills; it was also the favourite plane for Dorme, Heurteaux, Nungesser, Navarre and quite a few others in the skies over Verdun. Commandant de Rose was making up a combat group consisting of four escadrilles with six Bébés each. The plane did in fact however have a structural defect: the lower wing tended to fold up under the pressure from an over-abrupt manoeuvre.

More than 7200 examples were built in France, some under licence by de la Fresnay, Savary, CEA, Duperon-Niepce-Felterer, Borel, SAFCA and Lioré et Olivier. The American expeditionary corps used some as did the Royal Flying Corps. In fact Germany also built copies based on a machine captured almost intact and Trompenburg and Siemens improved on them.

They were replaced in operations by the arrival of the Spad VII in great numbers and were then used as two-seaters in the training centres under the designation Nieuport 80.

Technical Specifications
Wingspan: 24 ft 7 in (upper wing) 24 ft 3 in (lower wing)
Total Length: 18 ft
Height: 7 ft 9 in
Wing surface: 139.880 sq ft
Maximum take off weight: 1 056 lb
Payload: 352 lb
Max. Speed: 103 mph
Rate of climb: 6 560 ft in 8 ½ min
Operational ceiling: 15 100 ft
Flying Time: 2 ½ hrs

Type 12

Developed form Type 10 with a bigger engine, it appeared in the summer of 1915, with a 100-, then 130-hp (XIIbis) Clerget rotary engine. The observer in the rear cockpit had a Lewis machine gun; the pilot had a Vickers firing through the propeller arc. A few examples appeared in the units before they were re-equipped with the Bébé.

Technical Specifications
(compared with the Type 10's)
Wing surface: 247.480 ft²
Maximum take off weight: 1 804 lb
Payload: 660 lb

Above.
In-flight shot of a two-seat Nieuport Type 12bis with a 130 hp Clerget engine. Officially designated C2 (two-seat fighter), this plane could be armed with two machine guns served by both crew members.

Opposite.
Adjudant William Thaw aboard his Nieuport 11. He was an American volunteer engaged in the Foreign Legion and was one of the first members of the La Fayette Escadrille.

Opposite, below.
Charles Nungesser posing in front of his Nieuport 11 decorated with his personal insignia.

Below.
Nieuport 11 equipped with Le Prieur rockets.

Above.
Although officially classified as an A2, the Nieuport 14 was in fact a two-seat bomber which could carry four 120-mm projectiles. It had only a short career in the three escadrilles of the Aéronautique Militaire.

Opposite.
Nieuport 24 or 27 in flight. From this angle, the differences between the two models are almost impossible to make out since they are in fact on the landing gear and the tailskid, which was simplified.

Above.
Nieuport 24bis.

Type 14

This was a day-time two-seat bomber powered by a Hispano 150-hp in-line engine and armed with a Lewis machine gun in the rear cockpit. It gave rise to Type 15 which itself was quickly replaced by Type 17.

Max. Speed: 98 mph (87 ½ at 9 840 ft)
Rate of climb: 9 840 ft in 22 min
Flying Time: 3 hrs

TYPE 16

A version of the Bébé powered by a 110-hp le Rhône engine giving it slightly better performances.

Technical Specifications (compared to the Type 11's)
Total Length: 18 ft 6 in
Wing surface: 139.880 ft²
Maximum take off weight: 1 210 lb
Max. Speed: 97 ½ mph at 6 560 ft
Rate of climb: 6 560 ft in 5 ½ min
Service ceiling: 15 750 ft
Flying Time: 2 hrs

Type 17

Called the "Super Bébé", this plane appeared

at the beginning of 1916 and was fitted with the wings of Type 16 increased to a surface area of 158.710 ft², hence its name "Nieuport 15 metres". It was more robust that its predecessors and was powered by either a 110-hp le Rhône rotary engine or a 130-hp le Clerget engine. Its visibility was improved by moving the lower wing and the lower wing spar was reinforced; it was very agile and for the period had outstanding performances.

More than 4 300 examples were built. At the beginning it had a Lewis gun mounted on the upper wing though later it had a synchronised cowling-mounted Vickers machine gun.

N 57 was the first unit to be equipped with them before it equipped more than twenty fighter escadrilles from mid-1916 onwards. The test escadrille for synchronised firing through the propeller arc was N 3 and because of this it was given the first examples in April 1916. These were N° 891, 901, 917, 939, 962 – Deullin's usual mount – 980 and 1209.

Technical Specifications
Wingspan: 25 ft 11 ½ in
Total Length: 19 ft 6 in
Height: 8 ft
Wing surface: 158.710 ft²
Maximum take off weight: 1 232 lb
Max. Speed: 106 ¼ mph
Rate of climb: 10 820 ft in 10 min and 13 120 ft in 19 ½ min
Service ceiling: 17 380 ft
Flying Time: 2 hrs

Type 17bis

On this version the engine power rose to 130 hp which gave it a speed of 110 mph for a total mass of 1 166 lb. It was Nungesser's favourite plane: he appreciated its climb rate to 9 840 ft in 7 ½ minutes.

Type 18

This three seater with 150-hp Hispano engines and a wing surface of 552.634 ft² with a total mass of 4 070 lb was built at the end of 1915 but in the end nothing came of it.

Type 20

Using an 80-hp le Rhône engine then a 110-hp engine, this plane was equipped with bigger ailerons to improve agility.

Technical Specifications
Wingspan: 29 ft 6 in
Total Length: 22 ft 11 ½ in
Height: 8 ft 9 in
Wing surface: 247.480 ft²
Maximum take off weight: 1 655 lb
Max. Speed: 98 mph
Rate of climb: 6 560 ft in 12 min 15 sec

Type 22

Planned for October 1916 but remaining as a project, this more massive version, called

Top.
Nieuport 24 bis.

Above.
A line up of Nieuport 24 bis from N 97.

Opposite.
The Canadian ace of aces Lieutenant William Avery "Billy" Bishop, posing in front of his Nieuport 23 in 1917, the number of which has been rather crudely rubbed off by the censorship.

Opposite.
Nieuport 24bis N°3612 from Escadrille N 99 in 1918, next to some Spads.

the Type 23, was fitted with a 160-hp le Rhône engine, but the Spad VII's and then the XIII's success limited the use of this machine and the following ones.

Type 24

A biplane with a 120-hp le Rhône engine.

Technical Specifications
Wingspan: 26 ft 11 in (upper wing) 25 ft 7 in (lower wing)
Total Length: 19 ft 3 in
Height: 7 ft 9 in
Wing surface: 158.710 ft²
Maximum take off weight: 1 203 lb
Max. Speed: 110 mph (97 mph at 19 680 ft)
Rate of climb: 16 400 ft in 21 min 30 sec

Type 24bis

A single seater with a 150/170-hp le Clerget engine and improved aerodynamically by a circular cross-sectioned fuselage; it was rather successful.

Opposite page.
Nieuport 24 from a USAS training unit with a particularly spectacular "fish" camouflage scheme!

Opposite.
Nieuport 27.

Below.
Lieutenant E. Le Maître and Captain J.C. Bartolf in front of Nieuport 17 N° 2474 during this biplane's trials at Langley Field in the USA in 1917. *(Library of Congress)*

Type 27

Identical airframe to the Type 24 with a few differences including a 120-hp le Rhône engine.

Technical Specifications
Wingspan: 26 ft 10 in
Total Length: 19 ft 2 in
Height: 9 ft 3 in
Wing surface: 158.710 ft²
Maximum take off weight: 1 287 lb
Max. Speed: 115 mph
Service ceiling: 18 200 ft
Range: 156 ¼ miles

The Voisin Bombers

Opposite and below.
Voisin LAS.

The Type L used to set up the first bomber group was, like a lot of planes going into service during the Great War, a two-seat biplane which could carry an extra load of some 220 lb on top of the crew in the nacelle. The tail was borne on four tubular spars and the landing gear comprised two pairs of wheels in tandem. Equipped at first with a low-powered engine, it could fly at 60 mph for three hours at an altitude not above 10000 ft, or more often less depending on the load it was carrying.

This rustic machine was made of metal tubes. The wings were fabric-covered as was the tail. Its main failing was the pusher engine, though the observer-bombardier's field of vision at the front was exceptional. Moreover the floor of the nacelle was fitted with a triplex glass panel improving the downwards view. The pilot fared less well because his view was slightly obstructed by the wings. Although he could see downwards thanks to a glass panel, he could not defend himself from a rear attack the because of the propeller arc. This configuration remained unchanged right through the war and any modifications concerned especially the power plant and its logical consequence, an increase in the fuel and oil capacity. The solidity of the airframe, its resistance to the weather and the possibility of carrying a large load, made the plane an effective machine for service in the bomber units. But these machines only had one spark plug and one magneto per cylinder which explains why certain breakdowns forced the plane to land at once. Breguet, Nieuport and Esnault-Pelterie whose designs had been thrown out in October 1914 were ordered to build Voisin biplanes. The Voisin Type L with a 70-hp Gnome engine or an 80-hp (Type 2) le Rhône engine equipped Escadrilles V 14 and V 21 at the beginning of the war. With a wingspan of 43 ft 11 in and a length of 31 ft 1 in for a wing surface of 534.234 ft² it could carry about 220 lb of 155-mm shells used as bombs. Sixty or so machines were used by the military aviation plus a few examples intended for Russia which were quickly requisitioned.

Voisin Type LA

This model with a 130-hp Salmson Canton-Unné water-cooled engine appeared in September 1914. The prototype flew in February fitted with a 120-hp Salmson engine.
Voisin Type LAS
This version with a higher engine appeared in April 1915; more than a thousand were built, not including those built under licence in the United Kingdom and Russia. It equipped the bomber groups, like for example Escadrille VB 103 which had Voisin LAS N°475 in July 1915.

Voisin Type 3

Specialising in bombing, this machine was well-liked by its pilots but its lack of speed made the builder look for a more powerful engine. Building the 150-hp Canton-Unné was turning out to be difficult and as a result this version was finally abandoned.

Voisin Type 7

Appearing in mid-1916, this model was assigned to the reconnaissance units if possible, its 180-hp Renault engine ensuring it was more reliable than the previous models. More than 100 examples were built.

Above.
The **Voisin LAS N° 1342** used by the training centre of Avord.

Opposite.
Voisin LAS n° 1338.

Below.
A group of French zouaves poses in front of a Voisin LAS.

Bottom.
Voisin Type 4 or "Voisin Canon" being presented to Greek officers on the Thessalonica front.

Voisin Type 4

This version was armed with a 37-mm Hotchkiss canon instead of the machine gun which meant the upper wing had to be moved forward to maintain the centre of gravity. The plane was used in the bomber units for protection. Two versions (L and LA) existed alongside each other with the same armament.

Voisin Type 5

Equipped with a 140-hp Salmson Canton-Unné engine, the payload on this model was increased by 176 lb to the detriment of its flying qualities which did not make it popular. More than 450 examples were built however, mainly for night bombing. Its theoretical payload was 521 lb for four hours' flying time at a speed of 63.75 mph and at 6 560 ft, reached in 23 minutes. Variants were produced under licence in Italy, equipped with locally-built engines including the 160-hp Isotta-Fraschini.

Technical Specifications
Wingspan: 48 ft 4 ½ in
Total Length: 31 ft 1 ½ in
Height: 12 ft 6 in
Wing surface: 484.200 ft²
Weight (empty): 2 186 lb
Maximum take off weight: 3 080 lb
Armament: One Hotchkiss machine gun

N° 615. — SALONIQUE. — Officiers grecs devant un avion.
SALONICA. — Grecian officers standing in front of an aeroplane.

during the First World War

The « orphan » planes

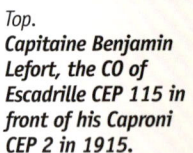

Top.
Capitaine Benjamin Lefort, the CO of Escadrille CEP 115 in front of his Caproni CEP 2 in 1915.

Above, right.
The turret placed on the upper wing of the CEP 1 was abandoned on the CEP 2.

Above and below.
Caproni CEP 2.

The Caproni CEP

As the General Staff was looking for a multi-engined night bomber, it chose the Italian three-engined biplane, the Caproni (CAP) 3 on condition it was built in France, by Robert Esnault-Pelterie who had to adapt it to French standards, hence the name CEP (Caproni-Esnault-Pelterie). Equipped with two 80-hp le Rhône side engines and a central rear pusher 130-hp Canton-Unnè engine, it had a wing surface of 1 420.320 ft², could carry a payload of 605 lb at a maximum speed of 75 mph for a seven-hour flight.

The machine's more than mediocre performances made the builders look for a more powerful engine and the later versions were strictly the same as the Italian versions. Two escadrilles, 115 and 130 used the REP1 then the original Caproni 3 from November 1915 onwards for the CEP, and from November 1917 for the CAP.

The Deperdussin Monocoque

This was a single-engined two-seat monoplane designed by the engineer Béchereau who especially studied aerodynamics. Like the other planes of the 1912-13 period, the wings could be warped. It had a classic tail, the landing gear had a nose skid to prevent nose-overs and a skid at the rear. The observer sitting over the wings could not see the ground. Subsequently the builder was firmly encouraged to build Caudron G 3s. It was 23 ft 11 in long, with a wingspan of 36 ft 9 in and was used by one escadrille, 36, from October 1914 to February 1915.

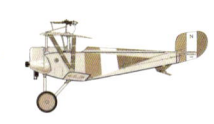

Opposite.
Caproni CEP 2.

Below, left.
One of the aviation aces from before the war: Marcel de Brindejonc des Moulinais in front of a Dorand DO 1.

Below
Dorand DO 1. Built by the Army's workshops, this armoured two-seater was used by a single unit, the Escadrille n° 22 (DO 22) just before the beginning of the conflict and for a few weeks only. Little successful because they were too heavy, even with their armour plating deleted, DO 1s were removed from the front lines in October 1914…

Below.
The gunner station of a Deperdussin monoplane Type TTS tested at the beginning of year 1914. Specially designed to fight the Zeppelins, this prototype was finally not mass-produced.

during the First World War

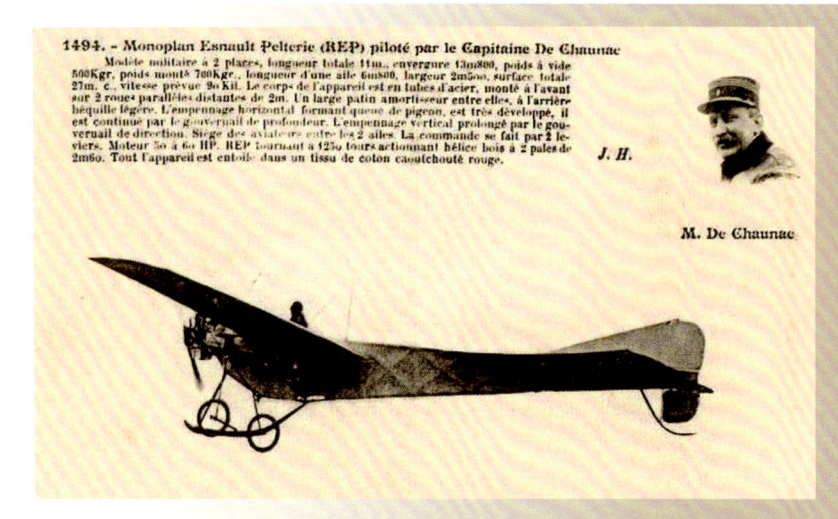

Above
REP monoplanes.
The Type K 80 two-seater surrounded by cyclists was certainly painted red.

Below.
Henri Farman HF 15 N°6. This postcard was in fact retouched as originally the aircraft is on the ground, its tail unit resting on a support to place it in firing position during the tests led by Lieutenant Mailfert (pilot) and Sergent Davost (gunner) in October 1913.

Dorand 001 (DO1)

Designed by Capitaine Jean-Baptiste Dorand, these two-seat biplanes with tractor engines and staggered wings held in place by a host of struts did not leave any happy memories among the crews who were all too glad to exchange them for Maurice Farmans after using them for three months.

Henri Farman HF 20/21

There were quite a few differences between this model and the Maurice Farman 7, including a more modern shape. The booms supporting the tail indeed formed a V, at the end of which were attached the rudders and elevators. The forward nacelle was clear of any obstacles underneath and the undercarriage comprised a double bogey, each bogey being attached to the lower wing which supported the two-seat nacelle. The upper wing was longer than the lower. The power plant was an 80-hp Gnome pusher engine. They equipped Escadrilles HF 1, 7, 13, 19, 28 and 32 between August 1914 and May 1915 but in spite of their more modern look, the builder was invited to halt production and while waiting for the Farman 40s to come out, to copy the Maurice Farman products which were less fragile.

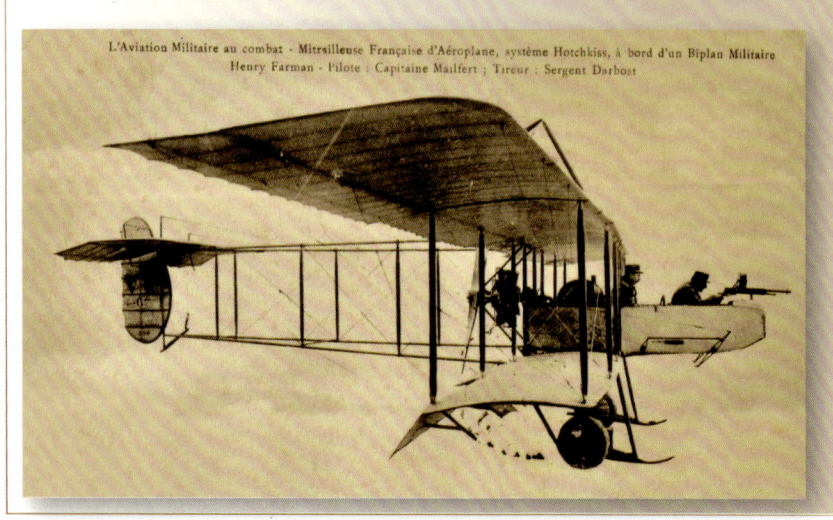

Morane Saulnier AC or MoS 23

This mid-wing single seat fighter cross braced with steel tubes was derived from the Type V. It was a very fine plane with a very big propeller boss, armed with a 7.7 mm Vickers firing through the propeller, powered by a 100-hp, or 120-hp Rhône rotary engine. Appearing in mid-1916, 30 examples were ordered and called monocoque, but it was not popular with French pilots because it was delicate to handle; it did however have a career in the RFC where it was called the "Bullet".

Technical Specifications
Total Length: 23 ft 1 ½ in
Height: 8 ft 11 ½ in
Wing surface: 161.400 ft²
Maximum take off weight:
Max. Speed: 111 mph at ground level and 109 mph at 6 560 ft.
Rate of climb: 19 680 ft in 6 min
Flying Time: 2 ½ hrs with a full load of 1 447 lb

Spad SAC 2

The first machine designed by Louis Béchereau, this two-seat single-engined biplane made of wood, featured an observer's position in a hinged bucket located in front of the propeller and protected from it by a grill. This bucket was supported by two struts attached to the landing gear. The machine was not chosen by the crews because the all-too original position was uncomfortable, psychologically, for the observer. 40 examples were ordered in September 1915 with a power plant of one 80-hp le Rhône engine, then 110-hp after December.

Technical Specifications
Wingspan: 29 ft 9 in
Total Length: 25 ft 3 in
Max. Speed: 88 mph for the 110-hp and 70 mph for the 80-hp engines

Above.
Spad SAC N°9 showing how the front part of the fuselage swung down to allow access to the engine.

Opposite.
Derived from the SA 1 which was virtually not produced (possibly fifteen aircraft), the Spad SA 2 was essentially characterized by its new Lewis machine-gun mounting, its parallel wing leading and trailing edges and its modified tailplane. Besides the French Aéronautique Militaire, over half of the hundred aircraft produced was bought by Russia.

REP (Robert Esnault Pelterie)

This builder's products were the logical result of machines designed ever since 1907, after the tandem type landing gear of the earlier models was abandoned.

REP Type K

This was a high wing monoplane with heavily wired tips above and below the wing, with lateral control achieved by wing warping. The fuselage was fabric covered with welded triangular cross-sectioned metal tubes, with a large tail and fin. The main quality of this two seater supplied to the Army was its strength. Its fuselage was made of steel tubes and its wings kept their shape, which meant that the airframe was heavier which was not compensated by any increase in power. Its 80-hp Gnome engine did indeed give it mediocre performances. Moreover, the pilot and the observer were placed above the wings and could not see enough. The armament was typically a rifle. The machine was withdrawn from operational service in 1915, two escadrilles, 15 and 27 having used it between 30 August 1914 and the beginning of 1915.

Technical Specifications
Wingspan: 35 ft 9 in
Total Length: 25 ft 10 in
Weight (Empty): 666 lb
Max. Speed: 72 mph at ground level

during the First World War

From the Somme to the Rhine

"The best pilots, the best weapons and the best equipment in the world are worth nothing in an inferior aircraft"

John Slessor

"The value of an air force is the result of the average aptitude of its pilots and not just the exceptional qualities of some of them."

Colonel Guillemeny

The year 1916

Right.
A pilot aboard a Blériot XI on the airfield at Buc, in April 1916.

John Slessor could have added "the best tactics" because although the fighters patrolled over Verdun this was still done without any precise notion of collective manoeuvring and the fighting was often "hand to hand" combat, where ability or the best plane decided the outcome. The result represented the effort of those responsible for the future of military aviation whilst at the same time making an initial conclusion about the Battle of Verdun.

The first, urgent, conclusion consisted of maintaining the fighter group organisation for the new battle, in the Somme, that was on its way. Other improvements had been introduced earlier when Commandant Barès imposed a restriction to the number of plane types by holding on to only the most effective ones. In doing this he did not exactly endear himself to some of the aircraft builders who did not hesitate to run him down to the Minister of War, General Galliéni. Besides Galliéni was seriously ill which meant he was replaced by General Roques. The Battle of Verdun raised questions that needed thinking about; among them was the need to ensure liaison between infantry, artillery and the command by low-flying planes, to escort the observation planes when they went away from their own lines, and to give the observation planes balloons fighter protection; all this led to the setting up of an air command for each zone to coordinate the action at the front and keep an eye on the supply of ammunition and flying materiel coming up from the rear.

Finally there was the problem of the ageing materiel and replacing it with new, more effective models, since earlier trials had not revealed a big enough quality margin compared with the enemy's equipment. A lot of hope was put into the new fighters being tried out and in the three-engined accompanying planes. Where bombing was concerned, the aircraft were so out-of-date that they were used for nocturnal activities despite night fighters appearing on the enemy side. However, matters were in hand to try and re-establish at least a semblance of parity, bearing in mind that the

Right.
The Blériots XIs at the Avord Training Centre. This centre created in 1912 used more than 250 aircraft. The tricolour roundels appeared on French military planes after July 1912.

TRIAL BY SPIN

According to René Tognard in Pau on 28 October 1917: After taking up the Nieuport Bébé including a trial at altitude, he went on to the Acrobatic School on 9 November and had to show how he could get out of a spin: "We were three pilots taking the test, the first of which was to get out of a deliberate spin. After gathering us round a plane on the ground, the instructor explained how to do the exercise, with lots of gesticulations. The first to go went up to 5 000 feet, lost speed, fell into a spin which he stopped after a few turns, restarted his engine and went down at full throttle crashing straight into the ground; all during this time, the instructor was shouting his lungs off 'Pull up!' Nothing happened and while the ambulance went over to pick up the casualty, the second pupil took off to show he had understood how to do the manoeuvre!"

enemy was the victim of a blockade which was getting harsher and harsher, depriving him of certain supply sources.

Pilot training was modified by setting up an initial selection at the Dijon preparation school, for each of the three types and an improvement course adapted to each one.

The fighters had two specific courses: the acrobatics school and the air combat school at Pau (dual controls on Nieuport 18s and 23 Ms, solo on Nieuport 13 and 15 M), then the gunnery school at Cazaux, like the machine gunners. The bombers finished their courses, including night flying, at Avord and the artillery observers had improvement courses at Chateauroux. The aim of all these changes was to give the pilot arriving in his operational unit at least 50 flying hours' experience.

Looking for a reliable and powerful engine bore fruit with the discovery and the exclusive production of the new Hispano-Suiza 140 hp engine which the engineer, Birkigt, had developed in Spain. On the instructions of the Service Technique two of these engines underwent trials in which they were tested at full power for 50 hours at Chalais-Meudon in December 1915. Then an engine was mounted on a Nieuport for life-size testing before being mounted on a Nieuport 17. At the end of these trials, the decision was taken to mass-produce the engine in a factory set up at Courbevoie. This news was obviously hardly welcome to French engine makers whose products were far from having anywhere near the same endurance as this engine. It was just another item to add to the list of complaints against Commandant Barès, who had ordered 1 600 of them. The production series version which was rated at 150 hp was to power the Spad VII fighter designed by Béchereau, appearing in 1916.

But, as Commandant Féquant wrote: "a host of details had still to be dealt with" since the pilots and the mechanics had to be taught how to get the best out of this particular mount. The pilots fought among themselves to get hold of the first examples numbered in the 100 series, Lieutenant Armand Pinsard getting hold of one of the first, N° 122, with which he claimed a kill on 28 August. According to the records, Sergeant Chainat from N 3 conveyed N° 112 from le Bourget to Cachy on 18 August and Sous-Lieutenant Guynemer got N° 115 on 26 August.

Likewise an effort was made to improve the morale of the fighter pilots after the losses suffered during the Battle of Verdun. Two decisions were taken with this in mind: withdraw from the engaged units all the pilots who returned too often to the airfields with engine trouble or any mechanical problem not confirmed by the mechanics.

Then a memorandum from GHQ gave each escadrille

Above.
The mechanics and the pilot of a Voisin 7A2 at Avord in September 1917

Left.
Blériots XIs on the airfield at the school at Avord in September 1917. In the foreground, N° 173.

CHOOSING AN INSIGNIA

There was competition within each escadrille for the choice of the most symbolic emblem for both the material and the dynamism of the crews. Here are two examples:

The fighters adopted insignias evoking combat. Escadrille N 3 distinguished itself by choosing a stork. Captain Georges Bellenger, who set up the escadrille in 1912 when it was stationed at Belfort declared, "in this province of Alsace, to whose gateways you are going, be the storks of Alsace". In 1916 when he had to choose an insignia, Captain Brocard recalled this and had the profile of a stork drawn with its wings on the down stroke. The insignia was adopted in various shapes and sizes by the escadrilles forming the first fighter group calling themselves "les Cigognes" (the Storks) (3, 26, 106, 73, 67 and 167) after the Battle of Verdun. Noting that the need to fly slowly gave rise to special shapes, C 11 chose something different. When a convoy drove past along the edge of the unit's airfield, an officer noticed the insignia on one of the lorries – two paper hens partly superimposed, roughly forming the number "22". Dividing the number by two, he put this drawing forward to be adopted with two restrictions: it had to be red to be seen from afar and the eye of the animal had to be turned to the rear, the direction fatal surprises come from in combat…!

Above.
Adjudant Jacques Richard posing in front of a Caudron R4 from C 217 in 1917.

its instructions on how to choose the insignia that was to be painted on the aircraft fuselages for in-flight recognition purposes.

When out on observation duties, the planes were an easy prey; they finally started to receive armed twin-engined planes, of which the prototype, the Caudron G-4, was tested by the crew of Lieutenants Vuillemin (pilot) and Moulines (observer) at le Bourget in June 1915. Its equipment was completed by installing a radio for transmitting artillery spotting information and photographic materiel with a variety of lenses. Laboratory

Above.
Members of MF 55 training to fire a machine gun in 1916.

Above.
Fokker D.VII (N° 4464/18 built by QAW) belonging to Leutnant Hans Jungwirth from Jasta 78b.

Left.
A mechanic posing in front of a Spad VII from Spa 150 sporting the escadrille's insignia, the "Condor gliding with wings spread seen from three quarters front right", on its fuselage.

AN INSIGNIA VANISHES

On 1 November 1916, all ranks and all personnel serving in the air arm were forbidden from wearing an armband showing a propeller or a winged anchor, earlier worn on the right arm. On the other hand speciality insignias were created and are still in use today.

trucks for developing the shots as soon as the planes landed were also assigned to the escadrilles. The very problematic Hotchkiss machine gun was replaced by more reliable imported materiel. The H. or M. Farman observation planes were quickly replaced by the Farman 40, still with a pusher engine but its flights were escorted. As there was no ideal plane, construction under licence of the British Sopwith two-seater with a tractor engine started to be used for day bombing and observation, but the first ones built were fragile

Below.
A Letord from C 47 after an accident in 1917, the only year in which this escadrille used this type of machine.

A MASSIVE BOMBING MISSION

"Guynemer setting off on a Nieuport 17" (original photo caption)

A vast bombing operation in successive waves was mounted on 23 October against the Mauser armaments factory at Oberndorf which produced 240 000 rifles monthly. It assembled 35 bombers, or two escadrilles (MF 29 plus six planes, and MF 135 plus five) from Farman MF 11, and BM 120 with fourteen machines of which seven were armed for en-route protection. The fighter escort was provided by four Nieuports from N 124 plus some Sopwiths, making an armada of 60 machines in all. The Nieuports' short range forced them to abandon the escort when they crossed the Rhine, and which they joined again for the homeward trip. MF 29 went in first and lost two planes on the way with engine trouble. MF 123 also lost two through mechanical problems then another was shot in two by a shell which hit it full blast. Another one was shot down by enemy fighters and only one plane reached the target. The Breguet Michelins (BMs) protected by the fighters which shot down several Fokkers, were not lucky, three bombers and three protection planes being lost* and one other was badly damaged but managed to get back to base.

These losses were considered too heavy compared with the results obtained, and the Farmans and the BMs were relegated to night operations.

The N 124 Nieuport piloted by Norman Prince, running out of petrol, flew into high voltage wires on 23 October in the twilight when landing out in the country, breaking both his legs. He was transported to the hospital at Gerardmer where he died shortly afterwards. He had scored five kills in 122 combat sorties.

The Sopwiths that had taken part in that mission attracted the attention of the High Command which then authorised Captain Robert de Beauchamp and Daucourt to go and bomb Essen. Leaving from Vadelaincourt at 11 AM on 24 September with two Sopwith single-seaters, they returned at 5 PM having flown 500 miles over enemy lines at an average height of 4500 m. A new raid by de Beauchamp was authorised against Munich station for 16 November. Taking off at 8 AM, the weather conditions forced the captain to fly low until he reached the target at midday where he bombed the station, then flew on to land in Italy, at Dona di Piave at about 4 PM after a tiring eight-hour flight. He broke his propeller on landing. The High Command did however wonder if these spectacular raids which attracted such intense media coverage were worth risking the lives of a crew carrying only 40 kg of explosives.

---
1. Two crews from BM 120 and one from MF 123 (Adjudant Baron, pilot) were declared as having died for France on 12 October.

PERSONALISING PLANES

Once an escadrille had chosen its insignia according to the orders issued on 23 April 1917, it was not unknown for a plane to be given a distinctive sign so that a pilot could recognise his leader or partner. The fighters, particularly the "Cigognes", started this practice very quickly. Hence Guynemer's "le Vieux Charles". Commandant de Rose had a rose on his, enclosed in a hunting horn drawn by Scott. His nephew, Captain de Sevin adopted the same idea. Auger only had the word "Je" on his plane; Laulhé from Béarn from N 3 had "Beth ceil de Pau" (the beautiful sky over Pau), and Sergeant Décatoire had "Tiro-ti? Mi, j'iro" ("Will you go? I will go") in the northern patois. Captain Battle had a Jerusalem Cross painted on his and Captain de l'Hermite "Maï mourirem" (We will never die). Fonck's mechanic had a four-leafed clover painted on the top of the fuselage of both his planes. Captain Raymond chose "Ma Ninon", Dubonnet reproduced his firm's cat and the Japanese Captain Baron Shigeno inscribed "Ma Ninette" on his. Letters from the front tell of an observer who had christened his plane "Stéphane", an allusion to the poet "Mallarmé", which he found so suitable for his plane, "mal armé" meaning badly armed!

Above.
Adjudant Maxime Lenoir, from N 23 alongside his Nieuport. This former Hussar, licensed in December 1914, perished in action on 25 October 1916.

Above.
German infantrymen start dismantling the wings of a Nieuport which made an emergency landing behind their lines.

Below.
French soldiers inspecting a Rumpler C IV captured intact.

and already out of date and reached the front with the usual delays. Meanwhile the Doran AR with a Renault tractor engine was introduced but none too successfully. Caudron promised that the armed two-engined G-6 would be arriving soon, before the R-4 straight off the drawing board. The curiosity of the moment was the Salmson Moineau, a single-engined twin-propeller whose Canton-Unné engine was placed transversally inside the fuselage. The two escadrilles equipped with them were not over-enthusiastic about them.

The bomber escadrilles were the worst off, because the day-time bombers' vulnerability meant they were relegated to night bombing. The planes' small load capability had not been improved by the licence-built Capronis; they were underpowered (total rating: 350 hp with two types of engines, even though the original model was rated at 450 hp). Trials were carried out with a Paul Schmitt but the crews thought it was too heavy and difficult to park because of its large wingspan, nor did it offer any particular advantage over the Voisin which soldiered on as the standard machine.

During a secret committee meeting, the Minister of War informed the members that as at 1 June all plane losses had been made up for and that on the

SINGLE-SEAT FIGHTER RULES

Lieutenant Deullin summarised his long experience as follows in June 1917: "A single-seat fighter has to bring together all the qualities needed by a pilot and an observer. Above all as a pilot he has to be able to manoeuvre; he can't get enough practice at aerobatics: tight turns without losing height, spirals up and down, spins, reversals, rolls, loops, zooming, dives, etc. He will never be totally ready until he has done them all against an adversary who can do them just as well as he can."

Above.
"I'm sending you a shot of a plane which came down behind our lines..." An extract from the correspondence on this postcard showing the debris of a two-seat German Rumpler.

Above and right.
This Rumpler C. I. (N° 4593/15) from KG 6 was forced to land at Villeneuve-les-Vertus on 6 August 1916 by a Caudron G4 from C 47 aboard which was Adjudant René Fonck (Sous-Lieutenant-Observer Paul Thiberge), being the first kill for the French Air Force's future "ace of aces".

A FLYING LION CUB

On leave in Paris the pilot William Thaw from Escadrille 124 saw a small ad in the New York Herald for a lion cub, up for sale at 500 francs. Returning to his base, he got his comrades' consent to make the lion cub their mascot and to set up a purchasing commission. Thaw reached the Gare de l'Est (a Paris station) with his big cat on a lead and a ticket for a dog. A conductor appeared, demanding to know what "that animal" was. "It's an African dog" was the answer. Unfortunately the quadruped started to roar, and the conductor cried out "It's a lion!" He called the station manager and Thaw was obliged to get hold of a cage so he could have his "dog" travel with the luggage. The animal finally reached Luxeuil in good condition, was christened "Whisky" and got to know "Fram", the escadrille's dog, a real airman's dog who could do a somersault, an imitation loop!

French front there were now 60 Army Corps escadrilles, with ten planes each, 24 Artillery escadrilles with five planes each, 19 combat escadrilles with ten planes each and 21 bomber escadrilles with ten planes and each of them had four canon-planes, making a total of 1 120 front-line planes. He added that the number of planes was going to be increased.

On 25 August, there were nine names on the list of the holders of at least 5 confirmed kills, headed by Sous-Lieutenant Guynemer with fourteen planes and a Drachen, followed by Navarre with twelve planes, Nungesser with eleven and two Drachens then Chaput with

Left.
A coloured German period photo showing the wreck of a French biplane being inspected by German troops.

79

On this page and right. ***Various pilots from the military aviation school at le Cortoy, founded before the war by the Caudron Brothers.***

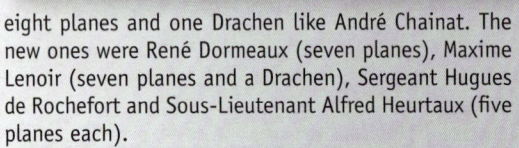

eight planes and one Drachen like André Chainat. The new ones were René Dormeaux (seven planes), Maxime Lenoir (seven planes and a Drachen), Sergeant Hugues de Rochefort and Sous-Lieutenant Alfred Heurtaux (five planes each).

The Somme (July-November)

During the Defence Council meeting, Joffre pleaded for the British to intervene in order to relieve his troops engaged at Verdun. The preparations announced in May then put off till June, finally started on 1 July whilst the fighting continued on the Meuse. At the same time, decisions were taken whose effects were only felt a certain time afterwards. The British army was responsible for most of the assault sector together with a French army under General Foch who was up in support and did all the rest. He had just published an "Instruction on how to use aircraft". When the Battle of the Somme started, the standard French fighter was the Nieuport 17 with a 110-hp engine armed with a 97-rounds Lewis drum machine gun. It replaced the Bébé but turned out to be quite inadequate when faced with the German fighters being put into service gradually from January 1917 onwards.

Morane proposed its Types N and I with a synchronised machine gun but General Headquarters decided on the Spad VII whose trials had shown how good it was. For this assault the whole "Cigognes" group mo-

THE TALLY

It was a good time for the fighters: Fonck got his first confirmed kill on 6 August against a Rumpler at Estrées-Saint-Denis; Dorme had eighteen, Heurtaux, 15, Guynemer added at least 14 to his score including a double on 23 September; Tarascon and Nungesser got nine of which three on 26 September; Tenant de la Tour and Sauvage eight; Lenoir, Loste and Mezergue seven; Flachet et Viallet six; Marcel Bloch, Chainat, Revol-Tissot, de Rochefort, Violet-Marty et Casale five; Lacour-Grandmaison, Sayaret et Soulier four; Pinsart, Jailler, Matton, Régnier et Madon three; Borzecki, Douchy, Derode, Guiget, Lachann, de Bonnefoy and de Marancoeur two; Narbezat, Blanc, Buisson, Camplan, Chaput, Coudouret, Covin, Guertiau, Langudeoc, Le Coq de kerland, Maunoury, Pendaries, Raymond, Rousseaus, Sardier, de Sevin, De Turenne and Lufbery one; and many others who were not mentioned in the communiqué. Maxime Lenoir became an ace on 1 August, but was killed aboard his plane called "Trompe la Mort" (dare-devil) on 25 October. On 17 November Commandant de Beauchamp fell in action over Verdun.

Among the individual exploits mentioned in the log books, that of Jean Casale, who became an ace on 27 December tells how, on 8 July, he set a Drachen on fire after missing two others. On 8 August, he and Lenoir ran into six enemy aircraft and put them to flight. On the 9th he forced an enemy plane to land hurriedly behind its own lines near Beaumont. On 2 September he shot down an enemy plane and did the same on the 28th.

ved to Cachy, near Villers-Bretonneux. It was placed under the command of Captain Brocard who was free to choose his pilots. To show how important this presence was, Foch reviewed the group the day after the planes arrived: some Spads VII already stood out amidst the Nieuports.

The British and French air forces clearly outnumbered the Germans and very quickly neglected the fact that the enemy could still do air reconnaissance. On the French side, this force assembled eight army escadrilles, twenty escadrilles from the army corps, the fighter group reserve at Cachy which had five Nieuport escadrilles including N 124 (1) reinforced by pilots coming from the training schools. It reached Cachy on

1. On 6 December the Minister of War exceptionally authorised M 124 to be called the ex-"American Escadrille" then, in November the "Escadrille des Volontaires" and finally the name "Escadrille Lafayette".

Below.
A moment of relaxation at le Crotoy: A land yacht on the school's airfield.

during the First World War

Right.
A Maurice Farman MF 11 from a pilot school.

Right.
The hazards of learning: a Blériot in a pitiful state.

23 October where Guynemer and the others had been untiringly flying nine-hour days. "A new plane, the 140 hp Spad VII, in the hands of Guynemer, literally astounded the enemy but was nonetheless still a horror for the younger pilots who spoke of it with respect", according to Captain Thénault, N 124's CO.

This was when the Balloon units equipped with M balloons and winches set up every 800 yards came into their own, as the German general, F. von Belok noted: "The sight of all those balloons suspended over the French lines like bunches of grapes was depressing because every single man, every single machine gunner thought they had been spotted, observed and would be submitted to very accurate shooting." This was confirmed by Lieutenant Combrond, observer on Balloon 39: "On 19 September I was particularly lucky to spot 35 trains and several German columns on the roads in the Péronne area." This information was immediately transmitted to Foch and enabled him to check a violent German attack the following day around Bouchavennes.

After six days' artillery preparation, British infantry launched the assault and ran into defences that had remained virtually intact despite the bombardment. At the end of the first day, the English attack already numbered some 20 000 dead and 40 000 wounded. The arrival of a few Model 1 "Tanks" in the Flers-Courcelette sector did not solve any problems because nobody had actually thought about how best to use them.

Too big, too slow, too heavy, too few! They got bogged down too easily and were an easy prey for the artillery. Meanwhile Foch's French troops had managed to reach the objectives that had been set but at a very heavy price.

Although the Allies dominated the skies brilliantly, their air superiority started to decline from September onwards because the Germans transferred part of their air force from Verdun to the Somme area and were resisting more and more fiercely, all the more so as their designers had started delivering aircraft which were now comparable to those of the Allies. On 23 September, Sous-Lieutenant Guynemer jotted down: "11.20: a Hun went down in flames here, 11.21: a Hun lost with his passenger killed, 11.25: a Hun down in flames 400 yards from the lines, 11.25 and a half a 75 took all the fabric off the upper left wing, hence a well executed spin. Went into the ground at 160 kph. The crate bounced and over turned. The Spad is solid. With any other I'd have been thinner than this piece of paper."

The observation aircraft carried out observation and photographic recce missions. These were done using cameras with 26 or 50 cm focus, fixed vertically between the observer's legs. He took photo after photo so as to cover as extensive an area as possible without interruption, and also vertical photos often combined with oblique photos taken during a fly-over. As well as supplying the high command with as precise a reproduction as possible of the terrain to be attacked, the main aim of the mission was to spot where the batteries were placed, and if possible follow where they moved to, and prepare the interdiction shooting. Once the artillery preparation started, they had to observe the results and check that the casemates or other targets had actually been hit and put out of action before the infantry attacked.

Bomber groups were given the task of operating against the communication lines to halt the arrival of reserves, attack stations, command posts at the rear and if possible moving troops, despite the dangers of daylight action.

Three bomber groups were involved in all. V 101 which had been withdrawn from the front at Verdun, moved from Behonne (Meuse) to Sacy-le-Grand (Oise).

THE PEUGEOT VOISIN SEEN BY A PILOT

According to Armand Viguier, "The Voisin Canton-Unné was going to be replaced shortly by a version fitted with a Peugeot engine. It had two faired tanks situated under the upper wing. It had a longer range but the drag caused by the tanks lowered its top speed by those few mph which the increased power offered by the engine could have given it. It did carry a few more bombs than the previous model but it was heavier on the pilot, didn't glide very well and was a long time taking off and landing."

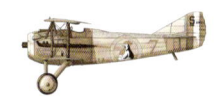

Opposite.
The pilots from the "Cigognes" (Escadrille N 3) in September 1916. From left to right and top to bottom: André Chainat, Matthieu Tenant De La Tour, Albert Deulin, René Dorme, Alfred Heurtaux and Georges Guynemer. Centre: Captain Brocart, the group's CO.

As soon as it got there, it attacked an ammunition factory on the night of 29-30 June, near Noyon. GB 3 came up and settled at Esquennoy; on 1 July it bombed the stations at Nesles and Roye and two of its canon-planes shot up the station at Tergnier. GB 5 moved to Palesne, near Pierrefonds on the eastern edge of Compiègne Forest, followed a short while later by first BM 117 then the whole of GB 5. Escadrille C30 flying G 4s, and MF 50 and MF 210 operated against the enemy communication lines. The main thrust on the front was given to GB 3 which attacked Saint-Quentin station on 1 July and four Farmans from MF 50 and two G-4s from C 30 dropped 38 120-mm shells on Laon station. On the 3rd, nineteen Caudron G-4s escorted by Nieuports from N 12, returned to these targets but lost one machine. GB 5, reduced now to only Escadrille BM 117, took part in operations against Ham, Chauny, Terngier and la Fère during the night of 10-11 July. In mid-July, Péronne was bombed during the night. As the Germans had reacted by bombing the stations at Longueau and Villers-Bretonneaux, Foch organised the counter-measures that were to be taken: balloon barrages, AA battery concentrations with their fire criss-crossing over the targets to be defended, night-fighters, black-outs. August and September were intensively active months and on each sortie three or four aircraft attacked the searchlights to protect the others' attacks. The large amount of activity did not compromise the efforts of the other groups which continued their attacks on both sides of the Rhine.

On 10 October, General Joffre explained what he had learnt from this campaign in a series of instructions recommending the formation of combat groups based on the Cachy Group model, reporting to the Commander-in-Chief, who decided what their assignments were to be. Four Fighter Groups were formed as a result: N° 11 given to Captain le Révérend, N° 12 to Captain Antonin Brocard, N° 13 to Captain Philippe Féquant and N° 14 to Captain Robert Royet Massenet de Marancour. Each group comprised four escadrilles with fifteen aircraft and as many pilots. Solo flying was forbidden and patrols of five planes staggered at different heights were organised.

Bombing activity declined between October and December because of the worsening weather conditions. The rain started falling during the second fortnight of October making the airfields unusable. Activity resumed in November with the bombing of German barracks. The German command in return inflicted a war contribution of 3 000 francs on Anisy-le-Château and 80 000 and then 100 000 marks on Laon. On 23 November, in full daylight, GB 3 and V 101 dropped 171 120-mm bombs on Grisolles airfield, north of Ham without loss. The airfield was devastated then abandoned by the Kaiser's air force. In December, only GB 3 and V 101 remained on the Somme front.

The communiqué at the end of the Battle of the Somme announced that from 1 July to 1 November, French troops had captured 1 446 German officers and 71 532 ORs, 172 medium-calibre cannon, 130 heavy cannon, 215 mortars and 981 machine guns. Since 1 July, the pilots had carried out 142 air raids of which 48 over enemy territory, dropped 5 426 bombs, shot down 228 enemy planes of which 96 fell behind the German lines, and 22 balloons. During 77 dogfights, French pilots shot down ten planes, dropped 970 bombs on the stations at Lens, Vouziers, Courcelles-sur-Nied and on the foundry at Algrange, near Thionville. This was the first time an attack was mentioned concerning the Briey Basin which supplied Germany with 76% of its iron ore consumption. However, with the onset of German daytime and full-moon night-time attacks in autumn by Gotha twin-engined bombers against industrial sites in Lorraine, the authorities feared that other sites would get bombed so protection escadrilles were set up in Lyon and at le Creusot in December, a decision which interested other towns which also set up protection escadrilles in the spring of 1917. Learning the lessons from this campaign which cost more than 1 200 000 men, on both sides, on 23 December 1916, General Foch added in his own hand and underlined it, the following comment on the report made by Commandant Pujo, his head of the aeronautical service: "Air superiority enables us to have artillery superiority which is indispensable if we are to have superiority in the present battle."

For his part the Receiver for the Aviation Budget reported that as at 1 December, the 2 023 planes in operational service included 196 school planes and 409 from the general reserve. The 1 418 planes assigned to the front line could be broken down as follows: 837 observers, 328 fighters and 253 bombers. The number

during the First World War

Opposite.
"Le biplace sort" (the two-seater comes out), illustration taken from a humorous series by Marcel Jeanjean.

of out-of-date planes still used by operational units, comprised 837 observers, or 488 Farmans and 314 Caudrons, 88 fighters and almost all the bomber fleet. Their performances were all inadequate. He also noted that out of 629 Spad VIIs ordered only 25 had been delivered whereas more than one thousand were needed, and that its big brother, the Spad VIII with two machine guns, was also expected.

The observers were still waiting for the 725 Dorand ARs which had been ordered ever since all the pusher-engined aircraft were being replaced by planes with tractor engines, like the G 4s or the Sopwiths. They gradually obtained some Caudron G 6s and were waiting for the first two-seat Salmson and especially the Breguet XIV which made its first flight on 21 November. The bomber situation was worse. A competition to choose the "Essen" bomber was held, as it had been the previous year, for the makers who came up with prototypes with two, three or even four engines but only two twin-engined planes passed the qualifying trials: Morane-Saulnier came first, then the twin-Renault 220-hp Spad. Colonel Barès proposed ordering 300 Morane-Saulnier twin-engined bombers for an estimated cost of 60 million francs; Parliament thought the expense exaggerated and refused to vote the money. There was one of these planes at the front, according to the memoirs of Commandant Armand Viguier (in "Une vie avec le ciel comme horizon" – A life with the sky as your horizon) who wrote "A twin-engined Morane came to our VB 107 group for trials and was handed over to Beaudouin from VB 109. When he took off alone, the plane did not remain level and nosed up so much that it crashed and caught fire". In despair, the night-bomber units started replacing their Canton-Unné Voisin 5s with Type 8s fitted with 220-hp Peugeot engines, and the day-time bomber units, equipped with Sopwiths, put all their hopes in the bomber version of the Breguet XIV.

Once the threat had gone, politics took over again and the Members of Parliament fiercely criticised the head of the Government, Aristide Briand who, to calm things down a bit, was forced to reshuffle the cabinet. General Roques was replaced as Minister of War by General Lyautey, recalled from Morocco. General Joffre paid for his contempt of politicians by being made counsellor without portfolio; this he refused and resigned on 26 December with a Marshal's baton to console him. He was replaced as early as 16 November as C-in-C of the Armies of the North and North-East by General Robert Nivelle who spoke good English, and who was appointed General-in-Chief of the French armies on 2 December. General Foch, in disgrace, was put into the reserve at Senlis.

Finally on 12 December, the Government set up a Ministry of Armament which had to decide what was a priority and what had to be built. During the year, some 7 549 airframes and 16 785 engines had been produced. Increasing the resources like this matched the effort that had been made by the training schools. They had trained a large number of recently licensed pilots, also recruited from among wounded soldiers who volunteered for the air force, after a rigorous selection process in which citations for bravery in action carried a lot of weight. A total of 2600 pilots came out of the schools, an average of 250 per school. The most active one was Chartres with 630, followed by Avord with almost 400; the others, Buc, Etampes le Crotoy or Ambérieu were average and Pau.

The training centre at Pau, in the middle of being reorganised, only produced 150 licensees, Juvisy (recently opened) 150 and Tours 200. These reinforcements meant other units could be created, including some for the heavy artillery, numbering from 200 or more, as follows: ten observation escadrilles in January, seven in February, two in April, one in May, October and November, and four in December.

One fighter escadrille was created in April, two in July, one in September, two in November and in December. The bombers had six new escadrilles in February. Theatres of operations abroad received observation escadrilles: four in Tunisia, one in Algeria, and a bomber escadrille in Morocco, where the agitation stirred up by the Germans led to the War of the Rif. Four escadrilles were sent to Romania which had joined the Allies on 17 August after hesitating for a long time. This does not take into account the escadrilles deployed on the Front of the Orient, nor those serving in Albania, Serbia and Italy.

In its 1/15 February issue, the magazine "L'Aérophile" published the annual German 1916 losses, those claimed and confirmed, compared with the French figures. From the German side, there were 739 French

2. 40000 men, or half the Moroccan garrison troops, had been brought to France and sent to the front, which encouraged Germany to subsidise the mutiny.

Opposite.
The aces from Escadrille N 3. From left to right: Tarascon, Lafargue, Dorme, Chainat, Brocard, X and Heurtaux.

and British kills and 221 losses. The French confirmation system gives 417 kills and 29 Drachens.

The monthly reports reveal some surprises: in January, Germany announced five losses whereas the French only had two kills. The most active period was from July to November, during which the French announced fifty kills or more monthly and even 70 in September. German losses stagnate at around 20 monthly during the same period. On the other hand, the kills claimed by Germany were on average higher at 80 monthly with a peak at 104 in October. It was true that these figures included British planes for which the details were not known.

The leading escadrille in the "Cigognes", N 3, which included the largest number of aces, fought 820 fights, obtained 82 kills (planes) and three Drachens. In the six months up till 1 July (Verdun), the tally was twenty planes and one Drachen shot down, and in the second semester (the Somme), twelve planes in July, fifteen in August, fourteen in September and twenty-four for the last quarter. Among the aces, Guynemer made 31 kills as at 17 February 1917, followed by Nungesser with 21, Heurtaux 20, Dorme 17, Deullin 11, Chainat 9, De la Tour 8, all of them from N 3 except Nungesser.

Navarre's escadrille, N 67, the first to take part during the attack on Verdun, with Captain de Saint-Sauveur as CO, carried out 1492 sorties, fought 319 fights and shot down 15 planes. During the Battle of the Somme it made 853 sorties, fought 200 dogfights and shot down ten planes. N 67 was the first fighter unit to earn the right to wear a *fourragère*, a distinctive sign worn by all members of the escadrille.

Below.
Pilots from N 442, the protection escadrille for Lyon with, centre, visiting them, Captain Baron Shigeno, a Japanese volunteer in the Foreign Legion, assigned to Spa 26 in which he obtained two confirmed kills and six probables.

during the First World War

The year 1917

Right.
Christmas card from C 43 with a full frontal of a Caudron G.4

Right.
German 12-inch (36 cm) diameter "Torpedo-bomb". This missile could be dropped from the big multi-engined bombers like the Gotha or the Zeppelin-Staaken or by Zeppelins

On 1 January 1917, the air force numbered some 2 066 officers and 18 850 ORs. The way awards were handed out was quite unfair because fighter pilots had an almost exclusive right to all the media coverage in the dailies and the specialist magazines. The title of "Ace", reserved for those who had fought and downed five or more enemy aircraft had been given to 21 airmen still alive as at that date, including three gunners with six kills each: Leon Vitalis, Lois Martin and Adolphe du Bois d'Aische. Georges Guynemer was at the top with 25 kills, followed by Nungesser with 21 confirmed kills who was in hospital wounded until May; then there was René Dorme who did not survive beyond 21 May, with 17 kills. Alfred Heurteaux already had 16 to his tally, made his 21st on 3 May before being sent on a special mission to America.

Yet the blatant injustice of lavishing publicity on the fighter pilots only did not hamper the activities of the other personnel of which some, in observation or bombing, had carried out more than a hundred missions.

The first six months of 1917 were the war's darkest. The air force didn't have enough Spads and the ones there were, were often grounded by teething troubles (1). There was as much criticism from the front as there was from the rear. At the front people were up in arms against the administration which was fussy and which didn't supply the spare parts needed for servicing the planes in time; there were also complaints about deliveries of out-of-date aircraft when technical progress meant that the materiel should have been replaced earlier. At the rear, decision-making was delayed by the barrage of authorisations maintained by an inflexible administration. Besides, using the system by which the artillery was run, based on how much it theoretically used up every month, was an obstacle to responding to what was actually needed at the front. Finally there was pressure from all quarters, as much from the manu-

---
1. The engine trials were carried out in warm weather with a different lubricant from that used on the front which didn't have the same viscosity. What was more, this viscosity diminished when the temperature dropped, so much so that in cold weather or high up, the engine seized up. It was Commandant Caquot who, after trials, found the problem and a solution for it.

Left.
Caudron G.6 of escadrille C 43. (DR)

Right.
The debris of several German bombs dropped over French Territory.

THE FARMAN 40 AS SEEN BY A PILOT

The pilot, Armand Viguier wrote in his memoirs: "One fine morning in May 1917, an unknown plane type landed on our airfield at Esquenoy. It was a Maurice Farman; it had a classic Farman airframe, but had a cruciform tail like the "Henry Farmans". The engine was no longer the usual Renault but a 220-hp Lorraine. Lieutenant de Greffier, who was in command of VB 107, gave me the new machine to test. This F-40 had its engine at the rear and was marvellous to fly. What was surprising was the silence. It had, it is true, two exhaust pipes. A few flying hours later I had my F-40 really in hand. I tried an engine cut-out at 10 000 feet. It flew as well as with its engine running. Letting yourself go down with nothing but the whistling of the slipstream through the plane's wires, feeling it obey you with suppleness, hearing the noises coming up from the ground sometimes, manoeuvring precisely to get into the wind, realising that you were neither too long nor too short, landing on the precise chosen spot, that was voluptuousness…"

facturers trying to impose their products as from the technical services holding on to models people at the front had chosen so that trials could be carried out, not to mention the complaisance between the builders and the technical services.

Finally something resembling a flexible organisation was set up so that the materiel was rationalised, limiting the choice of operational machines and ensuring new pilots were not assigned to units without being trained adequately in the training centres beforehand. Likewise units were no longer assigned to generals who didn't know how to use them rationally. These reforms were obtained by several talented organisers like Colonel Girod or members of parliament like d'Aubigny, and tended to reinforce the effectiveness of the whole air force in action.

Moreover the report from a team headed by General Guillemin sent to evaluate the disquiet in the air force, both at the front and at the rear, was handed in on 10 February. The crisis in the air service of the Army was caused mainly by Colonel Régnier who wanted the air force to work like the Artillery, managing stocks in the same way as they dealt with shells, and rationalising the command echelons.

Lieutenant-Colonel Barès became the unjustified victim of the intrigue contrived by his detractors in the ministries and among the builders: he handed over his job to Commandant Guillabert on 15 February. On 10 February Lieutenant-Colonel Barès was requested to command an infantry regiment, a transfer ordered by Lyautey, the new Minister of War, to placate the industrialists and certain GHQ officers and their recriminations. With the "hesitation-waltz" getting bigger, Guillabert was replaced on 20 February by an airman, Squadron Commander du Peuty. As a result of his report, General Guillemin was appointed the new boss of the Aeronautical Service at GHQ, with Colonel Régnier to assist him. This decision finally satisfied GHQ which insisted that the Aéronautique remain under the Army's control and opposed the idea, subsequently dropped, of removing the two RGAs from le Bourget and Versailles.

The German air force, mindful of how weak it was, exploited the tactic whereby their aircraft scuttled away as soon as they saw French fighters and only fought over their own lines; it harassed observation planes and bombers with group attacks. The appearance on the German side of effective machines with 180-hp engines made them difficult preys to shoot down.

Above and below. Sous-Lieutenant Georges Guynemer aboard one of his Spad VIIs, N° 254 ("Red 2") in January 1917.

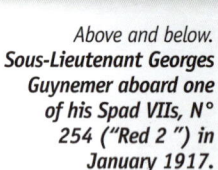

THE SIOUX IN TROUBLE

On 19 March, N 124 lost James McConnell, the last pilot of the original unit, then Edmond Genet was shot down by the flak on 17 April. On 23 May the French Second Officer Alfred de Lage de Meux was killed during a trial flight on a brand new Spad VII. Out of the 267 American pilots who volunteered for the French air force, 225 had their pilot's licence and 180 served on the front where 62 were killed, 51 of which in aerial combat; 19 were wounded and 15 taken prisoner. They scored a total of 199 confirmed kills of which 41 for Escadrille 124 alone. Although Raoul Lufbery scored 17 confirmed kills and most likely 70 probables, others like Thaw and Prince scored five and were mentioned on the aces list. When America entered the war against Germany and set up its own air force units with French materiel, Escadrille N 124 came under American command and was designated as the 103rd Aero Squadron.

The French air force had Sopwiths, Dorand ARs or Letords whose performances were scarcely better than the planes they had replaced. The fighters were used as stop gaps, changing bases as and when and where the need was greatest, in Lorraine to fight off the Gothas bombing the towns in the east, or in Champagne where a new offensive was building up, and supporting various offensives, without any particularly good results.

On 30 and 31 January, Paris and its outskirts were bombed by planes dropping 250 bombs causing 75 dead despite the action of the le Bourget protection escadrilles. In March the town protection escadrilles were assigned to Nancy (two escadrilles), Dunkirk and

Above.
The "Vieux Charles" was displayed at the Invalides in October 1917 after Guynemer had been killed. It was in fact Spad VII N° 254 with which he had scored 19 kills. After being exhibited in Salon-de-Provence at the Ecole de l'Air, this machine is now on display the Musée de l'Air at le Bourget, after being restored.

Right.
Charles Nungesser proudly wearing his decorations. There were further ones before the end of the war which he finished with a tally of 43 kills.

Below.
A pilot from the Lafayette Escadrille in front of a Nieuport 24. (SDASM)

AIR RAIDS OVER LONDON (MAY-AUGUST 1917)

The German bombers in Kampfgeschwader, or Kaghol, N° 3 under the High Command's direct orders, attacked the English coast then London from the spring onwards. This Kaghol, with a strength of four six-plane flights, each plane carrying 660 lb of bombs, started on 25 May with a daytime raid by 21 twin-engined Gothas based at Saint-Denis-Westrem, near Ghent, against Folkestone and other towns on the south coast, killing 95 people and wounding 260. Then 14 Gothas attacked London by day killing 162 civilians and wounding 732. The expedition's commander received the highest decoration for this feat, the "Pour le Mérite". Faced with this new danger, the British recalled three fighter units from the Continent, including the renowned N° 56 Squadron (the equivalent of the French N 3) to defend London. On 7 July a massive Gotha attack resulted in 57 further casualties for the loss of one Gotha shot down and four destroyed while landing. On 12 August, the last Gotha attack resulted in 78 civilians killed or wounded. These daylight attacks ended on 22 August, the day on which four out of the ten Gothas involved were shot down by British AA fire or fighters; the night-time attacks however were spread out from 3 September until the Armistice. In all the group lost 24 planes shot down and 37 lost in accidents for a theoretical strength of 30 planes.

a short while later to Belfort as well as those already assigned to defend industrial sites. In March likewise other escadrilles protected ports where troops and various other items of materiel were disembarking: le Verdon, les Sables d'Olonne, Quiberon, le Croisic, Eu-le-Tréport then in June Lion-sur-Mer and Marseilles. Le Bourget also had a specialised escadrille in April, Br 509 NE, assigned to protect the GHQ of the Armies of the North and North-East.

On paper at least the air force was stronger than it was at the time of Verdun, but the arrival of newly qualified pilots who weren't battle-hardened, the creation of several escadrilles commanded by inexperienced officers, the escadrilles at the front being reluctant to let their best men go, made for an air force that was in a weak state of which however the High Command was hardly aware. Marcel Haegelen was severe when he

Below.
Zeppelin LZ 89 (N° L50) shot down by five Spads from Spa 52 on 20 October 1917 near Bourbonne-les-Bains.

THE NIGHT OF THE ZEPPELINS

During the night of 19-20 October, thirteen zeppelins led by the CO of the German Navy airship units were scheduled to attack England in grey and misty weather. Two of them were unable to leave their hangar at Nordholz. The others (L53, 45, 54, 41, 44, 46, 47, 50, 55, 49 and 52) were in sight of the English coast at around 18.00 and went on with the air raid, killing 36 civilians and wounding 55 others in London. On the homeward trip, violent winds took hold of the armada, partly dispersing it. It was a disaster during the day. L 44 was destroyed by the 74th Half-Section's AA fire at Saint-Clément-les-Eaux, L 49 was forced to land by Nieuports from N 152 and its crew taken prisoner at Serqueux (Meurthe-et-Moselle); L 50 was driven by the wind and lost a nacelle when it touched the ground at Dammartin (Vosges) then disappeared in the Mediterranean, L 55 was destroyed in a crash landing in Germany, L 45 was forced to land at Laragne-Montéglin (Hautes-Alpes), near Sisteron and set on fire by its crew. That was the end of these large-scale raids, since a 50% loss rate was unacceptable.

wrote: "During the war, out of ten fighter pilots, one was an "ace", three others were brave but not talented enough. Among the remaining six, four should have been assigned to another arm, and the remaining two had neither the temperament nor the skill."

On 15 March, du Peuty, the former CO of fighter escadrille MS 48 and the new CO of the Service Aéronautique aux Armées, drew up a plan for 2 665 frontline planes as an emergency. He was insistent, remarking that there were only 75 Spad VIIs available in February, the operational planes being Nieuports 17 whose performances were not as good as those of the German planes. The bomber units suffered from the same deficiencies because the 250 planes in those units (Breguet-Michelins, Caproni-REPs, F-40s, Voisin 5s) had to work by night. The four escadrilles equipped with Paul Schmitts created in April to form a Group attached to GB 3, gradually converted to other types of planes. The army observation units with 900 planes (G-4s, Nieuport XIIs, F-40s) were, at the risk of being repetitive, in the same state, and replacements in the form of Sopwiths, Dorand ARs and Letords turned out to be only just that little bit better.

The Chemin des Dames (April-May 1917, including Craonne)

This was a two-stage concerted operation intended, in the mind of the new C-in-C Nivelle, to break through the German front. On 9 April, British troops launched

A FATAL MISTAKE

When the "Cigognes" group moved to Dunkirk the pilot, Nungesser, was delayed by engine trouble. Alone over Arras, he was attacked by an English plane taking him for a German. Very much in spite of himself, the ace ended up having to shoot down his attacker. Landing near the wreck, he inspected it and discovered that it belonged to a friend…

an attack against the German positions, relieving Arras from strong pressure and the Canadians managed to get hold of Vimy Ridge. But this initial success costing 11 285 killed, was short-lived. On the 12th, in morose weather – rain if not snow and violent winds – and on a narrower front than that of their British allies, French troops started an operation intended to test the strength of the German defences in the direction of Saint-Quentin. The pioneers had dug shelters and firing positions on this line of positions dominating the valleys, called the Hindenburg Line which couldn't be taken.

The main French attack planned by Nivelle developed from the Oise to the mountain at Reims on 16 April. Its ambitious objectives were Cambrai, Douai and Vervins. The assault captured most of the German front line whose ranks had been thinned out thanks to espionage, but it was brought to a halt in front of the second line of defence between Craonne and Berry-au-Bac. The rolling artillery barrage – massed shooting by cannon progressively increasing their range, calculated to preceded the troops into the attack (in this case the 6th Army under Mangin and the 5th Army under Mazel, or twenty divisions) by a hundred or so yards – went too far ahead of the infantry who were held up by muddy terrain and the bitter cold to which the 10th Colonial Division leading the assault was not exactly accustomed. The rolling artillery barrage ended up by going beyond the German lines whose infantry then pulled itself together, came out of its shelters and opened up, cutting swathes through the attacking lines of French troops. After only three days' fighting, French troops had lost more than 30 000 killed and 80 000 wounded for 5 000 German prisoners. Slightly further east, at Berry-au-Bac, the first French tanks, 128 Schneider CA1s, went up into the line but turned out to be too slow and vulnerable to artillery fire. Moreover 60 of them got bogged down or broke down, and although the rest of them tore down the lines of barbed wire, the infantry, for whom all this was quite new, weren't following behind them.

General Nivelle realised he hadn't made the much sought-after breakthrough and on the 19th gave orders to suspend his big offensive whilst maintaining localised attacks to improve the positions. The French army at the moment had some 130 000 men out of action, of whom 35 000 were killed or missing against 20 000 captured Germans. The English, who had been unable to get further than Arras, had also suffered heavy casualties. Only Mangin had moved forward, by about four miles and as a reward he was demoted. Public opinion was very disappointed by such feeble results while at the front such a useless sacrifice turned this disappointment into revolt.

Between 20 May and June, unrest spread to whole units who refused to go up into the line because they were fed up with offensives which were supposed to end the war quickly but which turned out to be great devourers of men for very little territorial gain. On 15 April, Commandant Paul du Peuty addressed the following message from GHQ to Commandants Brocard, le Révérend and Marancour: "From midday on 15 April onwards, the combat groups will resume their tactical offensive without restriction, the objective being the destruction of the enemy air force. No aircraft from the combat groups must be encountered behind the French lines. To do this, patrols will be made up of ten planes on average; they must never be less than five. Apart from the pilots to whom commandant le Révérend has given special orders, no one is to go up alone. The moment has come to make a big effort without thinking of being tired or our losses."

Although the fighters claim to have shot down 72 German planes for the loss of 17 of their own machines between 16 and 24 April, the reconnaissance planes numbered some 108 killed, wounded or missing from 16 to 30 April. They had to fly at low level looking for intelligence which would enable the artillery to get properly prepared. The French fighters were busy elsewhere and could not protect these planes which were accompanied by the inadequately armed protecting G-4s. On 16 April Captain Vuillemin from C11,

Left.
This Caudron R.4 N°1958 could be R 217 damaged on landing.

COURTESY ISN'T DEAD

Despite the brutality of the fighting, certain airmen did not forget good manners, as this weighted message demonstrates, dropped from a German plane on 20 August at Pévy (Marne) giving two pieces of information: the death of a Paul Schmitt crew in Escadrille PS 126 from GB 3, shot down at 07.55 over Pargny-les-Bois on the previous 29 July. This was the pilot Camille Desmaison and the observer Félicien Ferrieux whose graves rest in the cemetery at Crécy-sur-Serre after burial with full military honours. The message also announced the loss of Sous-Lieutenant Soliman Nazare Aga from the fighter unit N 82 flying a Nieuport shot down on the same day. This Persian pilot was well and truly on the N 82 roll but as a Sergeant. The message also indicated that its author was acting in response to similar French courtesy.

during the First World War

Nieuport 17

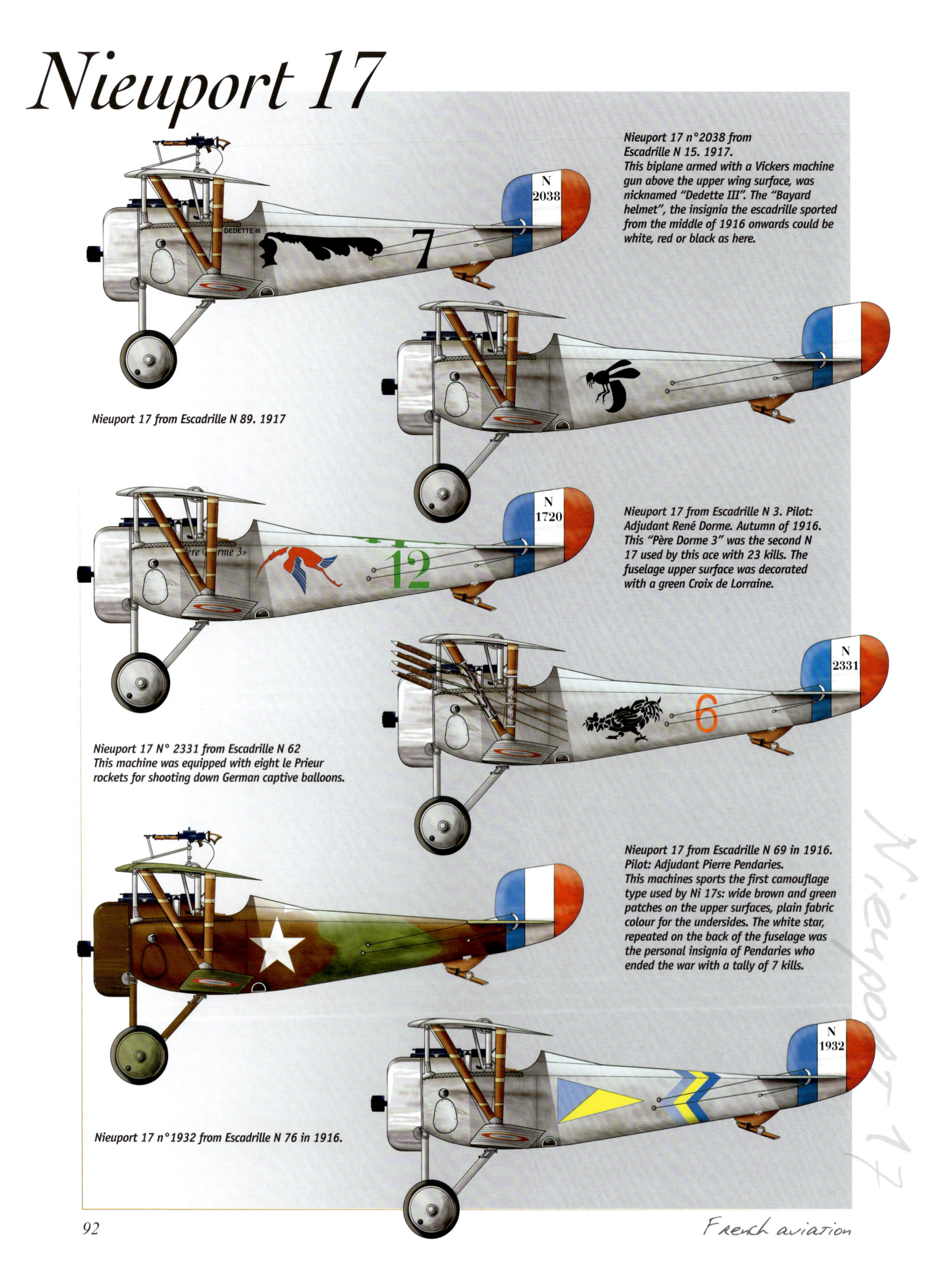

Nieuport 17 n°2038 from Escadrille N 15. 1917.
This biplane armed with a Vickers machine gun above the upper wing surface, was nicknamed "Dedette III". The "Bayard helmet", the insignia the escadrille sported from the middle of 1916 onwards could be white, red or black as here.

Nieuport 17 from Escadrille N 89. 1917

Nieuport 17 from Escadrille N 3. Pilot: Adjudant René Dorme. Autumn of 1916. This "Père Dorme 3" was the second N 17 used by this ace with 23 kills. The fuselage upper surface was decorated with a green Croix de Lorraine.

Nieuport 17 N° 2331 from Escadrille N 62
This machine was equipped with eight le Prieur rockets for shooting down German captive balloons.

Nieuport 17 from Escadrille N 69 in 1916. Pilot: Adjudant Pierre Pendaries.
This machines sports the first camouflage type used by Ni 17s: wide brown and green patches on the upper surfaces, plain fabric colour for the undersides. The white star, repeated on the back of the fuselage was the personal insignia of Pendaries who ended the war with a tally of 7 kills.

Nieuport 17 n°1932 from Escadrille N 76 in 1916.

French aviation

Nieuport 17 from Escadrille N 503 in 1916.
This escadrille was earlier called F 386 and was attached to the Army of the Orient and based in Greece, equipped mainly with Farman F 40s.

Nieuport 17 from Escadrille N 561 based in Venice in 1917. Pilot: Maréchal des logis André Loyseau de Grandmaison.
Designated N 92 I (I for Italy), then N 392, this escadrille was sent to Venice by the French Government in 1915 to protect Venice from Austrian air raids against the town after the Italians entered the war. This was because the Italian air force's resources were notoriously inadequate.

Nieuport 17 from Escadrille N 77. Pilot: Sergent Maurice Boyau. Summer 1917.
This former rugby international, born in Algeria, obtained his pilot's licence in February 1916 and ended the war with 35 confirmed kills, among which 21 Drachen balloons.

Nieuport 17 from Escadrille N 79. Fretoy (Oise) January 1917.
The insignia painted on the fuselage was the first style of "wolf's head" of the future SPA 79 whose traditions were adopted by EB 01.091, equipped today with Rafale B fighter-bombers!

Nieuport 17 from Escadrille N 90 in 1916. Pilot: Lieutenant Marius Ambrogi.
This ace who flew Spads and who specialised in attacking Drachens in the last months of the conflict, flew MB 152s during the Campaign for France in 1940 and added a German bomber to his 15 kills obtained during the Great War.

Nieuport 17 from Escadrille N 93 in 1917. Pilot: Lieutenant Gustave Daladier (12 kills on Nieuports then Spads).

Right.
Caudron R.4

Below.
Father Léon Bourjade as a missionary and as an airman.

Le P. Léon BOURJADE. — Officier Aviateur. — Missionnaire. — Nouvelle-Guinée.

Below.
Very spectacular accident of Caudron R.4 landing on a roof on 14 July 1917.

flying a Caudron G-6 at 600 feet over the trenches was shot at by machine guns on the ground: one bullet hit the left hand tank forcing the pilot to crash land. This escadrille started receiving three-seat twin-engined Letords armed with twin machine guns in the front and two machine guns at the rear.

But the German air force was also being reinforced by units now coming back from Russia where, ever since March, the revolution had been disrupting the Tsar's armies. It was also in the middle of being re-equipped with more effective materiel like the Fokker

THE ECCLESIASTIC'S ESCADRILLE

The joke told by a general about Abbé Léon Bourjade was made more in admiration than in criticism him since the abbé, a Sous-Lieutenant in the trench artillery and a volunteer for the air force on 15 March 1917, had trained as a pilot at Avord then at Pau on 17 June. Assigned to N 152 on 13 September 1917, he fought his first dogfight in December over Raon-l'Etape and obtained his first kill against a Drachen on 27 March 1918 near Gérardmer. Then he made a speciality of this, which the ground defences made especially risky. On 25 August he had scored thirteen kills, of which eleven were Drachens. When the war ended, he cried out: "So! This madness of attacking Drachens defended by twenty machine guns! I won't have to do it again!" He had fought 77 encounters in nearly 400 flying hours for 32 kills in eight months of operations and was fourth of the aces still alive. He returned to his life as a priest then as a missionary in New Guinea here he died of exhaustion in 1924.

D.VII fighter, or the Junkers or Albatros ground attack planes. Regrouping them into combat units made them very mobile and independent and enabled them to concentrate a large force very quickly, to the extent of even being able to strip other fronts. This German fighter superiority worried the French authorities who speeded up the arrival of the Spad XIII and asked for a change in combat tactics. The French fighters now patrolled in large groups of more than ten planes, staggered upwards looking for enemy planes, even over the German lines. This set up was difficult to command and the risk of collision was greater than the danger of meeting the enemy in the air. This tactic was revised on 10 May but too late to save the offensive which got bogged down at the cost of heavy casualties.

In the first weeks of the offensive the Royal Flying Corps lost almost all its 140 available planes to the Albatros D IIIs – 75 in action and 56 in accidents with 19 pilots killed, 13 wounded and 73 missing. Rein-

IN MEMORY OF THE INSTRUCTORS

Pilots withdrawn from the front because they were wounded or exhausted became instructors so they could pass on their experience to the pupils. This job was useful but not glorious, though it did have its dangers, since they had to allow the pupil to make mistakes in order to be able to correct them at the last minute, some times too late. This was the case of Albert Jacquin who was withdrawn from the front and appointed commandant of the Avord Training Centre. Licensed on 22 August 1912 N° 582 on Henry Farmans, he was giving his daily lesson to a pupil pilot on 24 August 1917 when one of the machines flying around the airfield collided with his. In the impact, the "boarding" aircraft's engine crushed the commandant's head, killing him. The pilot of the other plane got out unhurt.

forcements brought over from England included many pilots without any combat experience, equipped with out-of-date planes. This period remained in the corps' memory as "Bloody April" ending with the loss of 316 English airmen for only 119 Germans. The RFC lost 75 planes in the first week of April. In April alone, Manfred von Richtofen shot down 21 English aircraft, almost a quarter of his tally before he died.

On 7 May, Albert Ball, the ace with 44 kills, at the head of eleven planes from N° 53 Squadron came across a group of Fokker triplanes. In the confusion of the dogfight, he collided with Lothar von Richtofen's plane and crashed at Annoeulin, near Arras. From N° 56 Squadron only five planes returned to base at Vert-Galant. This accident prompted Hugh Trenchard, the RFC boss, to make Ball the first air hero and to publish the tallies of all those with more than five kills.

Even the German night-fighters were triumphant. A BE 2c from N° 100 Squadron whose flight had arrived in France on 21 March, was shot down during the night of 5-6 April during an attack on Douai, by the Albatros belonging to Lieutenant Frankl from Jasta 24.

To calm public opinion, the Government got rid of Nivelle and on 15 March 1917 brought in Philippe Pétain instead. The pilot, du Peuty (3) quickly ran into the same problems as Barès. In mid-May however he had set up a system to protect the observation units and managed to get the fighter units to cooperate with those of the Army corps. Moreover, a general fighter reserve was put at GHQ's disposal to be used as and when necessary so as to create a heavy presence during attacks with a restricted objective. This set up was part of a directive in July addressed to the armies. The change of command encouraged du Peuty to ask for a transfer.

The Battle of Flanders (Passchendaele – June-November)

This battle did not achieve the hoped-for results despite the loss of some 400 000 men. From June to November the Expeditionary Corps launched a violent offensive in Flanders. On 7 and 8 June the objective was to reduce the pocket formed to the south of Ypres

I'LL GO AND BOMB LONGWY

Infantry Captain François Lafont, Observation Escadrille F 41's CO, made this promise when his mechanic reminded him that his plane didn't fly high enough. On 25 September 1917, he embarked Lieutenant Observer de Nonancourt for artillery spotting over Douaumont; he had thought he'd be able to go to Longwy, but orders were orders. During the mission they noticed the slowest plane in their escadrille under threat from a large enemy patrol. They went to their comrade's rescue, fought alongside him and managed to get way from the pursuing enemy, then they returned to their observation. Then out of the mist came four enemy fighters who were shooting as though they were at a fairground… Lafont was hit in the head, the plane crashed at the bottom of a ravine at Couleuvre, near Douaumont; the crew was killed and the promise never kept.

2. Jasta, abbreviation for Jagdstaffel or fighter squadron with 14 aircraft, a part of the Fighter group or Jagdgeschwader N° 1 under Manfred von Richtofen.
3. In the autumn, du Peuty asked to be given a command at the front, like Barès, and was given an infantry battalion in which he was killed on 30 March 1918.
4. North America declared war against Germany on 2 April after a U-Boat torpedoed the *Lusitania* in 1915 and when Germany decided to resume the submarine war on 2 February 1917.

Below.
Caudron R.4.

during the First World War

Right.
On 29 August, a very violent tornado struck the centre-west of France and damaged quite a few aircraft hangers.

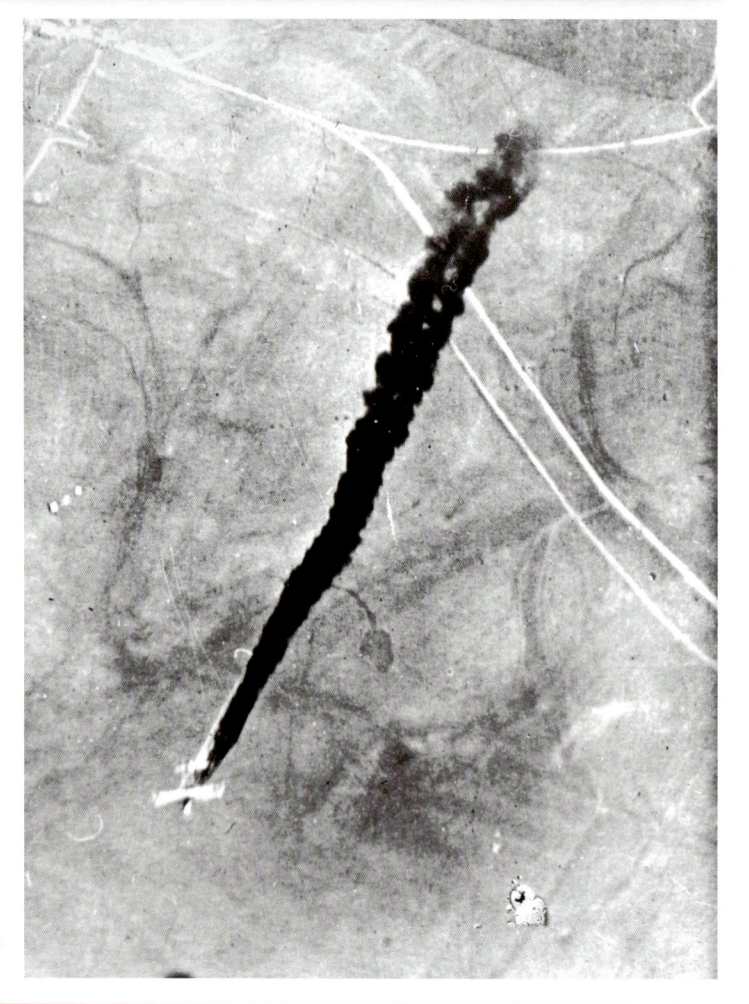

A NEW PLANE

Lieutenant Albert Roper, a pilot in N 68, had just obtained his first kill. He wrote: "To reward me, they gave me a machine which had just come out and which all the pilots dreamt of having: a Spad with a 200-hp Hispano engine which I went to le Bourget to fetch. It brought me back to our airfield at Toul at the speed of 144 mph, a record for the time." and a bit later "on 17 December 1917 I was appointed CO of a new escadrille with the job of forming a Nieuport escadrille by doubling up with N 90. This escadrille of 15 Nieuport 18 metres with two mechanics per machine had a total strength of 110 men". (from "Un homme et des ailes", Editions de l'Officine).

by the German positions at Messines. The RFC engaged 300 planes on 7 June but on 21 June two experienced squadrons were withdrawn from the sector and sent to defend London.

The battle then resumed around Ypres (also called the 3rd Battle of Ypres) led until November by the English helped by the French 1st Army. The English had assembled 825 planes of which 360 were fighters to tackle the 600 German aircraft. The Allies disengaged the Ypres Salient and managed to occupy the Passchendaele Crest 6 ¼ miles to the east Ypres on 6 November, covered by a concentration of 850 allied planes, including the "Cigognes".

This time the allied airmen ran into an independent German unit, the Jagdgeschwader 1, regrouping Jastas 4, 6, 10 and 11, soon to be known as "Richtofen's Flying Circus". The French night-time bombers took part, like Escadrille V 109 which had arrived in mid-June, based at Saint-Polnear Dunkirk, and joined at the end of June by the bomber escadrille Sop 108. They were joined in September by the escadrille of Voisin-Cannons, V 116. From 16 July to 31 August, 132 Voisins dropped 1 094 120-mm, 259 155-mm and 37 200-mm Gros shells on the stations at Cortemarck, Rouolers, Lichtervelde, Iseghem and on the German airfields at Averlee, Rumback and Thourout. Sop 108 took part from 27 June to 18 August in groups of six to ten planes, each carrying four 120-mm Gros shells but casualties were so high that they needed fighter protection. Their results were so poor they had to be removed from operations.

On 7 July, an LVG shot down by Guynemer (his 48th kill) crashed onto a 75-mm battery, the observer was

French aviation

IN MEMORY OF THE TEST PILOTS

Mass producing planes meant they had to be tested before being delivered to the front. Invariably these trials finished with some acrobatic stints – which were not without danger – to make sure the structure was solid. Two accidents have been taken as examples: Sous-Lieutenant Emile Stibick, civilian licence N° 1465 dated 23 December 1913 on Maurice Farmans, was the second pilot to claim a Taube with his gunner-mechanic David. As a fighter he took part in the defence of Verdun then went off to command an escadrille in Russia. He returned to France in the winter of 1917 when he was assigned to the builder's trials. On 26 August 1918, he was doing his last setting flight when it ended in a fatal accident. That was also the fate of Captain Roeckel, licence N° 916 dated 22 June 1912, in turn artillery spotter, long range recce flights specialist with MF 7 and fighter pilot, who was evacuated from the front because of his wounds. He died at Dunkirk on 18 August 1917 while carrying out trials on a fighter.

killed but the concussed pilot was recovered by a car sent from Escadrille 272, informed by the battery. "It was the tradition in the air forces to treat downed enemy airmen with courtesy", as Pierre Mariage wrote in his book "l'Adieu aux ailes" and "the escadrille's intelligence officer who spoke German, offered him something to eat and had some fried eggs and red wine served to him."

The Canadian pilot William Avery Bishop arrived then and joined N° 60 Squadron in March. He was an ace with 45 kills obtained in 112 sorties and had been awarded the Victoria Cross for a single action on 2 June against a German aerodrome far behind German lines. Although the Royal Flying Corps was the biggest force in the area, there was also the Belgian air force, based at Furnes-les-Moëres where the pilot Fernand Jacquet obtained his first kill.

The French communiqué summarised the French air force results for two months as follows: the fighters shot down 38 planes and two Drachens in July then 56 planes and four Drachens in August.

To these should be added forty planes destroyed beyond the front line in July and 59 which fell behind the German lines in August without there being any confirmation they'd been destroyed. Some 145 day-time sorties were made for 8 tons of bombs dropped in July and 233 sorties for 9.4 tons dropped in August. 261 night time sorties were made for 48 tons of bombs dropped in July and in August 265 sorties for 41.5 tons. On 11 September however Captain Georges Guynemer, heading the aces with 53 kills to his credit, was lost in action over Poelkapelle. He set off on a solo mission in the company of Sous-Lieutenant Benjamin Bozon-Verduraz but his partner lost sight of him during a dogfight with Jasta 3. Guynemer's body was found by a German patrol who recovered his pilot's card, but the English artillery preparation made it impossible for them to go and find the debris of the plane. Guynemer was avenged on 30 September by Fonck who shot down a biplane over Westrosebeck and according to legend, the enemy pilot was Wissemann (5), Guynemer's victor.

The observers worked hard in other sectors too. On 19 June, MF 44 hurried two F-40s on a photographic mission over Apremont and Epinoville (Meuse). Pilot-Sergeant Rogers together with Lieutenant Observer Robin was shot down by German fighters.

The failure of the Battle of the Aisne and its impact on the troops' morale, especially in the air force equipped with out-of-date aircraft, called for new measures in Parliament. On 8 August Parliament appointed the member, Daniel Vincent, (6) as Under-Secretary of State, director of the Aéronautique Militaire, to be responsible for aircraft production. He was in fact responsible for getting two departments which were at loggerheads to work together: the Service Technique de l'Aéronautique, and the Service des Fabrications. The first measure concerned increasing production by eliminating any hindrance to orders placed for materiel and eliminating also any favouritism shown to certain builders. Building out-of-date models had to stop, and arsenals building planes designed by the technical service engineers like the Dorands and the Letords (7) had to stop too. Finally the end users, the pilots and their crews, had to have their say too about how the airframes were to be fitted out and armed. The first batch, the Breguet XIV, entered service in the autumn with the day-time bomber escadrilles which quickly got rid of their Sopwiths.

La Malmaison (October)

A new offensive was launched on 17 to 22 October after intense artillery preparation to get hold of the fort of La Malmaison, just under ten miles to the northwest of Soissons and at the western end of the Chemin des Dames; it was intended to measure the troops' will to fight. The 6th Army led the attack on the 23rd then the infantry stopped once the first positions had been taken. Now aware of what was happening, the enemy thought the attack was over and launched its counter-attack just at the moment the artillery resumed its barrage preceding the second wave of the attack, cutting the Germans to pieces completely. Pétain got the Schneider and Saint-Chamond tanks to take part after the artillery had knocked out the enemy batteries. The tanks were able to show how effective they

Above.
This Rumpler CIV (n°1431/17) from FlAb 3, was captured with its crew on the airfield at Fère-Champenoise on 21 October 1917 after landing because of an engine breakdown.

---

5. It appears this lieutenant was shot down on 28 September by Captain Bowmann from No 56 Squadron at Poperinghe.
6. He was a Sous-lieutenant Observer in Escadrille V 116 and reporter for the Aéronautique's 1915 budget.
7. An engineer in the technical service and a creator of planes since 1912 which Dorand had built in its workshops under his name, then by the sub-contractor Letord.

during the First World War

were, opening the way for six infantry divisions who were right behind them. The Germans withdrew 6 ¼ miles abandoning 50 000 dead, wounded or prisoners. In the night of 1 and 2 November, they abandoned the Chemin des Dames as far back as Craonne. Cooperation with the infantry continued with AR-59 and Balloon 71 to capture Filian.

The Battle for Cambrai (November)

At the beginning of November a dozen French planes were seriously damaged when they landed because of the very violent winds and turbulence. On the 9th, the "Cigognes" group engaged in 58 dogfights and dropped 12 000 little bombs on Miserey, Moislains and Péronne and the wood at Vaux. During the night of 16-17, Cachy airfield was bombed and N 3's Bessonneau hut was completely burnt out with all the machines in it, as well as a lot of aircraft from Escadrilles 26 and 65 which were unusable; one man was killed and seven others wounded.

On 20 November, the British started the Battle of Cambrai. A force of 289 planes was engaged in support of the ground forces in the hope of greatly perturbing the enemy's communication lines and preventing reinforcements from being brought up. Planes were given the task of strafing the German forward lines in order to enable the troops to advance more easily, which was a first, which the enemy soon copied. But just like with the other offensives, despite the support given, a German counter-attack, backed by strafing aircraft, pushed back the English to their jump off point.

Politics had gone through three changes of government (Briand, Ribot and Painlevé) before Georges Clemenceau arrived on 20 November, his only aim being to make war to win the war. Ministries were turned upside down which had an impact on aircraft production as well as on the tactical decisions to come. The arrival at the front of the first American units of divisional size and the influx of troops for training meant people could start hoping for an early end to the war.

In 1917, the French builders delivered more than 23000 engines and 14915 airframes. The schools licensed almost 4730 pilots: Chartres supplied 1 141, followed by Etampes with 962, Ambérieu with 767, Avord, Juvisy and Tours with 400 each, le Crotoy 345, Dijon 278 and Buc seven. The general report for the year shows 1227 enemy planes shot down over the French lines, 479 over the German lines plus 27 destroyed and 583 planes presumed out of action.

The aces' roll included 21 with more than seven kills. Lieutenant Nungesser was in the lead with 30 kills, with sous-lieutenant Fonck close on his heels with 26. At the end of the list with eight kills, there was Sous-Lieutenant Omer Demeuldre (N 84), Adjudant André Herbelin (Spa 81) and Sergent Hector Garaud (N 38). Among the new comers Lieutenant Hay de Slade confirmed his fifth kill on 5 December.

The most active months were March to June, then October and December with on average more than 15 planes shot down over the French lines with 26 in December. During the month's operations Anglo-French pilots claimed 106 kills for the loss of 43 machines. The anti-aircraft artillery also claimed a few victories. Thus the 10th AA Section under Lieutenant Gorssike confirmed 13 enemy aircraft shot down between 26 September and 31 December 1917.

Opposite.
An almost identical scene but dealt with in a more humorous fashion by the artist Marcel Jeanjean.

The year 1918

The blockade had a big effect on the morale of the German people who were suffering increasingly from the severe restrictions and at the beginning of the year a series of brutally suppressed strikes shook its industries. The Russian Revolution, followed by the Armistice with Germany signed on 15 December, freed a large part of the German troops originally engaged on the Eastern Front. The Kaiser's HQ, which now had troops in reserve, decided to prepare a big offensive with the intention of breaking through the Allied front over a wide area. In France, Clemenceau was now becoming interested in aviation, and so as to take into account, or silence, critical members of Parliament, appointed Albert Caquot, a 36-year-old Ecole Polytechnique graduate, as Head of the Aviation Technical Service with orders to re-invigorate this service which was too subservient to the dictates of industrialists and rejected by the men at the front. It was thanks to him that the Spad XIII and the Breguet XIV with a 300 hp Renault engine started coming off the production lines quickly, raising production by 60%. He put an end to the 23 different models of planes just as he did to the 22 different types of engines making the industry concentrate on just a handful. To obviate a shortage of engines, he got other industrialists specialised in the building of heavy machinery like Flandrin, Mayen, and Parent involved and monthly production rose from 2700 units at the end of 1917 to 4000 in October 1918.

An assessment of French aircraft activity between 1 December 1917 and 15 February 1918, or 77 days, was as follows: 22 518 sorties for 104 enemy aircraft shot down for certain and 93 planes out of action for a loss of only 38 French machines; 1 399 photographic missions brought back 21 328 shots. Captive balloons totalled 3 593 hours in the air. 192 tons of explosives were dropped on Ludwigshafen, the Briey and Sarre Basins, and the Metz-Thionville, Trèves, Sarrebrück and Fribourg depots. During the night of 29-30 January, the Capronis from GB 2 bombed Friedrichshafen during a six-hour return flight in winter weather.

During January, British airmen, including those in the Navy, claimed 140 enemy aircraft shot down and the French 81. Between 11-20 February, 16 enemy planes and two captive balloons were destroyed by the fighters, four other planes by AA fire and 43 other damaged enemy aircraft were sent crashing behind their own lines.

On the eve of the German attack, the French air force had a strength of eleven combat groups with four escadrilles each, three daytime bomber groups (GBs 3,4 and 6) and three night-time groups (GB 1, 2 and 7) following on from the conversion of six mixed GBs, in all a total of 27 escadrilles. The High Command chose to assign the daytime bombers to the battle on the ground, leaving the British with the task of carrying out the strategic bombing, because the Head of Aviation at GHQ said that "it was no use bombing Cologne if the Allied armies have been pushed into the sea by the Germans' big push on the ground". As the German bombers were increasing the number of raids against the metal works in Lorraine, the British air forces based at Ochey and the Breguet XIVs from GB 5 attacked the industrial centres of the Moselle and the railway marshalling yards in the Plain of the Woevre. The fighter tally, made at the end of February, listed some 52 pilots with at least five confirmed kills. At the top of the list was Fonck with 32 kills followed very closely by Nungesser with 31. At the bottom of the list twelve pilots had five kills.

CHASING ZEPPELINS

On 11 January in the evening, the air raid sirens sounded in Paris announcing the arrival of the zeppelins. In the CRP, the planes were brought out, one of them was piloted by Lieutenant Georges Bedora who had moved across from the infantry in 1916 and who was the brother-in-law of the pioneering pilot, Emile Aubrun. When the warning ended, Bedora and his gunner reached the base at le Bourget. When they landed at night, the aircraft broke up and caught fire. The two men were seriously burned and transported to hospital were they died the next day.

Opposite.
Sopwith 1A2s from the training centre for observers at Sommesous in May 1918. Created on 15 October 1917, this training centre was renamed the Centre d'Instruction pour l'Aviation d'Observation (CIAO) in October 1918.

The "Kaiserschlacht" (March to May)

Warning signs of an offensive were detected by French observation planes working behind the lines under heavy fighter protection. Foreseeing a German attack in Champagne, which the German dissuasive manoeuvre of flying spurious reconnaissance flights around Mourmelon seemed to indicate, Colonel Duval sought to destroy the enemy air force in this sector.

On 13 March at CAP 115 in GB 2, when taking off on a night flight, Captain Balleyguier, the Escadrille CO, had his right leg almost cut off by the rear engine propeller when he climbed aboard. He was quickly transferred to a hospital after receiving first aid from an American doctor who happened to be visiting the base.

After hesitating for a long time between Ypres and Verdun, Ludendorff decided to attack in the centre in front of Cambrai and started to make preparations, bringing reinforcements up during the night. On 20 March, on a long-distance sortie, GB 2 paid Mannheim and Ludwigshafen a visit under the command of Lieutenant Jacques de Lesseps.

The weather conditions were not favourable for continuous aerial observation along the front which on the whole was calm. On 18 March a German NCO pilot was forced to land and taken prisoner. When interrogated, he admitted that an attack was being prepared for 20 or 21 March. On the morning of the 20th, British aerial reconnaissance signalled that the troops in the trenches were being relieved by fresh troops. In fact it was with the utmost secrecy that large convoys had brought these troops liberated by the Armistice back from the Russian front and a number of units had been specially trained before being assigned to the area.

The German air force had also been reinforced and above all had had all its equipment renewed, more than half its strength now being the Fokker D. VII with some observation units had been converted into assault units, flying armoured aircraft whose two cowling mounted machine guns pointed 45° downwards.

Lots of escadrilles had also been brought together for this offensive whose main thrust was against the British positions. There were more than 1 000 aircraft of which 72 reconnaissance escadrilles (336 planes), four for photography, 28 for ground attack (112 planes) and 51 fighter escadrilles (475 planes) and 18 bomber escadrilles, not counting von Richtofen's Flying Circus in toto. Facing the front held by the French, there were only 367 aircraft shared out in 40 reconnaissance escadrilles (157 aircraft); five artillery cooperation escadrilles, 18 fighter escadrilles (168 planes) and three bomber escadrilles.

On 21 March, Ludendorff launched the "Imperial Battle" or the "Kaiser's Battle" (Kaiserschlacht) which programmed three series of interventions during which the Germans inaugurated a new tactic. It was based on the idea of using specially trained, heavily armed groups of free-shooters who, as soon as a breakthrough was made, were moved elsewhere by trucks, leaving the traditional infantry to exploit the breach they'd made. The first intervention, code-named Michael, on the British front was at first in the Montdidier sector from 21 March to 6 April; then there was the Georgette offensive which was to break through in Flanders between Armentières and La Bassée between 9 and 29 April, and the last was on the French front on the Chemin des Dames. In all, the Germans took a hundred thousand prisoners and captured more than 2 000 cannon without however obtaining a definitive breakthrough. However, although they weren't aware of the fact, they had lost the initiative.

The Battle of Saint-Quentin-Amiens (21 March-5 April)

At 04.40 in overcast weather, a deluge of steel from 6 200 cannon firing poison gas shells fell for five hours a²long the 56-mile front between la Scarpe and the Oise, the line where the British and the French troops met; then the 63 division-strong German infantry went over to the attack, supported by a thousand planes. This offensive was divided into three sectors:

The first axis, called Michael 1 given to the 17th Armée, aimed for the sector between Scarpe and Somme heading towards Bapaume and d'Albert. In support, this army had seventeen reconnaissance escadrilles,

Opposite. Escadre and escadrille commanders in 1918, a reproduction of a period painting by J.-F. Bouchor. From left to right: Joseph Battle (SPA 103), Captain Jean d'Indy, Commandant Victor Ménard (N 23) Captain Xavier de Sevin (SPA 26) and Captain Joseph Peralda, commanding the aeronautical park.

---

1. On 20 March, a captive balloon washed up near Vitry-le François. Its basket contains, among other things, the plan of an offensive in Champagne expected on 26 mars. Big manipulation !

seven ground attack escadrilles, thirteen fighter and seven bomber escadrilles all spread out over thirty-one aerodromes in the Lille sector.

The second, led by the 2nd Armée, aimed for Péronne and Nesle, supported by sixteen reconnaissance escadrilles, eleven ground attack, ten fighter and three bomber escadrilles spread out over thirty three aerodromes to the east of Cambrai and Saint-Quentin.

The third, called Michael III and aimed at Ham and Noyon and was given to the 18th Armée, supported by sixteen reconnaissance escadrilles, eleven ground attack escadrilles, twelve fighter and six bomber escadrilles.

As it turned out, the British soldiers had been allowed to go away on leave, since some of them had been in action now for eighteen months, so much so that the sector wasn't very well defended. Moreover the Germans had 173 escadrilles or more than 730 planes, of which 326 were fighters, against 579 British planes of which only 261 were fighters, and lots of those pilots had only relatively little combat experience.

Confronted with 56 German divisions, the British were outnumbered four to one, and the use of poison gas shells meant the soldiers couldn't fight where they stood. The front gave on the first day in, forming a large pocket. 17 English squadrons abandoned their airfields, setting fire to the lame ducks. For example on the 24th, N° 63 Squadron left Merville and moved to Arras.

The onslaught was however contained by the 3rd British Army which abandoned Bapaume. The 2nd German Armée, which had been ordered to push towards Amiens, bypassed Péronne and forced the 5th British Army to withdraw; the 18th German Armée worked its way along the Oise, went beyond Saint-Quentin, invested Ham and got close to Noyon. Fortunately the German general, Oskar von Hutier, dallied in front of Montdidier on the 24th instead of rushing into the 12 ½-mile breach. On the 25th, the French 3rd Army under Debeney intervened and checked the advance on the 28th although Montdidier had fallen the day before. The offensive was contained to the north but to the south, between the Oise and the Somme, the English army was overwhelmed and fell back on Amiens though the Australians checked the German advance at Villers-Bretonneux on 4 April. After fierce fighting, Ludendorff resigned himself to the fact that the attack would have to be halted. In ten days his troops had advanced 37 ½ miles, taken some 90 000 prisoners, picked up a lot of booty and taken the towns of Péronne, Bapaume, Noyon and Montdidier. On 23 March however GB 8 intervened in strength in the Montdidier region and halted the German advance on Paris.

The reconnaissance aircraft were able to get a good idea of the extent of the attack very quickly and the 1st Division moved quickly to new operational airfields. The Féquant and Ménard fighter groups arrived on 24 March under the direct command of Commandant le Révérend who had been appointed to the post on 10 February 1918. The Féquant group comprised three combat groups with the 11th, 13th and 17th Fighter groups and two day-time bomber groups, GB 3 and 4. The Ménard group had three combat groups made up of GC 15, 18 and 19, and three daytime bomber groups, GB 5, 6 and 9. GB 5 carried out daytime bombing raids and photographic reconnaissance missions between Laon and Vouziers. GB 2 and the Capronis bombed the enemy ammunition depots and supply centres every night.

Thanks to this arrangement, the French air force managed to recover air superiority in four days. Of the 1 232 British front line aircraft at the beginning of the Ludendorff offensive, 1 000 had been destroyed in the four weeks after it started: 195 had disappeared, 695 were destroyed and 147 set on fire during the withdrawal. In exchange the British pilots claimed 354 confirmed kills and 188 probables.

The reconnaissance aircraft were the targets of a very aggressive German fighter force which had very effective new machines. Mis-

A FEW FORGOTTEN ADVENTURES

Adjudant-Pilot Pierre Halphen, an ex-balloon corporal captured by the Germans at Maubeuge who escaped after thirteen months' captivity, qualified as a pilot in 1916 was assigned to the CRP, but was killed during a protection sortie round Paris, a victim of fog near Argenteuil on 30 January. The American pilot, William H. Tailer from Escadrille Spa 67 was killed on 5 February. On 18 February, the Belgian Adjudant-Pilot Willy Coppens, having taken off in a Hanriot HD 1 from les Moeres, decided to fly over Brussels to say hallo to his parents. He returned without hitch after a two-hour flight. Belgian Sous-Lieutenant Thieffry, who had fallen behind enemy lines near Ypres on 23 February, was taken prisoner.

LES AVIONS DE LA GUERRE_ «Bréguet» en pylône.

Opposite.
A ground loop for this Breguet XIV from BR 111.

during the First World War

sions were carried out with two planes or more closely escorting the observation aircraft. On 3 April a battery spotting mission used one Dorand and two protection Salmsons from Sal 1, at the time re-equipping with Salmsons which had left Corbeaulieu. After flying over Pierrefonds, they went over the lines towards Mont Renaud where they were attacked by four Fokker D.VIIs. The Dorand flown by Corporal Paul-Yves Busser with Aspirant le Ray as observer came under crossfire and dived for the ground. The pilot who had been hit several times managed to land the aircraft behind the French lines but the plane keeled over.

The French bomber force lost Captain Paul Moulines from BR 11 during a mission on the night of 26-27 March, mortally wounded by ground fire while flying the plane low. The observer, Lieutenant Lecreux was taken prisoner.

On 3 May, Lieutenant Omer Demeuldre from Spa 84 fell in action over Montdidier during his third fighter patrol of the day after obtaining thirteen confirmed kills and 30 probables. A series of dogfights took place over the Montdidier sector on 6 May between five staggered patrols under Nungesser, Chaput, Guérin, de Turenne and Thomas, and a group of Germans which ended in five German planes shot down for the cruel loss of Jean Chaput, the ace with sixteen kills. Seriously wounded by three bullets in his thigh in the fight against six adversaries, he shot down two and managed to reach his airfield where he died. As only one of the planes fell behind French lines it was the only kill that was confirmed.

THE BIRTH OF AIRMAIL

By decree dated 26 February 1918, Georges Clemenceau founded the Inter-Ministerial Commission of Civil Aviation and ordered the Minister of Trade, Industry and the Post Office to promote the use of the plane as a way of carrying mail. The minister decided to experiment with the route between le Bourget-Saint-Nazaire where American troops were disembarking. This was a service inaugurated by the twin-engined Letord N° 932 belonging to Adjudant Houssays on 17 August 1918. On 15 May, a Toulouse industrialist was already working on an airmail route Toulouse-Casablanca. It was American airmen however who opened up the first airmail route, between New York and Washington on 15 May using the Curtiss Jenny seaplane N° 38262. In Canada, Captain Brian Peck opened the first official service on 24 June.

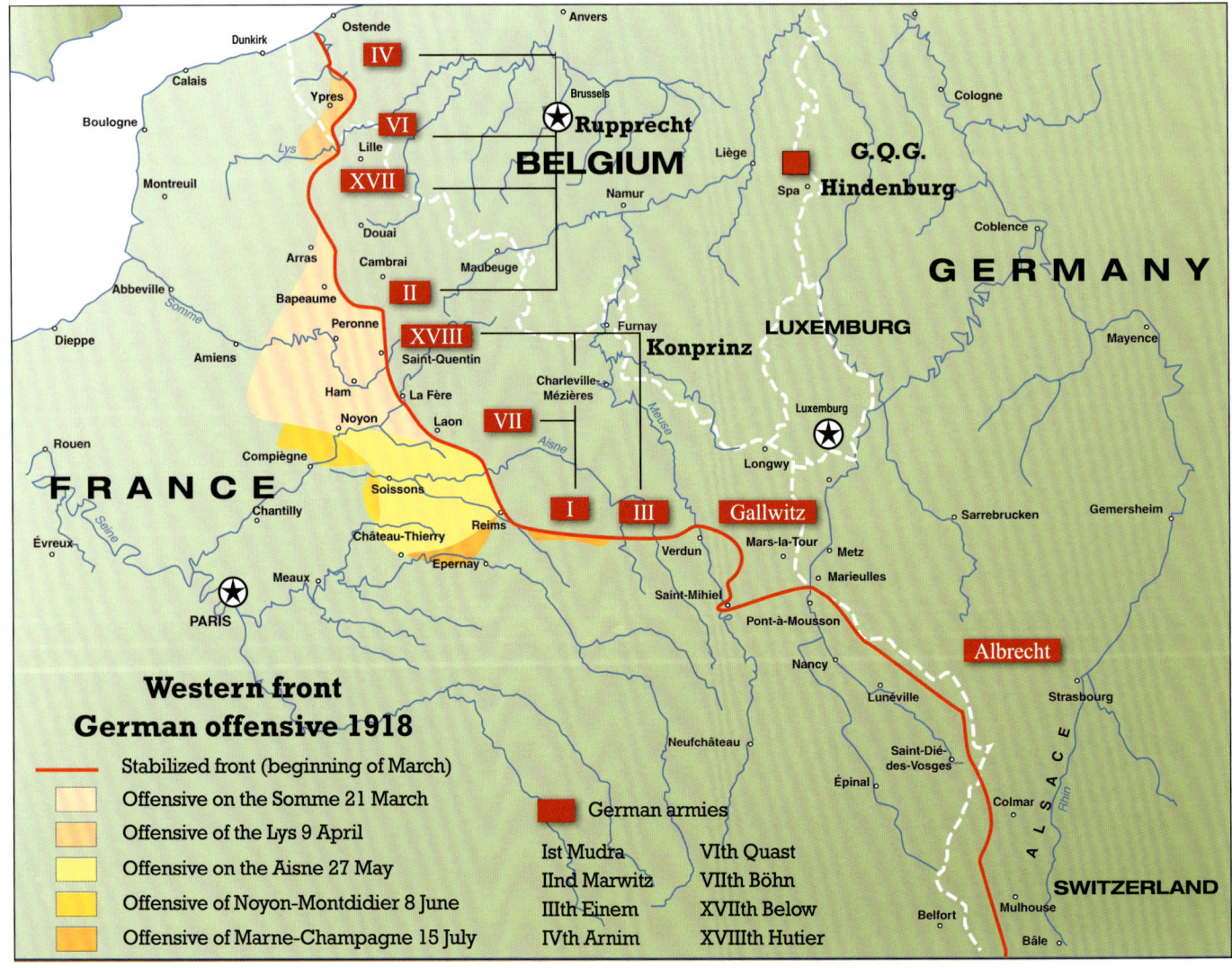

Western front
German offensive 1918

- Stabilized front (beginning of March)
- Offensive on the Somme 21 March
- Offensive of the Lys 9 April
- Offensive on the Aisne 27 May
- Offensive of Noyon-Montdidier 8 June
- Offensive of Marne-Champagne 15 July

German armies

Ist Mudra — VIth Quast
IInd Marwitz — VIIth Böhn
IIIth Einem — XVIIth Below
IVth Arnim — XVIIIth Hutier

Above.
The pilot Yves Busser from Escadrille AR 1 in 1918, posing in front of his Dorand AR.

tish. It was five miles deep and 14 ½ miles wide. The front stabilised along a line going through Givenchy to the south, Bailleul in the centre and Ypres to the north, making a salient. Taken by surprise, the Allies called up reinforcements which halted this thrust on the Flanders Hills on the 27 April. Particularly heavy fighting took place around Mount Kemmel from 25 to 27 April. The British army lost 82 000 men and the French, the ones responsible, 35 000 for German losses amounting to 109 000 men.

GB 2 renewed its night time attacks on Mannheim and Ludwigshafen on 3 April, then on 12 and 23 April with more than 80 aircraft they attacked railway targets. Thus five Voisins and ten Capronis were sent in against the stations at Laon, Hirson, Marles, Montcornet and against the airfield at Clermont-les Fermes. The station at Montcornet, the target for four Italian Capronis, received 3 000 lb of explosives and two Handley Pages attacked Amagne-Lucquy (Ardennes). In VB 114, Pilot-Captain Michel Mathieu, licensed in August 1910 with 173 bombing missions under his belt, was lost with Lieutenant Rivalleau during another mission on the night of 2-3 May.

Offensive on the Chemin des Dames (25 May-13 June)

Converging intelligence forecasted an imminent German attack against the Chemin des Dames, planned since 1 May and involving 43 divisions. Having been unable to obtain a decisive victory in Picardy, Ludendorff launched the 7th German Armée towards Soissons in a two-pronged attack. One was called York and aimed at far-off Soissons; the other was called Blücher and was aimed at Fismes. Both of them ran into the 6th French Army which reeled from the shock and allowed a pocket to develop, threatening Villers-Cotteret to the west and Epernay to the east.

On 30 May the attacking troops had reached the east of Château-Thierry, from Brasles to Jaulgonne. The following day, a vigorous French counter-attack forced the attackers to fall back but Château-Thierry was taken. On 2 June, thirteen German divisions rushed to le Matz. There was a lot of activity in the air because of the good weather conditions.

On 19 May Lieutenant Raoul Lufbery from the American 94th Aero Squadron with eighteen kills fell in aerial combat over Maron. He jumped from his burning machine and fell 2 600 feet to the ground just missing the river Moselle nearby. On 27 May, Lieutenant Georges Félix Madon, Spa 38's CO, claimed four German planes shot down over Reims, but GHQ only confirmed two of them whose pilots were NCO Wilhelm Weniger and Leitenant Karl Hentschel. The other two were an infantry plane to the north of Fismes and a fighter near Craonne.

The dogfights were not over for all that because the Gneisenau offensive, a new attack by the German 2nd and 18th Armee, tried to break through the front to the south of Montdidier on 9 June towards Compiègne and recover some more square miles.

The 3rd Battle of Flanders (9-27 April)

This battle, called Georgette, had a twofold objective: the 4th German Armée aimed to reach the North Sea by crossing the Yser near the distant objective of Dunkirk and ran into the 2nd British Army and the Belgian Army. The 6th German Armée had to break through the front to progress towards Saint-Omer against the 1st British Army, reinforced by a Portuguese division being trained in what was supposed to be a calm sector, during an assault whose primary objectives were the towns of Hazebrouck, Steenworde and Poperinghe. The advance on Ypres was quickly halted but to the south, four German divisions, or 100 000 men drove in the front held by the 20 000 Portuguese, who were relieved the following day.

At four in the morning a violent artillery barrage destroyed all links with the rear and at 7 o'clock, the assault overwhelmed the defence, quickly went round Hazebrouck and created a pocket. On both sides of the Lys, the German offensive advanced some 12 ½ miles. The attackers captured 100 cannon and made 6 585 Portuguese prisoners.

At the end of April, the pocket was closed by the Bri-

THE DANGERS OF AIRSHIPS

The odyssey of a Navy airship CO is told here as an example. Airship V Z 3, based at le Havre under Lieutenant de Vaisseau Fleury, a pilot, returned to its hangar on 20 February 1918 after an observation sortie but the rudder no longer responded to the pilot's commands. Driven by the wind, the airship flew into the cliffs at Saint-Adresse and exploded. The pilot and his radio operator were killed outright; a quartermaster managed to jump to the ground and broke his arm. Unfortunately the explosion of bombs on board caused thirty or so extra casualties.

during the First World War

Opposite.
A seriously damaged MF 50.

Opposite.
A group of Annamite Tirailleurs alongside a Dorand AR2.

Thierry, a photo mission specialist, assisted by Captain Davenne and Corporal Fontame in a Spad-bi on 17 August.

The fighters which were active in all the sectors did have some successes: the American Frank Baylies from N 3 had eleven kills, Berthelot, Bosson, Gasse, Gérard and Moissinac obtained five; Barcat, Boyau, Bourjade, Chaput, de Chavannes, Hasdenteufel, Marinovitch, Nuville, Parsons, Pezon, Hay de Slade and de Sevin added four kills to their tallies, plus 102 other kills obtained by 59 pilots. The official roll listed new entrants like Adjudants Lionel de Marmier and Fernand Chavannes, both from Spa 112, Major William Thaw from Spa 163, Lieutenant Paul F. Baer from Spa 80 and Adjudant Ed-

AMBULANCE AIRCRAFT

The medical personnel were very worried by the numerous wounds, some of them very serious, the soldiers at the front received. Transporting the wounded from the trenches to the field first aid post often caused terrible suffering frequently leading to the man's death. Another trial was imposed on the wounded when they were transferred from the field post to the nearest hospital, not to mention another trip for further, longer treatment. In 1914 already, Senator Emile Raymond, a doctor and a licensed pilot, backed by Ch. Julliot of the Ligue Nationale Aérienne, was lobbying in favour of ambulance aircraft. Julliot, mobilised and in charge of an ambulance, gave a lecture on 10 January 1918 called "Ambulance aircraft and the war" in front of an audience of army doctors and surgeons. He recommended using the Breguet XIV to evacuate the seriously wounded since, he said, vehicles took an hour and a half to drive 20 km whereas planes took only fifteen minutes. He reminded his audience that the surgeon, Truffier, had noted that 17 out of 18 soldiers with abdomen wounds died if they were operated after eight hours. He mentioned the example of Dr Chassaing who had carried out tests at the windmill at le Laffaux on 6 November 1917, transporting patients some 60 km away in 35 minutes. As a conclusion he declared that inestimable service could be expected from the ambulance plane. The idea was taken up and found its resolution in Morocco and in the Levant a short while after the Armistice.

Above.
A nosed-over Dorand AR1 from Escadrille AR 33 bearing the famous Gallic red francisc, adopted as its emblem at the end of 1916 and commonly called the "Hâche d'Abordage" (boarding axe) after the CO's family name, A. -for Alfred- Bordage). This unit briefly used Dorands from mid-1917.

He was therefore deprived of a four-fold victory but found himself in the same situation at la Main-de-Massignes on 17 July, except that this time only one kill was confirmed.

On 31 May, Lieutenant Léon Hébrard from CAP 130 hit an ammunition train at night in Guignicourt station (Aisne) which continued to explode for several hours. Then the fighting picked up with the losses – to mention but a few – of Captain Pierre Pène, an infantry liaison specialist, and of Lieutenant Brun from Sal 10, during one of these missions; of Adjudant Auguste Baux from Spa 103 killed on 17 July; of Sous-Lieutenant Marrin-Berrier, shot down during a photographic mission, his plane on fire; of the crew Lieutenant-Pilot Henri Dupont and Sous-Lieutenant Schalbar from Br 219, shot down during a dogfight on 1 July against three German planes; of the crew Adjudant-Pilot Marcel

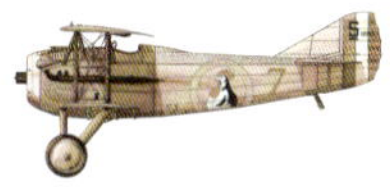

THE END OF A "SUPER ACE"

On 21 April, the "Red Baron" took off with his patrol of six Fokker Dr. 1 triplanes, with a few Albatrosses in dull weather for a flight over the Somme region. Two RAF (the new name for the RFC since 1 April) two-seat aircraft were in the area. Three German triplanes dived in for the kill but the merry-go-round attracted other machines including some British Camels. Lieutenant May's machine with both its machine guns jammed tried to scuttle away, but Manfred von Richtofen saw him and made it his business to shoot him down. This was not at all to the liking of Captain Brown of N°209 Squadron who got himself onto the tail of the Baron and fired. The triplane took the shots and crashed to the ground killing the pilot near Sailly-le-Sec (Somme). The kill was also claimed by some Australian machine gun crews in the trenches. It was the end of a great fighter with 80 confirmed kills.

Opposite.
Hauptmann Baron Manfred von Richtofen, the First World War ace of aces with 80 confirmed kills. He is wearing the "Pour le Mérite" cross, commonly called the "Blue Max", the German Empire's highest award.

mond Pillon from Spa 102. They completed the list of the aces dominated by Fonck with 44 confirmed kills (he claimed he had 68...), followed by Nungesser with 34.

The bombers also contributed to the fighting, but not without losses, like that on 9 June when two crews from Br 120 were lost in an in-flight collision; one of the planes was piloted by Sergeant Boulanger with Sergeant Millioud, the other by Lieutenant-Pilot Ménaud with Maréchal-des-Logis Fernand-Yves Ropartz.

The first lessons

The series of alerts and successes obtained by the German attacks made the General Staff take important decisions which were put into effect in mid-March. The reason for this catastrophe – the Franco-British dual command – ended on 26 March at the Doullens conference when England finally accepted General Foch as the man to co-ordinate the action of Allied troops on

PILOT HENRI TRÉMEAU'S SOUVENIRS*

He wrote in his book "J'étais pilote de chasse au dessus des tranchées" (I was a fighter pilot over the trenches): Morning (23 March) hedge hopping patrol before Roye for 1 ¼ hours. Reconnaissance patrol over Lassigny-Dives-Evricourt, Hill 125, Epinoy-Dives-le Franc-Mont-Renaud. In Lassigny the wooden barracks situated near the house are burning. Dives appears to be the centre of the lines. Evricourt-Epinoy-Dives-Le-Franc have been occupied by our troops. At 16.15 at Suzoy, a German attack immediately halted by violent shooting from our artillery. Mont Renaud, the chateau and the park are on fire as well as the wood depot to the south of the chateau along the railway line. A lot of French troops came up as reinforcements. Enemy artillery not very active. A few heavy calibre shells on the edge of the woods, to the west of Dives-le-Franc. No enemy air force activity. Returned at 5 p.m.

Below.
Letord 1 n° 134.

Letord 2 n°254 (?).

---
* Editions Gilles Platret 2011, 170 pp (iIllus.).

during the First World War

Above.
Lieutenant René Fonck aboard one of his Spads in SPA 103.

Above right.
Alexander I, the King of Greece (profile) visiting the Grand Parc Aéronautique of the Armies of the Orient in February 1918, behind a Spad VII from Escadrille 506 bearing the red chevron that was painted on the tail of some of the machines. The black mosquito painted on the fuselage was however a personal insignia.

the Western Front. In May Colonel Duval, promoted to general, took command of the reformed 1st Air Division comprising two day groups and three night groups working directly with the High Command in massive coordinated operations. The day groups were the Ménard group whose HQ was at Montagne near Amiens with a four-group fighter wing and a three-group bomber wing. The Féquant group whose HQ was at Beauvais-Tillé was added to them, made up of a four-group combat wing with and a two-group bomber wing.

The night groups were made up of Chabert's group whose HQ was at la Ferté Millon, made up of GBs 1, 7 and 8 as well as Villomé's group at Villeneuve-les-Vertus with all the Capronis from GB 2 (CAP 115 and 130, and V 101 flying Voisin 10s, and the Italian GB 18 with three escadrilles), and finally the Laurens Group at Montagne, with GBs 8 and 10. The division's fighters were made up of 24 escadrilles (or 432 planes) and its day bomber force 15 escadrilles of Breguet XIVs (or 225 planes), escorted by four escadrilles of Caudron R XIs (60 planes). The whole represented a considerable force of some 43 escadrilles (717 planes).

In the same period in May, General Duval proposed a front line programme of 2 870 planes in 298 escadrilles to General Pétain: this programme was sent to the new Secretary of State for the Aéronautique in the form of: 32 army corps escadrilles, 62 divisional escadrilles, 90 fighter escadrilles, 66 bomber escadrilles, 40 for the heavy artillery and eight for the heavy long-range artillery. These escadrilles' strength was moreover increased to 18 instead of 15 planes and Caproni R 11s were given the task of close-quarter protection for the Breguet XIV daytime bomber escadrilles. He also recommended that a daytime fighter and bomber instruction centre (the Centre d'Instruction de l'Aviation de Chasse et de Bombardement – the CIACB) and for observation also (the CIAO) be set up in which the pilots and crews training at the rear carried out a training programme together before being assigned to operational units. This was a relief for the operational units who no longer worried about training the newcomers.

THE CANON SPAD

*O*n 18 May, De Sevin went out with two Spads from his SPA 26, flown by Naudin and Puget. He shot down a two-seater with his canon in the Montdidier region, but then spotted a single Albatross operating within his lines at 15 000 feet. Suddenly he saw it dive on Puget, who was himself diving on three two-seaters, shooting him down with the first burst. Abandoning Puget out of action, he rushed over to Naudin whose guns jammed and who was forced to flee. De Sevin was engaged in a fight to the death. The German fired first and burst the water sleeves on the French plane but de Sevin fired off a round from his canon and sent him spinning a way like a rabbit. On this subject, Marcel Haegelen, 21 years old and 22 confirmed kills, among which twelve Drachens, wrote: "for the armament: increase the effectiveness of the shooting by using rapid fire canon."

NIGHT FLIGHT TRAINING

*I*n the first week of July 1918 an instruction centre started working at Pars-les-Romilly, for night fighter instruction. The trainee pilots on Nieuport 120-hp two seaters were chosen from the night bomber crews. They were shown that interceptions were possible, the Breguet XIV "decoy" having been attacked successfully each time. Therefore on 8 October, GHQ published a project organising seven night fighter groups, each group comprising a flight of twelve planes and a company of 120-cm searchlights. Subsequent events rendered this ambitious project pointless. The crews from the observation units also had a special training centre where emphasis was laid on photography.

The Chemin des Dames (part 2) 27-May to 13 June and the limited offensives (5 June to 15 July)

Regular reconnaissance didn't uncover anything in the sector chosen by the Germans who had not given up on the idea of an offensive against Paris. They silently concentrated a force of some 300 000 men, all massed in the Laonnois massif with its rugged relief, in an apparently sleepy sector facing the 6th Army spread out between Anizy-le-Chateau and Craonne. On the 27 May in the morning, preceded by a short and violent bombardment with gas shells, the attack developed between Soissons and Reims along the French front whose own reserves had been sent over to Flanders and Picardy to help the British. On the night of 27-28, the Night Bomber Group N° 11 (GB 1, 7 and 51) sent 49 planes to the region. In retaliation, the German air force attacked the airfield at Cramaille (Aisne), burning a Bessonneau hut and the ten Spa 88

French aviation

MAKING UP A STRATEGIC BOMBER FORCE

The British Government decided to create a fleet of heavy bombers as soon as the industrialists could produce aircraft that could carry out reprisal raids behind enemy lines. This force, the 41st Wing, got together with N° 16 Naval (Experimental) Squadron in the east of France in October 1917 and then carried out some air raids. The plane chosen was the Handley Page 0/400, a twin-engined night-time bomber powered by 250-hp (then 360-hp) engines; it could carry a ton of bombs (sixteen 112 lb bombs) with a flight endurance of eight hours. The headquarters of this independent force were in Nancy and the machines of N°216 Squadron were based at Ochey on 9 May, Xaffévillers for N°97, 100 and 215 Squadrons in August 1918, the planes only being delivered in sufficient numbers in June 1918.

Below.
The carriage for one of the long-range cannon called the "Big Berthas" which bombed Paris.

Spads inside it and destroying the village of Beugneux, thinking that the French Bomber HQ was based there. The attackers quickly found the weak point on the Vauclerc Plateau held by the British and overwhelmed the French Colonial Division. By the evening the Germans had reached the Valley of the Vesle, taken Fismes, and its army warehouses, ambulances and depots. The advance reached a line along the Aisne on 25 May, the Chemin des Dames on the 27th; on the 28th the thrust intensified, Soissons was taken and the next day Fère-en-Tardennois fell. The Germans were getting closer to Paris, but everywhere they were held off, suffering very heavy casualties. The road to Paris was open when the German long-range heavy artillery started firing on the capital.

This advance threatened the airfields used by the night bombers which evacuated the Cramaille, Arcy-Saint-Restitue and Château-Thierry sector. All the advanced firing positions were suppressed. The bombers made a considerable effort to hinder the German advance and some Voisins even bombed the German columns in the daytime. Escadre 12 (the Ménard group) attacked the station at Péronne on 2 May; the Féquant group was given the task of attacking the troops rushing to the Marne from the front. Only the night-time GB 8 did not take part in the hunt. It was working over the Somme which would soon become the new jump off point for the Germans, which is precisely what happened, on 9 June.

The combat groups literally rushed at the enemy columns and bombed and strafed everything they could but they also ran into the enemy groups equipped with excellent machines, fighting in the same way as the French. Flying in groups

THE END OF "BIG BERTHA" *

The German advance threatening Paris was accompanied by regular heavy artillery shots intended to create panic in the streets, worsened by the showers of shells fired blindly from 23 March onwards. It is in fact a three cannons battery especially adapted by Krupp in Essen, each of these cannons weighing about 738 tons, with a 118-ft long barrel and a range of more than 75 miles. More than 380 shells felt on Paris, notably on the Good Friday (29 March) on the church of Saint-Gervais making 92 deaths, and the suburbs of Paris during 44 days resulting in the death of 256 persons and by injuring 625 others. Although this battery is moved by rail from Crépy to Fère-en-Tardenois, it is identified by the aviation on 10 and 11 August.

* It was in fact the Wilhelmgeschutze (William's canon) with a practical range of about 80 miles firing 210-mm shells, of which three examples were based in the Saint-Gobain forest near Crépy-en-Laonnais, then moved to the north of Château-Thierry after 1 May.

Opposite.
German gunners on the 420-mm Gamma howitzer. Nicknamed the Dicke Bertha (Big Bertha) or Fleissige Bertha (Keen Bertha), this canon could send a 1 760 lb-shell at a rate of ten shells every hour. In all, 12 Kurze-Marine-Kanonen (the official name) were built.

THE MEMOIRS OF GUNNER-SERGEANT ANDRÉ DUVAU *

"One fine day, off we went to get closer to the areas we had to bomb; we reached Gourgançon, to the west of the camp at Mailly. Not a brilliant airfield, not set up: tents were pitched near a gentle stream whose water was so cold that I only bathed in it once. I had the opportunity to take part in a dogfight, at Connantre not far from Sézanne, where General Duval, the Director of the Aéronautique at GHQ told us that the end of the war was expected for the end of the following spring. This was good news for us, coming from such a source."

---

* From "Br 29, Souvenirs d'escadrille", a publication by the Service Historique de l'Armée de l'Air, 1976, 70 pp, ill.

---

of six or nine machines, the Schlachtstaffeln (assault squadrons) attacked isolated planes, wiped out the laggards and caused heavy losses. On 30 May, the attackers reached Château-Thierry but were checked on 5 June. To the east the German thrust was contained from Reims to Château-Thierry by two French armies. Ludendorff was trying to push home his success in spite of his exhausted troops, by reducing the French salient from Compiègne to Villers-Cotterets with a new offensive, called Gneisenau, launched along the Oise on 9 June.

The Battle of the Matz (9-12 June)

From 9 to 12 June, a new German attack intending to reduce the Compiègne salient started against the Lassigny Massif; it was called the Battle of le Matz.

---

2. His destiny is mentioned in the book by Pierre Mariage, who was an observer in AR 272, under the title "L'Adieu aux Ailes" published by Editions France Empire, 1967 in the Chapter "Escadrille AR 272 on Mount Renaud", page 109.

At four in the morning, the German infantry attacked along a 26-mile front between Monchel and the Oise. The French centre gave, and opened up a 10-km deep pocket. At 10 o'clock the Germans were at Ressons-sur-Matz, Cuvilly and Mareuil. On the 10th, the capture of Thiescourt Wood enlarged the pocket. On the same day at 14.00, GHQ confirmed that the French counter-attack, planned for the 11th, would be supported by combat aircraft and bombers. Group 12, uniting GBs 5, 6 and 9, bombed enemy troops at Cuvilly, Orvillers and Mortemer on 9 June. GB 8 also carried out this mission even though its airfield at Bettencourt had been bombed the day before and 3 planes from V 113 and part of the buildings had been destroyed. As a reprisal V 113 set fire to the base at Estrées-en-Chaussée after bombing the artillery piece that was shooting at Paris; but the Lassigny Massif was taken by the enemy which forced the French to evacuate the plateau at Carlepont (Oise). On the 10th and the 11th, eleven tons of explosives were dropped from a low altitude on the roads near Ressons-sur-Matz, Orvillers, Elincourt and Marquéglise. But the Germans worked out where the bombers had come from and three nights running they attacked the airfield at Plessis-Belleville. In Group 12, in a single day, Escadrille 127 lost six of its Breguet XIVs out of the seven engaged and the seventh returned with the observer seriously wounded. Fortunately, General Mangin's offensive checked the German advance once and for all on 12 June.

The air division was reinforced from 9 June onwards by the English 9th Air Brigade with two Wings of five fighter squadrons and three bomber squadrons. The observation escadrille AR 272 announced the loss of Captain Meiffre (2) killed by ground fire while hedge-hopping on a recce mission over Mont Renaud. His observer, Ménétrier, emerged unscathed from the wreck in Chiry Wood.

A frightful assault on Reims was halted by the Colonial Corps and elsewhere the German advance was halted, just short of Compiègne by a French counter-attack on 11 June.

Some of the French escadrilles, especially the obser-

SUPPLYING BY AIR

On 17 July a battalion was encircled in the Pourcy region following the big push. They held out but started getting short of ammunition and supplies. The CO managed to inform Brigade HQ of the situation who sent planes in spite of heavy artillery fire. A short while later aircraft dropped 250 loaves, 250 cans, biscuits, bullets and grenades. On 28 July, the crew of Adjudant Forquet (pilot) and Sous-Lieutenant Penigaud (observer) in a Salmson 2A2 from Escadrille SAL 106 left to drop supplies of food and ammunition for the battalion at Vandières encircled in the park of a château, which had asked for help. The delivery went off all right but on the homeward run the plane fell to German gunfire killing the crew. This use of aircraft in this way quickly became standard.

THE DEATH OF GARROS*

On 20 August Roland Garros turned up at SPA 26's airfield at Hétomesnil, wearing the uniform, with white gloves, of an officer of the 27th Chasseurs à Pied Battalion to resume his duties after managing to escape from a German prisoner of war camp. The next day he made his first test flight, just like a pupil pilot coming back to learn his lessons again, wearing the glasses he'd brought back from Germany because he was short-sighted. On 2 October, Garros and de Sevin went out together; the former went into the action and the latter had to get him out of it. Garros attacked a patrol of six Fokkers. De Sevin got him out then Garros turned back into the fight, de Sevin dived in turn and both intrepid fighters shot down their adversaries. On 5 October, in the morning, Garros went off on patrol with five comrades and started a fight against a patrol of Fokkers but soon a second enemy group turned up. Garros attacked five times and de Sevin got him out each time. At about 10.30, Garros, still protected by his team mate went off in the direction of Vouziers, above a flight of Fokkers on their way home. A group from Spa 48 hurried up to help the two Frenchmen and Garros' plane, which sported a huge 30 on the upper wing, was not seen again in the melee. Impossible to find him. One of 48's pilots saw a Spad from far off attacking three Fokkers head on; two veered away at the last moment but the third held its course and the Spad exploded. Garros' grave was found at Vouviers several months later.

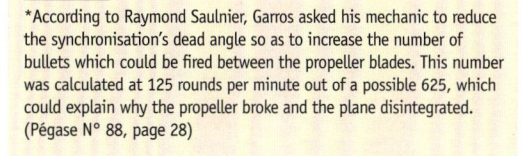

*According to Raymond Saulnier, Garros asked his mechanic to reduce the synchronisation's dead angle so as to increase the number of bullets which could be fired between the propeller blades. This number was calculated at 125 rounds per minute out of a possible 625, which could explain why the propeller broke and the plane disintegrated. (Pégase N° 88, page 28)

Opposite.
Roland Garros photographed on 3 October 1918, two days before his death.

GROUP 12'S CITATION

The Squadron Leader commanding Group 12 is happy to pass on the congratulations from the 1st Air Brigade's Commanding Officer to all the units under his command for the good work carried out on 29 August 1918. The crews went up to 9 miles behind enemy lines twice at low altitude (between 4 920 and 8 200 ft). They fought several dogfights and came out victorious thanks to the units' good group work and Escadrilles 239 and 240's effective protection. Eight enemy planes were shot down for certain. 82 020 lb of bombs were dropped on Anizy-les-Châteaux where a large number of convoys were sheltering (visible on the photographs taken by Group 13).

Below.
Departure of Guynemer aboard his Spad.

vation ones, just seemed to melt away in this battle of annihilation. On 29 May, the Féquant group attacked in the Fismes region, thirty sorties in three days, then towards the mountain at Reims. On 30 May, the Ménard group operated in the Fère-en-Tardenois sector, dropped 9 ½ tons of bombs and used up more than 10 000 cartridges. On 2 June the battle moved away towards Oulchy-le-Château. The Ménard group dropped 19 tons of bombs on the 3rd and lost two crews against two kills. On 4 June, the Germans were on the edge of the forest at Villers-Cotterets, some of their units having managed to sneak into positions sheltering from the canon-fire; they were driven out by attacks from GB 3 and 5 dropping 17 tons of explosives and firing off 5 000 cartridges thus relieving the 28th Infantry Division which was positioned there as cover.

New decisions see the light of day

On 13 June the heads of the Aéronautique in the Army Group of the East informed the English bomber force of their plan of action. They would have to keep a watch on the railway lines from Sarreguemines to Cologne and from Sarrebrück to Namur, and attack the enemy airfields. The targets of this strategic bombing were the stations at Metz-Sablons, Thionville, Bettembourg and Sarrebrück as well as the factories at Hagondange, Rombach and Knutange. The reality was actually slightly different because the English had also decided to go and bomb German towns in retaliation for the repeated attacks on English towns.

Given that the German attacks followed on from each quickly but in different sectors, far away from each other, the air division was separated into two mixed brigades on 15 June to make it more flexible; meanwhile it was also strengthened. The 1st Brigade was commanded by de Goÿs and comprised the Combat Wing N° 1 and the Bomber Wing N° 12. The 2nd Brigade was commanded by Féquant with Combat Wing N° 2 and the Bomber Wing N° 13. They were put at General Foch's disposal. Combat Wing N°3 under Commandant Ménard comprised fighter groups with four escadrilles each, the N°15 under Commandant Glaize, N° 18 under Captain Sabatier and N° 19 under Captain Deullin. Combat Wing N° 2 under Commandant Féquant also comprised three fighter groups, all on Spads, N° 13, 17 and 20.

The day bombers groups, GB 3, 4, 6 and 9, were entirely equipped with Breguet XIVs. The night bomber escadrilles with their Voisin Renaults were doubled up to form new escadrilles making up GB 10 (VBs 101, 116 and 133) and GB 51 (VBs 135, 136 and 137) which were added to the GBs 1 and 7 from Wing N°11 and to the GBs 8, 10 and 2 from Wing N° 14.

Note that on 14 June Combat Wing N° 1, stationed at Amiens, was ordered to position itself to the north of Paris so as to back up the great offensive Mangin was preparing on the Villers-Cotterets and Soissons front.

CITATION IN THE ORDER OF THE ARMY FOR THE DAYTIME BOMBER FORCE (EXTRACTS) *

From 27 March to 27 May [it] took part in the Battle of Picardy, dropping 132 tons of bombs. From 29 May to 9 June [it] took part in the operations between the Marne and the Aisne, dropping more than 191 tons of bombs. [It] particularly distinguished itself on 4 June by stopping a German attack in its tracks by bombing the assembled enemy troops getting ready for action in the ravine at la Salière. Since 6 July it has powerfully contributed to making crossing the Marne very difficult for the enemy, breaking the enemy's footbridges with its bombs; it has vigorously chased the German troops in their retreat dropping 147 tons of bombs.

* Includes GB 5 (Br 117,120,127), GB 6 (Br 66,108, 111), GB 9 (Br 29, 123,129) and the «escadrilles de protection» (protection flights) R 239 and 240

NIGHT RECONNAISSANCE IN A FARMAN 50

On 25 September, the crew from VB 110 consisting of Lieutenant Bizard (pilot) and Captain Garnier (observer) and Aspirant Rives (machine gunner) was chosen for a night reconnaissance over the stations at Montcornet, Rosoy-sur-Serre, Liart, Mézières, Sedan, Amagne-Lucquy, Châtelet-sur-Retourne and back to the airfield at Villeneuve-les-Vertus. They took off at 9 pm for at least a 3 ¼ hour flight at 1 200 m. but the Farman 50 got caught in searchlight beams and an enemy single seater got close near Châtelet-sur-Retourne.

The adversary kept high up on the F 50's tail. It was then that the gunner realised how ineffectual and unpractical the Farman's armament was. Bizard slipped away to get closer to the French lines but the fighter's burst hit the plane broadsides on. The pilot was hit; he told the gunner, who had no idea how to fly, to take over the controls, and then collapsed. After a few ups and downs, the plane ended up by reaching an airfield and landing more or less well. On the ground the pilot, thrown out by the impact, was dead. The cadet managed to get the seriously wounded observer out. They were taken prisoner, looked after and evacuated to the rear.

The 15th Fighter Group with four four-escadrille groups (SPAs 37, 81, 93 and 97) occupied the airfields a mile to the north of Roissy-en-France, the 18th Group (SPAs 48, 94, 153 and 155) was based along the National Road N° 2, the 19th put its Escadrilles 73, 85, 95 and 96 to the west of Road N° 17 in front of the Louvres sugar factory, and SPAs 37, 93 and 97 were near the village of Roissy, SPAs 48, 94 and 155 at Mauregard. Strangely enough these country airfields are now part of the Charles de Gaulle Airport at Roissy-en-France.

In mid-June, the High Command wanted to have an air force unit at its disposal, a group of escadrilles for long range reconnaissance, able to respond quickly to all sorts of needs; three Breguet XIV escadrilles – the 45, 220 ad 249 – were chosen and put under the command of Captain Paul-Louis Weiller. He was given the job of finding out what was going on behind the enemy lines and of taking photographs of anything that seemed important. Such a task was not without risks since Weiller in his Breguet XIV had to shoot down two enemy aircraft on 9 July. This unit also had a photo laboratory on wheels, developing and assembling the shots at night which then were put in front of Foch or his chief of staff, General Weygand, early in the morning. At the time the general was in favour of a general offensive from Verdun to Ypres.

The Battle of Champagne (15-17 July)

The German lines were now 9-miles from Amiens, 31 miles from Calais and above all only 40 miles from Paris, bombed by planes and by heavy artillery. Ludendorff wanted to have done with it all and in a final effort, take Paris. The battle raged from 15 to 17 July and marked the check to German ambitions, because an allied counter-attack now became possible. Called Friedensturm (the assault for peace), the German attack on 15 July covered a 90-km front on either side of the Reims salient. At midnight on the 15th, and for four hours, 8 000 cannon crushed the French positions at Château-Thierry and the Argonne. Informed beforehand by prisoners captured before the attack, GHQ had withdrawn the troops from the trenches in the front line and a wall of fire defended the new positions. German troops managed to cross the Marne near Epernay, but in Champagne, Gouraud's army drove in their front and seriously threatened the whole of the disposition for the German attack.

The German air force had recovered; its new fighter, the Fokker D.VII, now made up two thirds of the Ger-

THE BREGUET XIV AND THE ARMISTICE

On 11 November the German Major von Geyer, a member of the Armistice Commission, got on board Breguet XIV N° 5546 from Escadrille Br 35 flown by Lieutenant Minier, to take the Armistice conditions from Tergnier to Spa and the German GHQ. The plane, bearing a Lorraine cross, had had its equipment removed and flew long pennants from its struts.

Above.
Crash of the Breguet 14B2 n° 1229 from Br 55.

Below.
The wreck of Breguet 14B2 N° 1300 from Br 134. The escadrille's insignia, the third, was an eagle's head inspired by a hallmark identifying old objects.

Opposite.
A Breguet 14 in flight.

Below.
Overturned Breguet 14 from Br 43. This type of plane was the last to be used by the escadrille during the war, the first examples being delivered in May 1918, replacing the Sopwiths.

man fighter strength; its performances equalled those of the Spad XIII. The Kaiser's bomber aircraft, directed until then against London now appeared in full daylight. French bomber activity was directed against the bridges over the Marne, twelve of which were made up of barges sunk to escape photographic detection from the air, leaving the night bombers to act over the main sector of operations. A new group, the 13th, made up of GBs 3 and 4 using Breguet XIVs under Commandant des Prez de la Morlaix, was added to the daytime bombers. Bombs dropped from the planes wrecked the bridges the Germans had thrown over the Marne and threw whole units into the river. A few days later with the Germans retreating, the day bombers threw themselves at the column bottlenecks and dispersed the retreating troops. It harassed any enemy troops, the enemy convoys, the trains, the stations, the cantonments and the airfields.

One wing dropped up to 31 tons of bombs. In less than three months it dropped 611 tons of bombs, used up 218 000 cartridges, took 797 photos, fought 105 dogfights, shot down 45 planes and damaged a further 25.

In July the tally of the allied aces put Fonck first with 59 kills, followed by the Englishman Mannock with 50 kills; Nungesser was third with 39 kills, then Madon 36, the Englishman Dallas 34, the Italian Barrachini 29. In all, 40 pilots had at least 10 kills, ten because they needed that number to appear on the list. There were also the Belgian Coppens, dubbed Chevalier de Houthulst by his King with 20, and the Americans Frank Baylies 12 and David Putnam 10.

Re-conquering territory

Foch decided to launch a general counter-offensive comprising two interim phases preceding the general attack which was to be energetic. It was a matter of first recapturing all territory lost since March, then getting rid of the various salients before launching an operation whose objective was to liberate territory now occupied for several years, and to break through into Belgium and push the enemy back towards his natural borders.

The Battle of the Ile de France (18 July to 4 August)

On 18 July the French artillery showered thousands of shells nailing the Germans to the spot in the Villers-Cotterets sector. Foch launched his counter-offensive on the Marne in which American troops under Gene-

Opposite.
The personnel and the Breguet 14s of Br 43 during the last months of the conflict.

ral Pershing took part; it turned out to be successful. To avoid disaster, the German troops tired out by their advance, turned and faced them, then withdrew in front the allies who had plenty of aircraft and 500 light tanks up in support. The German army went back over the Marne, slipped away and retreated northwards. A vast pursuit movement got under way which shook the whole front. The enemy retreated, but not before committing exactions on the civilian population and destroying everything.

On 1 August, Mangin's army took the German positions on a 40-km wide front, reached Soissons and forced the enemy to pull back in disorder to the north of the Vesle. Ludendorff lost 30 000 men captured together with 700 cannon. Foch, promoted to the honorary title of Maréchal de France on 7 August, now took the initiative and reduced the pocket at Château-Thierry, then the one at Montdidier. On 8 August, the Allies completely broke through the Picardy front with the help of tanks and recovered all the terrain. The English carried on with their attack on the Scarpe and the French to the east on the Ailette, which forced the Germans to fall back on the Hindeburg Line by 20 September. This line consisted of a line of trenches, criss-crossing all over the place, 7 ½ miles deep in some places with joining tunnels, cemented casemates and fortified villages giving what was thought to be total security. From 21 March to 15 August the bombers dropped 2 536 tons of bombs on the stations, railways, factories, military gatherings and buildings belonging to the enemy, or 858 tons by day and 1 678 tons at night. On 13 August during the night, Escadrille F 110 flying the brand new Farman 50 deplored the loss of the plane flown by Lieutenant Astier carrying Brigadier-Gunner Foulot and Lieutenant-Observer-Bombardier Rabardel, specialists in reconnaissance and bombing.

The Battle of Santerre (or Amiens, or Montdidier) (8-30 August)

This was the beginning of a 100-day offensive which spread from Albert to Montdidier, or 15 miles, where seven divisions were engaged, supported by four others held in reserve and 400 tanks. Amiens was clouded in thick fog when the attack started, without any artillery preparation, the Canadians and the Australians at 4 o'clock and the French at 5. On the evening of 8 August, the British were at Chipilly and Beaumont-en-Santerre and the French at Villers-aux-Erables and at la Neuville-Sire-Bernard. Aircraft supported the advance closely, particularly the fighters which strafed the enemy positions. Beyond 30 August, the pursuit went on with the capture of Péronne by the Australians and the New-Zealanders and Saint-Quentin, then they took Quéant which forced the Germans to fall back on the Siegfried Line (Saint-Quentin-la Ferre) – in other words, abandoning all the territory conquered in the spring. This battle cost the lives of 42 000 dead among the Franco-British of whom 15 000 Canadians, and more than 70 000 Germans, and 30 000 prisoners.

Above.
Close up of the Renault engine on a Breguet 14.

Above, left.
A Breguet 14 in flight.

Opposite.
Breguet 14 N° 83xx with especially faded camouflage.

during the First World War

Above.
A Letord 4 (?) possibly from Escadrille 122 landing.

Above.
The accident of Breguet 14B2 N° 1229 from Br 55.

The observation units were not forgotten, witness the citation awarded to an escadrille on 12 February 1919: "Fought on all the fronts of Alsace, in Flanders, and earned the praise of all the commanders who worked with it. From October 1917 to November 1918, in 2 500 flying hours, its crews carried out 200 reconnaissance missions, of which 34 were more than 18 miles behind the German lines, bringing back 1 600 photos. They spotted 900 enemy batteries and directed destructive fire on more than 300 of them. They fought in more than 40 dogfights."

The Saint-Mihiel Salient and the Meuse (12-30 September)

This 32-hour battle engaged 250 000 men, of whom 216 000 were Americans, supported by more than 1 450 balloons, a balloon company, 3 100 cannon and 267 light tanks, against 13 German divisions set up in concrete trenches. It covered a 40-mile front between

Above.
A Sopwith 1A2 (N° and unit unknown) whose landing gear broke on landing. Although of British origin, this biplane was built mostly in France, in both bomber and reconnaissance, and single- or two-seaters versions.

Above.
Albert Guillaume, from Escadrille Spa Bi 2 in front of a Spad two-seater, the machine that was received at the end of 1917 and which gave the escadrille its new designation, previously AR 2. This escadrille's insignia represents three women's legs to resembling a Celtic triskelion... or an aircraft propeller!

114

French aviation

Les Éparges and the Moselle. The objective for the 15th Colonial Infantry Division was Les Éparges. On 12 September American troops attacked after an artillery preparation, with the 1st US Army on the southern front in the direction of Thiaucourt which was taken on the way. On the 13th another attack concerned the north and south of the salient towards Vigneulles-les-Hattonchâtel and the conquest of le Mont Sec. The 2nd Colonial Corps pushed in the direction of Saint-Mihiel, captured 4 000 prisoners and settled on a line running from Haumont-lès-Lachaussée-Woel-Doncourt; the 15th Division occupied the Côtes de Meuse, les Eparges then Champlon, Saulx-en-Woëvre, Saint-Hilaire, Wadonville and Avillers. The Saint-Mihiel salient was reduced for the loss of 7 000 men, taking 13 200 prisoners and 400 canon.

Air cover from more than 1 450 planes of which 600 from the air division and 300 from the independent groups, was in a way just like a great offensive during which the air division was used like cavalry, charging the enemy, ferreting it out of its shelters, machine gunning anything that moved, bivouacs, gatherings, convoys, all knocked out by machine guns and bombs. Escadre 12 took part in the action, even in the night of 25-26 September when the bad weather had not allowed any flying to be done in daytime! It attacked the enemy airfields at Saint-Loup, Leffincourt, Blaise, Mont-Saint-Martin and Amagne-Lucquy (Ardennes). Coordination with the ground troops still left a little to be desired but the results were nonetheless spectacular.

Bombing at night was carried out with very few losses. The crews were well trained and operated in

Above.
Salmson 2A2. Note the short landing gear and the grill fitted with gills on the frontal engine ring.

Opposite.
A crew from Sop 43 in front of one of the escadrille's Sopwith 1A2s.

Opposite.
Sopwith 1A2 N° 4127 from Sop 43 in the autumn of 1917. The horseshoe on the fuselage was originally an emblem on at least one Sopwith before being adopted as the unit insignia in 1917.

during the First World War

Above.
Salmson 2A2 in flight, maybe from Sal 17 or from Sal 58.

Below.
An officer on horseback riding past a line up of Spad XIIIs from Spa 93 in 1918.

the sectors which they were familiar with. Night-time beacons on the roads were effective and the Voisins' Renault engines ticked over without any snags. They were used to shooting at low altitudes and often returned peppered with shots from the ground.

The generalised offensive

The results obtained at Montdidier encouraged Foch, who had been promoted to Maréchal de France on 7 August, to prepare an overall offensive. Germany still had 205 divisions but its assault troops had been decimated. Facing them the Allies lined up 194 divisions plus the 20 in the American Corps.

The Battle of Champagne-Argonne (25 Sept.-11 Nov.)

The orders for the attack were given on 3 September and expounded on the 8th. They concerned three successive offensives: one on either side of the Argonne towards Mézières; one to the north of the Oise against the "Siegfried Line"; and the third in Flanders against the positions at Passchendaele towards Bruges. Preparation started on the 8th and drew on seven army corps, plus the 1st US Army, concentrated over 18 miles from Prosnes and Vienne-le-Château, in the Marne. The objective was to break through the German defences. The artillery preparation began on the 25th at 11 pm and the offensive started at five the next morning against an enemy taken completely unawares.

On 26 September, Foch attacked on both sides of the Argonne, supported by 500 light tanks along a 18-mile front from Forges to the Meuse and brought back 20 000 prisoners and 300 cannon, with a gain of 9 ½ miles in the first five days, then again on the 28th in Flanders and on the 29th in the Saint-Quentin sector beneath a formidable air umbrella. The British breached the front and the French got hold of the massif at Saint-Quentin.

The town was liberated on 1 October, Cambrai on the 9th, followed by Laon on the 13th; the Hindenburg Line was crossed once and for all. The second phase began on 14 October between the Meuse and the Moselle and caused a huge breach in the German defensive lines; the last phase consisted of getting hold of the German defences at Buzancy, crossing the Aisne and thrusting forward towards Sedan, which was reached on 6 November. The offensive was pushed home vigorously and Lille was liberated on 17 October.

The Kaiser, worried by this situation which had now become dangerous, got rid of Ludendorff on 26 October and ordered Hindenburg to contain the disaster and withdraw as many troops as possible to defend the Reich. Reims was freed and the enemy driven back nearly forty miles away. All throughout the offensive the Breguets carried out daytime sorties in groups of 150 to 200 planes protected by fighters

Opposite.
Personnel from Spa 67 posing in front of one of the escadrille's Spad XIIIs in 1918.

Below, left.
The nacelle of a Voisin 8 with a 47-mm canon from Escadrille VC 468. This unit was assigned to the protection of Paris (the CRP) and was designated Escadrille 396 until June 1917. On the left the gunner Boisney and beside him Maréchal-des-Logis de Pérignon.

Above.
Captain Georges Chardenot aboard a Salmson-Moineau SM 1 from Escadrille F 58 in 1917.

or by three seat twin-engined Caudron R.XIs, the first true escort fighters. The Germans were powerless to stop these huge raids and incapable of launching any themselves. Their troops were subjected to strafing whilst their Gotha bombers tried flying beyond their lines but became easy preys for the allied fighters.

The Fokker D.VII biplanes however caused serious losses among the French bombers but the replacement rate quickly made up the losses, because the French industrialists were supplying them in large numbers whilst the enemy could not compensate for the losses he was suffering. Ever since it had been created on 18 May, the air division alone, with its 600 planes, had shot down 637 planes and 125 Drachens and dropped 1 300 tons of bombs.

Aircraft played an important role during this period and now the first American units were taking an active part in the fighting. First Lieutenant William Potter from the 20th Aero Squadron was killed at Stenay on 10 October. Among the fighter unit losses was that of SPA 152's Sous-Lieutenant Henri Garin, a missionary priest who already had three kills to his credit, shot down while cruising as observer for Abbé Bourjade on 29 October. He had been licensed on 31 August 1918. Peace negotiations started as early as 26 September but were rejected by the Allies. On 5 November, the whole German front fell back on the Antwerp-Meuse line. On the 7th, German representatives presented themselves to the French forward positions with the task of negotiating an armistice. On 9 November under pressure from events and the population, the Kaiser abdicated and sought refuge in Holland. Foch who was preparing an offensive for 14 November on the Lorraine front, between Metz and the Vosges, could only bow to the wishes of the Allied politicians to end it all as quickly as possible. In order to avoid the catastrophe of fighting a war on its own soil, Germany accepted all the conditions dictated by the victors and in the forest of Compiègne, not far from Rethondes, the delegation signed the documents which were later called the "Diktat" by the regime which rose out of the revolution which had swept away the Kaiser.

Germany had to hand over 5 000 cannon, 25 000 machine guns, 1 700 planes, 5 000 locomotives, 150 000 wagons, 26 large battleships, all its submarines and four zeppelins as well as handing over all its captured territories, and reimbursing all the damage caused by its troops, the famous "war reparations".

When the war ended, French frontline aviation units comprised:
- The 1st Air Division made up of six combat groups with four escadrilles each comprising eighteen Spads, five daytime bomber groups with three escadrilles of 15 Breguets, four protection escadrilles of fifteen Caudron R XIs, in all 43 escadrilles and 717 planes.
- Autonomous combat units made up of seven groups of 4 to 5 escadrilles of eighteen Spads and twelve army escadrilles of fifteen Spads, 42 escadrilles and 720 planes.
- The night bomber group created on 13 February 1918 uniting three GBs (GBs 1, 2 and 3) with three escadrilles of fifteen Voisin 10s, plus the bomber groups – one GB with three escadrilles of fifteen Farman F 50s and one GB with two escadrilles of ten Caproni 3s – in all fourteen escadrilles and 200 planes.
- The observation units with a strength of 148 escadrilles with ten or fifteen planes (Breguet XIV, Salmson 2A2, Spad 11 or 16 two-seaters, Caudron R XI and Voisin 10).

For the bombing only, activity in 1918 was as follows:
In the first quarter, 100 tons of bombs were dropped for the loss of eight crews; in the second quarter 850 tons for the loss of 27 crews; the third quarter, 880 tons for the loss of sixteen crews and the last complete month – October – 281 tons for the loss of two crews.

In GB 1 (Escadrilles 114, 110 and 25) from 27 March to 8 November there were 106 nights of missions, 2 134 sorties to attack 749 objectives, 109 night reconnaissance missions with 530 tons of bombs dropped for 113 targets destroyed. In GB 7 (Escadrilles 118, 119 and 121) from April to 9 November during 94 nights of missions, there were 1 525 sorties, 125 reconnaissance missions at night to attack 304 targets with 358 tons of bombs dropped and 43 depots, railway lines, airfields destroyed for the loss of 54 killed, 57 wounded and 35 missing among the flight crews.

during the First World War

An assessment of First World War Aviation

With the escadrilles, the schools and the pools, at the time of the Armistice, the French air force had a strength of 19 396 planes; 3 737 were in the front line compared with a theoretical 3 900, not counting the 1 000 seaplanes in the Navy air arm, the 40 airships and more than 100 Caquot balloons. Of about 20 000 planes in all, 7 620 were at the front with 4 398 in 288 escadrilles among which 158 observation units; 3 222 others were in the pools and 604 at the depots; 3 404 served with the training schools or in the factories and 148 formed the coastal and AA escadrilles.

British air units lined up 2 600 planes of which 1 800 were in France on a 94-mile front along which there were also 500 French and 75 American planes. At the beginning of the war the French air units had a hundred or so operational aircraft but at the end of the war the total was 70 times more. The four British squadrons which came to France in 1914 had given rise to an operational force of some 1 785 aircraft in 1918, with a total of 3 600 aircraft, all categories included, based in France.

When the Armistice was signed the German air force consisted theoretically of 275 squadrons and 2590 aircraft of which 1800 in the front line. As at 1 December 1918, the number of flying personnel in the air force was 12 919 men; war casualties therefore represented some 61% of this strength. In all the French air force shot down 2049 planes and 357 Drachens for certain and 1901 planes identified as almost certainly destroyed. There were 180 French aces who had at least five kills to their credit; at least a quarter of them were killed in action.

In spite of its recently acquired reputation, the French air force was only represented at the Victory parade by Fonck, on foot and carrying the Air Force's standard alone. This omission, attributed to the Generals, was felt very badly by the whole of the Air Force which had wanted the escadrilles to fly past during the parade.

Aircraft factory production stood at 3 460 aircraft in 1915, 7 552 in 1916, 22 751 in 1917 and 34 219 in the first nine months of 1918. During the last months of the war, the factories were turning out some 2 800 planes a month, or 100 per day, or the equivalent of the whole 1914 strength. The overall total was 51 700 aircraft produced of which 3 300 delivered to the American Expeditionary Corps, 2 200 to Great Britain, 2 000 to Russia and in smaller numbers to a host of other countries.

The personnel employed by the factories went from 12 650 workers on 1 January 1915 to 30 960 on 1 January 1916, 68 920 on 1 January 1917 and 186 003 on 2 November 1918. The aircraft engine industry, for a long time restricted by the specifications of the rotary engine rated at less than 150 hp, managed to build reliable 300-hp engines and was even preparing 500-hp engines for 1919. It turned out 3 481 engines in 1914, 6 849 in 1915, 13 874 in 1916, 20 805 in 1917 and 40 308 before 11 November 1918.

The consequences for the country

It seems to be necessary to remind people about the sacrifices the French population made during this war, since the suffering that went with the war did not disappear overnight when the war ended. Of all the belligerents it was France that paid the heaviest toll with 1 393 000 dead, mainly among the rural population, or 1 per every 29 inhabitants (1) (in reality more than a quarter of the men aged between 18 and 27), nearly three million wounded, 680 000 war widows and nearly a million orphans.

The cost of the war amounted to 156 billion old francs of which a large part was borrowed and which now had to be repaid quickly even though large portions of the country had to be rebuilt. The Germans moreover had followed a policy of systematic destruction, clearing factories of their stocks of raw materials and machine tools, blowing up bridges and railway lines, cutting down fruit trees in the orchards, flooding coalmines. Entire villages had been wiped off the face of the earth; rich areas had become treeless and houseless wastelands. Large towns like Reims, where only twenty houses were left standing, Soissons or Verdun, were in ruins. In Picardy there were some 120 000 hectares of battlefield were the dead had piled up, and where there were hundreds of thousands of unexploded shells.

Gradual demobilisation also caused renewed suffering when the factories had to slow down production and or even lay off personnel because of cancelled or reduced orders. A lot of goods like planes and trucks were put up for sale at knock down prices thwarting sales of better machines. The 1939 mobilisation was to bring trucks back out of the depots still with solid bandaged tyres which hadn't budged since 1920, not to mention the weapons...

Summary of casualties (wounded and killed) on the Western Front (in 000s of men)

Year	French	British	Total	Germans
1914	1108	101	1209	847
1915	1100	247	1347	533
1916	874	623	1497	969
1917	459	749	1208	818
1918	964	829	1793	1473

* Great Britain lost one man out of every 66 inhabitants, Italy one out of 72, and Germany one out of 38.

The development of commercial aviation

Among the many demobilised crews, many returned to their earlier activities. According to the records of the Amicale des Personnels Navigants (the flight crews association), 145 ex-air force pilots and 21 mechanics had a job in commercial aviation.

Others sought fame as test pilots or as receivers like Maurice Arnoux with five confirmed kills, Lucien Bossourot, Edouard Corniglion-Molinier and Gustave Douchy; or as long distance pilots like Paul Codos, Dieudonné Costes, Marcel Doret, Georges Pelletier-Doisy. Others became land clearers, like Didier Daurat, Maurice Noguès, Paul Vachet or Georges Winckler. Finally some were pioneers like Alexis Maneyrol with gliders, Joseph Thorel with mountain flying... sometimes after years of wandering, like Pierre de Fleurieu, a fighter pilot in SPA 95 with four kills, a bank clerk in 1920 before becoming the manager of an airline, like Henri Bardel.

Others chose the civil service to work for aerial navigation like Alphonse Du Bois d'Aische, a gunner with six kills, or Paul Cornement, a pilot from 1913. Among those who remained in the service, some reached the highest positions, the archetype being Joseph Vuillemin, a soldier from the class of 1903, pupil pilot in 1913, general of an air army in 1937, Chief of Staff for the Armée de l'Air in 1938.

Finally parliamentary life tempted some of them like Pierre-Etienne Flandin, a pilot and deputy in 1912, assigned to MF 33 in 1915, and who was several times a minister; or Laurent Eynac, a deputy, Sous-Lieutenant Bombardier in V 110 in 1916, then first Air Minister in 1928. Both of them had a long career; or again René Fonck, the ace of aces, a deputy from 1919 to 1924; or Alfred Heurtaux, Sous-Lieutenant pilot in 1915 with 21 confirmed kills, deputy in 1919 then major-general in the Armée de l'Air.

All of them contributed in one way or another to making aviation more effective, safer and more accessible to the public. The huge progress made during those four years was forgotten except in commercial aviation, the only sector to benefit. The tactical lessons however were studied by the various European general staffs – Germany more than the others – putting into practice a large number of these lessons, especially where the cooperation between motorised armies and air forces were concerned.

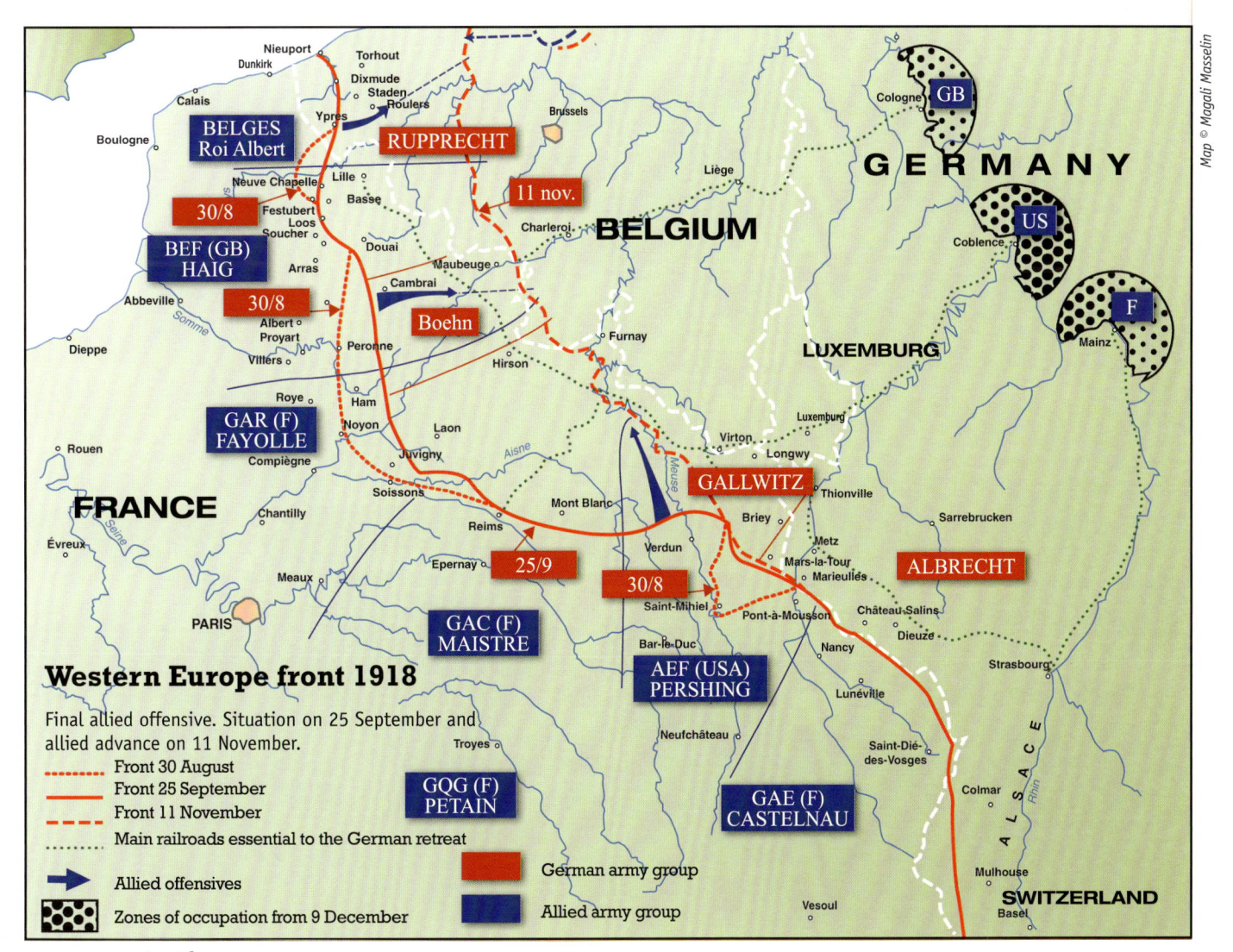

The human cost

During the war, 17 189 pilots were licensed, of which 6 900 in 1918. Out of the 5 300 officers and 102 500 men in the air force, the losses were 1 145 officers killed or missing, or more than 21 % of the strength, 3 600 other ranks (there were pilot soldiers), or 4 745 dead, or 3.5 % of the strength. From 4 August 1914 to 11 November 1918, 1 945 pilots and observers were killed in the combat zone, 1 461 missing whose death was certain, and 2 922 wounded. In the interior area, losses stood at 1 927 pilots and observers. All in all 7 757 flight crews died during the war.

Western Europe front 1918

Final allied offensive. Situation on 25 September and allied advance on 11 November.
- Front 30 August
- Front 25 September
- Front 11 November
- Main railroads essential to the German retreat
- Allied offensives
- Zones of occupation from 9 December
- German army group
- Allied army group

during the First World War

Breguet

FRENCH AIRCRAFT

Above.
Breguet 14 A2 N° 831 from Br 227 without its armament on the dorsal mounting.

After a long absence during which successive Breguet prototypes were not chosen by the Service Technique, the industrialist brought out a machine which was finally mass-produced, starting a long career, both military and civil. It was built in response to a Ministry of War specification in the summer of 1915 requiring a so-called powerful plane capable of carrying 660 lb of bombs for 375 miles at a speed of 75 mph. A rival of the Paul Schmitt, its original design started in 1916 with a 220-hp Renault engine, pushed up to 275 hp in February 1917 then 316 hp. The first flight took place on 21 November 1916 and production started on 22 February 1917 after an order was placed for 150 aircraft on 6 February, increased to 100 on 4 April. Quantity production was speeded up by using sub-contractors: on 25 April a licence for 200 planes built by Darracq, 50 by Farman on 8 June, 230 by Schmitt on 18 June and others. It was clearly innovative with the structure of its fabric-covered fuselage made of Dural tubing, sulphur-welded inside the melted aluminium joints to make a gusset.

Type 14

Two-seat single-engined biplane produced in a reconnaissance (A2) or a bomber (B2) version. At the end of 1917, there were 2 600 examples on the order books and in all 5 300 were built by December 1918.

Technical Specifications for Breguet XIV A2 (B2)
Wingspan: 47 ft 1 in
Total Length: 29 ft 6 in
Height: 10 ft 9 in
Wing surface: 527.240 ft²
Weight (Empty): 2 354 lb
Maximum take off weight: 3 520 lb (4 672 lb)
Payload: 682 lb (1 205 lb including thirty-two 17 ½ lb bombs)
Max. Speed: 118.75 (103 mph)
Rate of climb: 16 400 ft in 21 min 45 sec (13 120 ft

Above.
On 19 May 1918 in the Somme, the engine of a Breguet 14 A2 from Br 227 has caught fire.

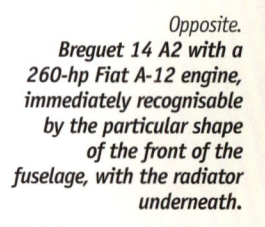

Opposite.
Breguet 14 A2 with a 260-hp Fiat A-12 engine, immediately recognisable by the particular shape of the front of the fuselage, with the radiator underneath.

1916-18

Opposite.
Breguet 14 A2 N°162x from Br 201. This machine, bearing the escadrille's insignia (an Alsatian knot inside blue oval edged with red) on its fuselage, was damaged in an accident in 1918.

Opposite.
A period postcard (touched up) of a Breguet 17 showing its "footprint" (a black patch) on the right hand extrados of the upper wing and which was to be found on all camouflaged machines of this type.

AÉRODROME DU BOURGET
LE BRÉGUET — Type XVII C. 2

in 26 min and 16 400 ft in 47 min 30 sec)
Service ceiling: 20 000 ft
Flight Time: 3 hrs
Armament: one synchronised cowling mounted and one or two machine guns in the rear position
Optional radio and photographic equipment
On 1 October 1918 there were 450 of these machines on the front.

Type 16

Two-seat night bomber biplane whose prototype flew for the first time on 1 June 1918 with a 450-hp Renault engine, but production did not begin before the Armistice.

Technical Specifications
Wingspan: 55 ft 9 in
Total Length: 31 ft 4 in
Height: 11 ft 2 ½ in
Wing surface: 790.860 ft²
Weight (Empty): 2 783 lb
Payload: 2 486 lb (not including fuel) of which 1 100 lb of ordnance
Max. Speed: 100 mph
Rate of climb: 13 120 ft in 51 min and 10 sec

during the First World War

Breguet

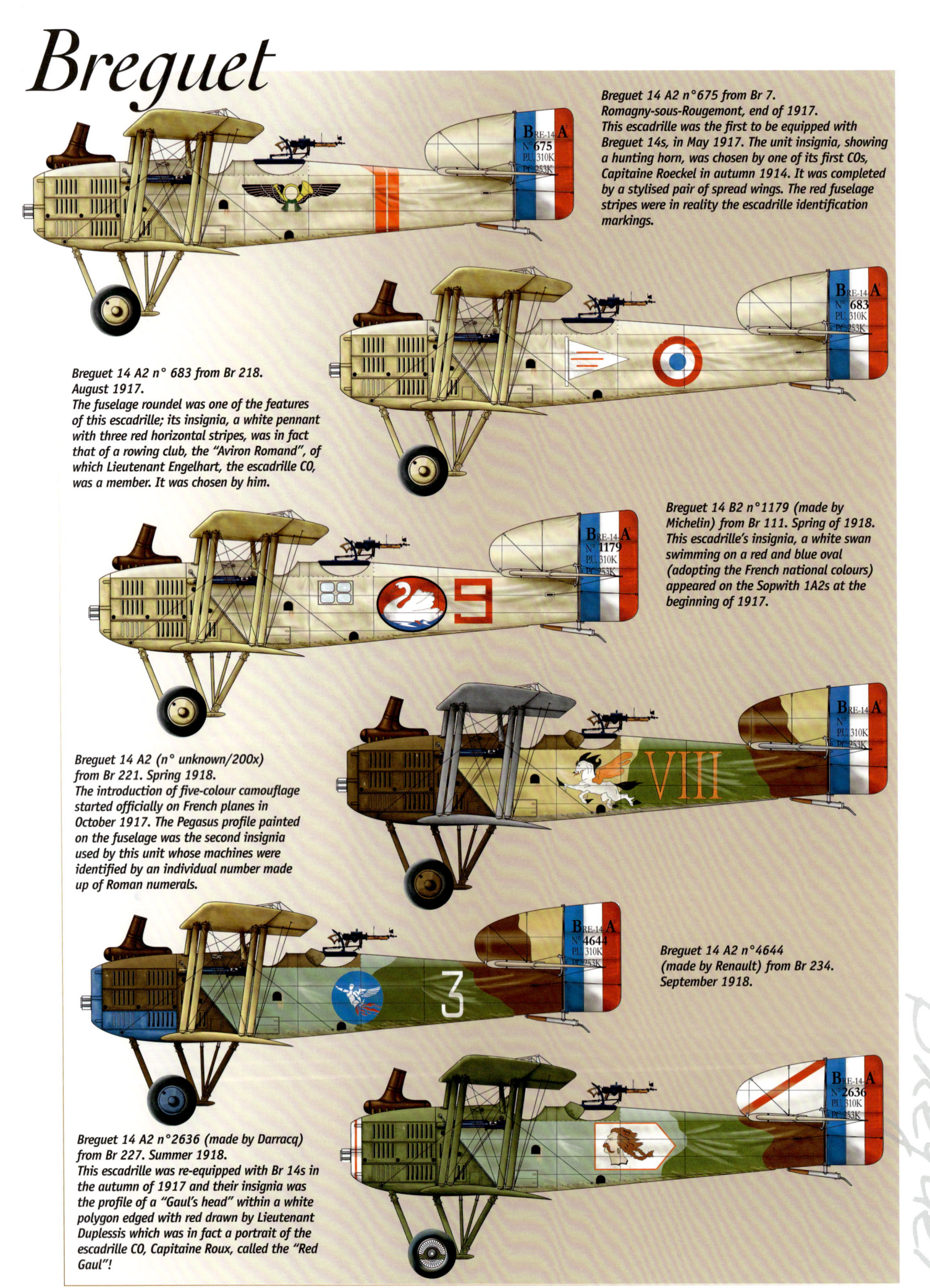

Breguet 14 A2 n°675 from Br 7.
Romagny-sous-Rougemont, end of 1917.
This escadrille was the first to be equipped with Breguet 14s, in May 1917. The unit insignia, showing a hunting horn, was chosen by one of its first COs, Capitaine Roeckel in autumn 1914. It was completed by a stylised pair of spread wings. The red fuselage stripes were in reality the escadrille identification markings.

Breguet 14 A2 n° 683 from Br 218.
August 1917.
The fuselage roundel was one of the features of this escadrille; its insignia, a white pennant with three red horizontal stripes, was in fact that of a rowing club, the "Aviron Romand", of which Lieutenant Engelhart, the escadrille CO, was a member. It was chosen by him.

Breguet 14 B2 n°1179 (made by Michelin) from Br 111. Spring of 1918.
This escadrille's insignia, a white swan swimming on a red and blue oval (adopting the French national colours) appeared on the Sopwith 1A2s at the beginning of 1917.

Breguet 14 A2 (n° unknown/200x) from Br 221. Spring 1918.
The introduction of five-colour camouflage started officially on French planes in October 1917. The Pegasus profile painted on the fuselage was the second insignia used by this unit whose machines were identified by an individual number made up of Roman numerals.

Breguet 14 A2 n°4644 (made by Renault) from Br 234. September 1918.

Breguet 14 A2 n°2636 (made by Darracq) from Br 227. Summer 1918.
This escadrille was re-equipped with Br 14s in the autumn of 1917 and their insignia was the profile of a "Gaul's head" within a white polygon edged with red drawn by Lieutenant Duplessis which was in fact a portrait of the escadrille CO, Capitaine Roux, called the "Red Gaul"!

French aviation

Breguet

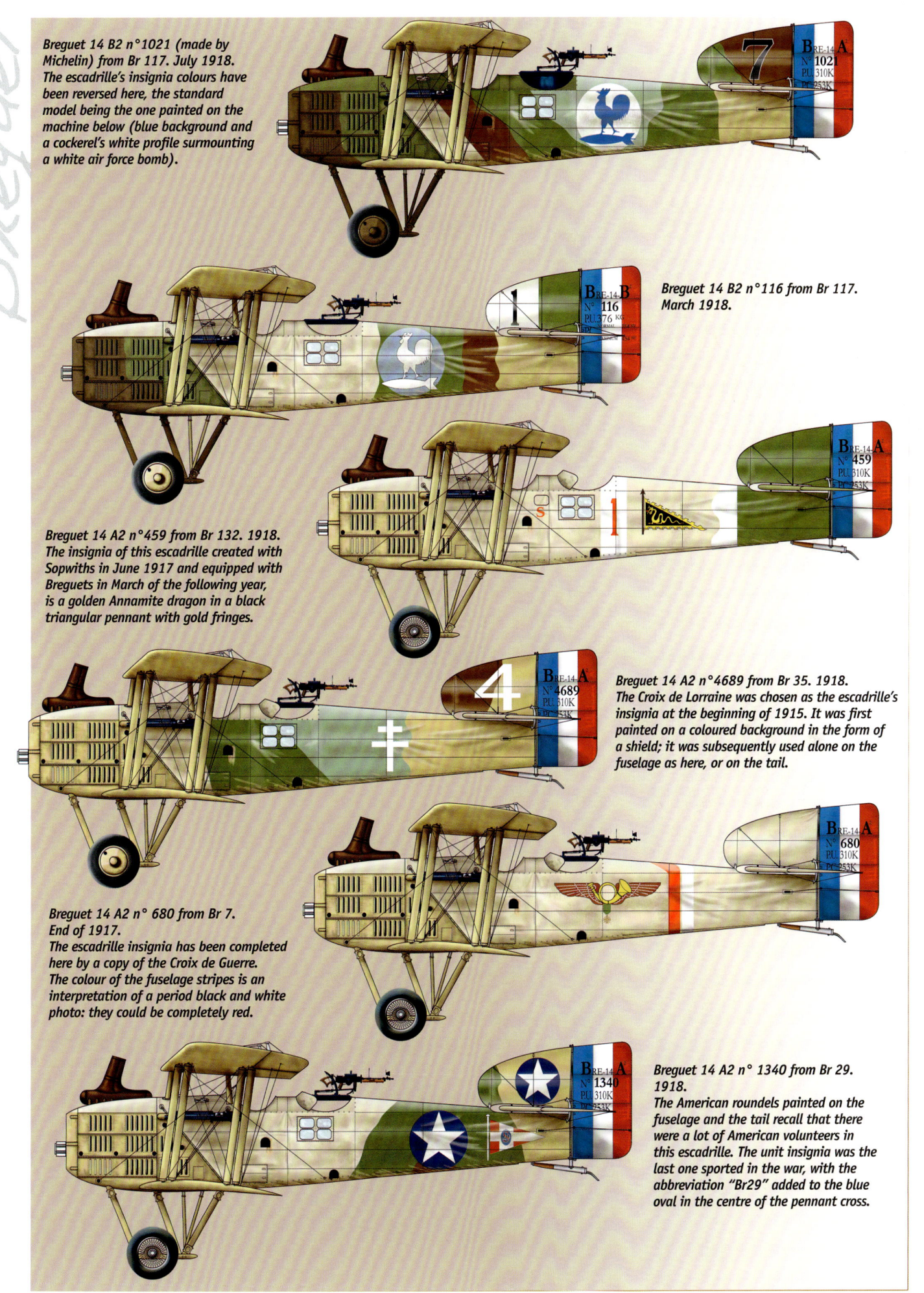

Breguet 14 B2 n°1021 (made by Michelin) from Br 117. July 1918.
The escadrille's insignia colours have been reversed here, the standard model being the one painted on the machine below (blue background and a cockerel's white profile surmounting a white air force bomb).

Breguet 14 B2 n°116 from Br 117. March 1918.

Breguet 14 A2 n°459 from Br 132. 1918.
The insignia of this escadrille created with Sopwiths in June 1917 and equipped with Breguets in March of the following year, is a golden Annamite dragon in a black triangular pennant with gold fringes.

Breguet 14 A2 n°4689 from Br 35. 1918.
The Croix de Lorraine was chosen as the escadrille's insignia at the beginning of 1915. It was first painted on a coloured background in the form of a shield; it was subsequently used alone on the fuselage as here, or on the tail.

Breguet 14 A2 n° 680 from Br 7. End of 1917.
The escadrille insignia has been completed here by a copy of the Croix de Guerre. The colour of the fuselage stripes is an interpretation of a period black and white photo: they could be completely red.

Breguet 14 A2 n° 1340 from Br 29. 1918.
The American roundels painted on the fuselage and the tail recall that there were a lot of American volunteers in this escadrille. The unit insignia was the last one sported in the war, with the abbreviation "Br29" added to the blue oval in the centre of the pennant cross.

during the First World War

Caproni

Above.
Caproni CAP 2 Bn 2 from CAP 115.

Below.
Caproni Ca 33 from Italian XVIII° Gruppo operating in France during WW1.

This was a twin-boom biplane with three 180-hp Isotta-Fraschini engines, one of which as a pusher, derived from the 1915 prototype (Type 3) with 100-hp Fiat engines. It was supplied to two escadrilles using the CEP and 80 examples were built. The crew comprised two pilots, an observer-bombardier installed in the front, and a machine gunner installed in a rear turret, above everything so he could fire both to the front and to the rear. The crew were exposed to the slipstream and had to put up with temperatures exceeding -30°. Some versions received Fiat engines rated at 260 hp giving a little more speed and a climb to 6 560 ft in 14 minutes 34 for a little reduction in payload.

Simple repairs were possible in flight and the plane flew correctly with only two engines out of three working. But the plane was heavy and cumbersome, using a lot of people and the view downwards was not very good. The first ones to be used by the French were licence-built versions by Esnault-Pelterie, hence the name CEP, the first examples of which were convoyed to Dijon in October 1916. Then Italy delivered some 160 original Caproni planes. In all about a hundred of these planes were used. In 1917, the increase in power made it a formidable plane but the French crews didn't like very much.

Technical Specifications
Wingspan: 74 ft 6 in
Total Length: 32 ft 11 ½ in
Height: 12 ft 7 in
Wing surface: 1 029.086 ft²
Maximum take off weight: 8 580 lb of which 880 lb of bombs
Military Payload: 440 lb of bombs with the possibility of 880 lb
Max. Speed: 84.37 mph dropping very quickly with the altitude to 68.75 mph at 11 480 ft
Rate of climb: 6 560 ft in 24 min and 11 480 ft in 50 min
Flight Time: at least 4 hrs

Caudron

Type G.6

Deville, the engineer, had served as an observer on a G.3 before entering Caudron to improve the G.4 in the summer of 1915. He drew the plans of this two-seat, twin engined G.6 biplane, which came out at first with two 80-hp le Rhône engines. The production series machines used two 120-hp le Rhône engines and entered service in 1917. The plane's configuration was different from that of the G.4 because its fuselage was more standard. More than 750 were ordered but only 512 were actually delivered to the cooperation escadrilles, some of them being built under licence by Letord. It was said that Jules Védrine used one for bombing trials.

46 which claimed to have shot down 34 German planes in eight weeks, but the plane turned out not to be very manoeuvrable and was structurally weak.

Above and below.
Caudron G.6 N° 4508 from Escadrille C 43

Technical Specifications
Wingspan: 56 ft 5 in
Total Length: 28 ft 2 in
Height: 9 ft 7 in
Wing surface: 394.892 ft²
Maximum take off weight: 3 174 lb
Max. Speed: 101 mph at ground level, dropping to 90 mph at 6 560 ft and 85 mph at 13 120 ft
Rate of climb: 13 120 ft in 25 min
Flight Time: 3 hrs
Armament: two Lewis 7.7-mm machine guns and 2 200 lb of bombs

Technical Specifications
Wingspan: 69 ft 4 in
Total Length: 38 ft 1 ½ in
Height: 11 ft 8 ½ in
Wing surface: 779.024 ft²
Maximum take off weight: 5 082 lb
Max. Speed: 87.5 mph at ground level
Rate of climb: 6 560 ft in 18 min
Flight Time: 3 hrs

Type R.4

A twin-engined biplane powered by two 130-hp Renault engines or two 140-hp Hispano engines; it had a classic fuselage, appeared in June 1915 and 249 examples were built. Designed for bombing, it was more often used for photo reconnaissance. The first example was delivered to the front on 1 October 1916 and 53 of them were in active service on 1 August 1917, as combat three-seaters. The main undercarriage was made up of two double wheels under the wings and one anti-nose-over wheel (or a bogey) under the fuselage; this was often removed before operations. The first R.4s were given to Escadrille

during the First World War

Caudron G.6

AÉROPLANE CAUDRON Type G-6 "CORPS D'ARMÉE"

Type R.XI

This three-seat escort and reconnaissance biplane appeared in March 1917. It was in fact an improved version of the R.4, powered by two 215-hp Hispano engines. This machine was used a lot for artillery cooperation and bombing because it could carry a large load and was easy to fly, even in bad weather. It was also used as a daytime escort plane for the Breguet XIV bombers thanks to its two machine guns in the front and another one firing downwards. 370 were produced but the problems with the Hispano engine made it less effective. The first R.XIs were delivered at the end of 1917 to Escadrille 46, which had been flying on Letords until then, Escadrilles 239, 240, 241 and 242 being equipped with them before July 1918. On 1 October, 54 of these machines were in front-line service.

Technical Specifications
Wingspan: 58 ft 9 in (upper wing) 55 ft 8 in (lower wing)
Total Length: 36 ft 11 in
Height: 8 ft 8 ½ in
Wing surface: 583.730 ft²
Maximum take off weight: 4 767 lb
Payload: 891 lb
Max. Speed: 118 mph at ground level, 115 mph at 6 560 ft, 108 mph at 13 120 ft
Rate of climb: 6 560 ft in 8 min 10 sec, and 16 400 ft in 39 min
Flight Time: 3 hrs
Armament: five 7.7-mm Lewis machine guns

Below.
A front view of a Caudron R.4 showing the large wingspan very clearly.

AÉROPLANE CAUDRON Type R-4 "CORPS D'ARMÉE"

Opposite.
This shot of the right-hand side of a Caudron R.4 shows the host of struts and wires on the wings very clearly, especially the lateral supports for the engine nacelles.

Type C.23

Designed by Deville, this plane made its first flight in November 1917 with two 80-hp le Rhône engines, replaced later by 120-hp ones. 1 000 examples were ordered in February 1918, powered by Salmson Canton-Unné water-cooled engines rated at 240 hp, but only 54 had been built by 11 November 1918 and were reserved for bombing Berlin. This heavy machine was not very agile.

Technical Specifications
Wingspan: 80 ft 3 in
Total Length: 45 ft 6 in
Height: 9 ft 9 in
Wing surface: 1 140.560 ft²
Maximum take off weight: 9 174 lb
Max. Speed: 90 mph at 3 280 ft
Flight Time: 5 hrs
Armament: 3 machine guns and 1 320 lb of bombs

Below.
Caudron R.XI from Escadrille R XI-46 damaged in 1918 with part of the upper right hand wing torn off.

Opposite.
Caudron R.XI N°4xx alongside some Voisins.

Opposite.
Caudron C.23. Although 1 000 examples of this bomber had been ordered originally, only fifty or so were actually built and they were reserved for bombing Berlin.

Below.
Starting the engines of Caudron C.23.

Dorand

Opposite.
A spectacular shot of a Dorand AR 1 (N° 0x?) held on its flight line by a single man.

Below
Dorand AR 1 (N° 1256?) from Escadrille AR 41. This escadrille also used some Salmson-Moineau SM1s in 1917 and some Letords before being re-equipped with Salmson 2s in 1918 and being re-designated as SAL 41.

Below.
Photo: Dorand AR 1 from Escadrille AR 253 whose insignia painted on the fuselage was a yellow sphinx on a blue disc.

Type AR

This was a two-seat biplane with the wings staggered backward, designed in 1916 by Colonel Jean-Baptiste Dorand who was head of the Service Technique and built by the Chalais-Meudon workshops then sub-contracted to Farman and Letord. The AR stood for reconnaissance (A) and 190-hp Renault pusher engine (R).

The machine was also powered by a 240-hp Lorraine-Dietrich engine. The AR 2 version had the same specification except for the wingspan which was slightly smaller.

Technical Specifications
Wingspan: 43 ft 8 in
Total Length: 30 ft
Wing surface: 539.829 ft²
Maximum take off weight: 2 926 lb
Military Payload: four 26-lb bombs
Max. Speed: 92 mph at 6 560 ft

Opposite.
Dorand AR 1 N° 1776.
(US Army)

Farman

Opposite.
Close-up of the front part of a Farman F 50 showing the underwing bomb racks and the searchlights.

Type 50

Designed to replace the Voisin bomber, this twin-engined aircraft made its first flight at the beginning of 1918 and started operational service in August. 45 examples were delivered to Escadrille F 25, 110 and 114. This biplane with unequal wings was powered by two 275-hp Lorraine engines.

Technical Specifications
Wingspan: 74 ft 11 in
Total Length: 35 ft 9 in
Height: 10 ft 9 in
Wing surface: 1 093 216 ft²
Maximum take off weight: 4 664 lb
Payload: 1 650 lb
Max. Speed: 84.37 mph at 6 560 ft
Rate of climb: 6 560 ft in 12 min
Service ceiling: 15 580 ft
Range: 262 miles

Below.
Farman F 50.

Letord

The first twin-engined plane to be equipped with 150 hp Hispano engines, which enabled it to reach 84.37 mph at 13 120 ft, the Letord 1 was designed by the engineer Dorand. It was an all-purpose three seater; its undercarriage was braced to the fuselage and its wings were staggered backwards, two of the characteristic aspects of this type of design. It could carry a payload of 891 lb and climbed to 13 120 ft in 36 minutes. The following versions only differed by the type and the power of the engines.

Type 2

Equipped with two 200-hp Hispano engines, this model flew at 90 mph at 13 120 ft, reached in 29 minutes. The maximum ceiling was 16 000 ft with a payload of 888 lb.

Type 3

Designed in 1917 and powered by two 200-hp Hispano engines and armed with a canon, this plane was intended for escorting night bombers.

Type 5

A sesquiplan, without the front support, powered by two 220-hp Lorraine engines, and armed with two machine guns and 440 lb of bombs. Fifty or so examples were produced mainly for the army cooperation escadrilles and, if necessary, for bombing.

Type 7

Two-seat version of above with two 275-hp engines.

Type 9

Three-seat biplane with two 240-hp Lorraine Dietrich engines.

Technical Specifications
Wingspan: 29 ft
Total Length: 36 8 in
Height: 12 ft 1 in
Wing surface: 669.272 ft²
Maximum take off weight: 5 550 lb
Payload: 1 210 lb not including fuel
Max. Speed: 100 mph at 6 560 ft

At the top.
Letord 1 from Escadrille AR 50 in 1918.

Below.
Letord A N° 155 without any unit insignia in 1918.

Below.
Letord 4 A3 n° 724.
(SDASM)

Morane

Opposite.
Morane AI.

Below.
Morane AI. (US Army)

Type P

This parasol-winged two-seater powered by a 110-hp le Rhône engine was quite an improvement on the Type L/LA. After trying it out in March 1916, the Aéronautique Militaire had 565 examples built, plus different variants which increased the total to more than 1 200. A single-seat version was also used.

Technical Specifications
Wingspan: 36 ft 8 in
Total Length: 23 ft 6 in
Height: 11 ft 4 ½ in
Wing surface: 193.680 ft²
Maximum take off weight: 1 606 lb
Max. Speed: 101 mph
Rate of climb: 6 560 ft in 8 min
Flight Time: 4 hrs

Armament: one machine gun on the upper wing operated by the pilot and one machine gun operated by the observer in the rear cockpit

Type AC

Single-seater derived from the Type V of which only a few were built while waiting for the Spad VII. 30 examples were shared out throughout the fighter escadrilles.

Technical Specifications
Wingspan: 32 ft 2 in
Total Length: 23 ft 2 in
Height: 8 ft 11 in
Wing surface: 151.400 ft²
Maximum take off weight: 1 447 lb
Max. Speed: 111 mph at ground level and 108 mph at 6 560 ft
Rate of climb: 6 560 ft in less than 6 min
Flight Time: 2 ½ hrs

Type AI

A parasol variant of the Type AC appearing at the beginning of the summer of 1917 and equipped with a 150-hp single valve Gnome rotary engine. 1 200 examples were ordered under the military designation Mos 27 for the version with a machine gun and Mos 29 for the one with two machine guns. Series production started at the beginning of 1918. The first escadrille to be equipped with it was N 156 in January 1918, then N 161 and 158 in March of the same year. However, the unreliability of the engine and the plane's structural defects meant it was removed from operations after

1 050 machines had been built. They were assigned to advanced training centres powered by a 120 hp le Rhône engine and with their armament removed.

After the war a certain number of these Moranes were used for civil aviation. Albert Fronval who knew how to make use of the machine's excellent agility, made the most of it during the spectacular acrobatic displays he gave during numerous meetings, and setting some records like the one he broke at Madrid in 1919 where he made 629 loops in a row!

Technical Specifications
Wingspan: 28 ft 4 in
Total Length: 18 ft 9 in
Height: 7 ft 8 in
Wing surface: 142.032 ft²
Maximum take off weight: 1 428 lb
Max. Speed: 140 mph at ground level
Rate of climb: 16 400 ft in less than 16 min

Above.
Morane AI armed with a single machine gun and designated Mos 27.
(SDASM)

Below.
Morane AI (Mos 29) armed with two machine guns.
(SDASM)

Nieuport

Opposite.
Nieuport 28 N° 6168 from the 94th Aero Squadron of the USAS sporting the insignia of the unit, the famous "hat in the ring" on its fuselage. (SDASM)

Before the Nieuport 24 and 27 entered service, it was obvious that their performances had to be improved by fitting a more powerful engine, reinforcing the rigidity of the airframe and increasing the wing surface in order to take the greater mass of the new machine.

Type 28

A single-engined biplane fighter whose prototype flew on 6 May 1917 with a single-valved 160-hp Gnome engine; its wings were supported by parallel struts. It was also equipped with a 180-hp le Rhône engine (the Madon version) and covered with a more streamlined annular engine cowling. During the trials it flew at 130 mph and reached 16 400 ft in 16 1/2 minutes. It was very manoeuvrable and the example delivered to the escadrilles reached 132 mph at ground level but was outclassed by the Spad. Delivered from March 1918 onwards especially to the American units, its engine tended to catch fire and the fabric on the upper wing to tear when coming out of steep dive. Moreover the radiators burst too easily and the vibrations caused fuel leaks.

Technical Specifications
Wingspan: 26 ft 9 in (upper wing slightly staggered forwards) 25 ft 6 in (lower wing)
Total Length: 20 ft 4 in
Height: 8 ft 1 ½ in
Wing surface: 172.160 ft²
Maximum take off weight: 1 540 lb
Max. Speed: 126 mph at 6 560 ft
Rate of climb: 16 400 ft in 19 min 48 sec
Range: 250 miles

Opposite.
Nieuport 28 n° 6298.

Salmson

Type 2 A2

A two-seat biplane powered by a 260-hp Canton-Unnè engine used for reconnaissance, it entered service in 1917 and was delivered to more than 24 reconnaissance escadrilles; in all 3 200 examples were produced. On 1 October there were 448 Salmsons on the front.

Technical Specifications

Wingspan: 38 ft 6 in
Total Length: 27 ft 10 in
Height: 9 ft 6 in
Wing surface: 401.025 ft²
Maximum take off weight: 3 036 lb
Payload: 462 lb
Max. Speed: 117 mph at ground level, 110 mph at 9 840 ft
Rate of climb: 9 840 ft in 17 min
Service ceiling: 20 340 ft
Flight Time: 2 ¾ hrs
Armament: one cowling mounted Vickers machine or two Lewis at the rear for the observer

Opposite.
Salmson 2 A2 captured by the Germans and wearing the markings of its new "owners".

Below.
Salmson 2A2 N° 318, perhaps from SAL 1.

Salmson 2A2 N° 402x, most likely from SAL 254, whose cables have broken.

during the First World War

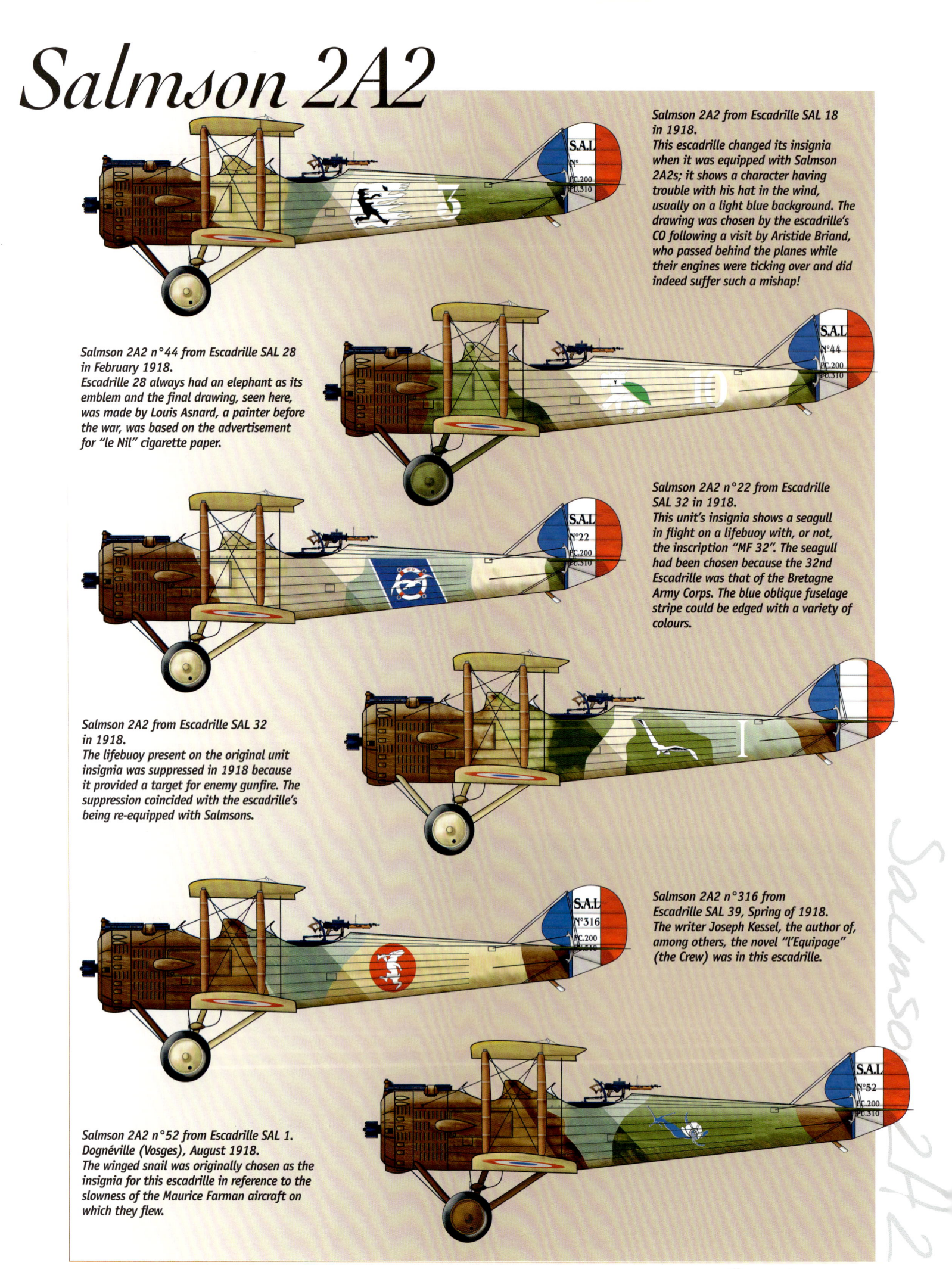

Salmson 2A2

Salmson 2A2 from Escadrille SAL 18 in 1918.
This escadrille changed its insignia when it was equipped with Salmson 2A2s; it shows a character having trouble with his hat in the wind, usually on a light blue background. The drawing was chosen by the escadrille's CO following a visit by Aristide Briand, who passed behind the planes while their engines were ticking over and did indeed suffer such a mishap!

Salmson 2A2 n°44 from Escadrille SAL 28 in February 1918.
Escadrille 28 always had an elephant as its emblem and the final drawing, seen here, was made by Louis Asnard, a painter before the war, was based on the advertisement for "le Nil" cigarette paper.

Salmson 2A2 n°22 from Escadrille SAL 32 in 1918.
This unit's insignia shows a seagull in flight on a lifebuoy with, or not, the inscription "MF 32". The seagull had been chosen because the 32nd Escadrille was that of the Bretagne Army Corps. The blue oblique fuselage stripe could be edged with a variety of colours.

Salmson 2A2 from Escadrille SAL 32 in 1918.
The lifebuoy present on the original unit insignia was suppressed in 1918 because it provided a target for enemy gunfire. The suppression coincided with the escadrille's being re-equipped with Salmsons.

Salmson 2A2 n°316 from Escadrille SAL 39, Spring of 1918.
The writer Joseph Kessel, the author of, among others, the novel "l'Equipage" (the Crew) was in this escadrille.

Salmson 2A2 n°52 from Escadrille SAL 1. Dognéville (Vosges), August 1918.
The winged snail was originally chosen as the insignia for this escadrille in reference to the slowness of the Maurice Farman aircraft on which they flew.

136   *French aviation*

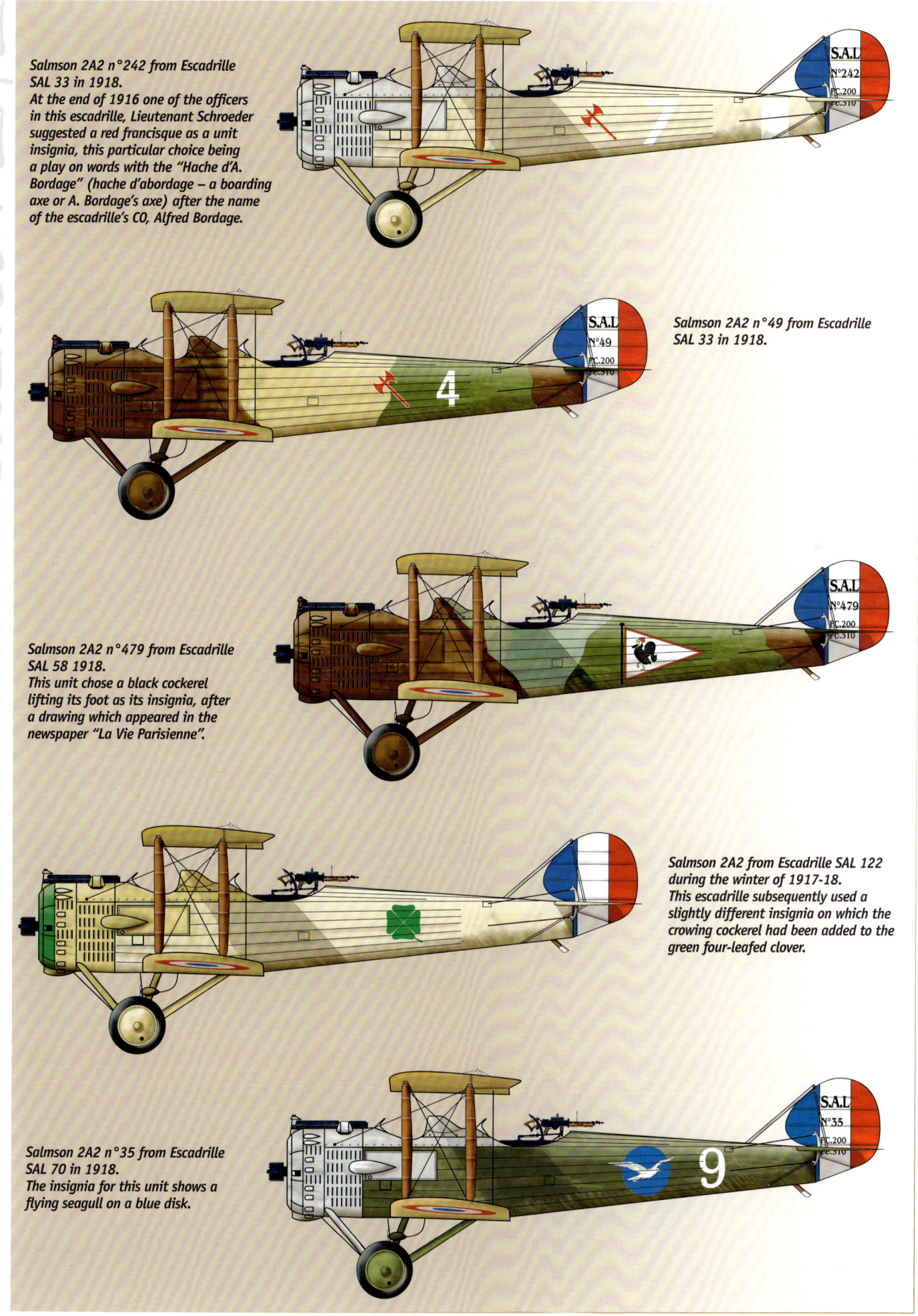

Salmson 2A2 n°242 from Escadrille SAL 33 in 1918.
At the end of 1916 one of the officers in this escadrille, Lieutenant Schroeder suggested a red francisque as a unit insignia, this particular choice being a play on words with the "Hache d'A. Bordage" (hache d'abordage – a boarding axe or A. Bordage's axe) after the name of the escadrille's CO, Alfred Bordage.

Salmson 2A2 n°49 from Escadrille SAL 33 in 1918.

Salmson 2A2 n°479 from Escadrille SAL 58 1918.
This unit chose a black cockerel lifting its foot as its insignia, after a drawing which appeared in the newspaper "La Vie Parisienne".

Salmson 2A2 from Escadrille SAL 122 during the winter of 1917-18.
This escadrille subsequently used a slightly different insignia on which the crowing cockerel had been added to the green four-leafed clover.

Salmson 2A2 n°35 from Escadrille SAL 70 in 1918.
The insignia for this unit shows a flying seagull on a blue disk.

during the First World War

Above.
Marceau Denecker in front of a Salmson 2 A2 from SAL 4 whose insignia, a red star, painted on the fuselage, can be clearly seen.

Opposite.
One of the external features of the Salmson 2 A2 apart from its large size, especially its wingspan, was its relatively short undercarriage.

Opposite.
91st Aero Squadron.

Sopwith

1½ Strutter

A single-engined two seat observation and combat plane equipped with a 110-hp or 130-hp Clerget rotary engine, it was developed in 1915 and appeared in the British RFC units in May 1916. The French air force did not have the equivalent and chose to make it under licence, using it as a jack of all trades, but the construction delays meant it was almost out of date when it reached the escadrilles. It was armed with a Vickers cowling-mounted machine gun and the observer at the rear had a Lewis gun on a turret. According to Captain Blaise "the Sopwith is swift and supple, defends itself well and can be protected by two-seat Sopwiths armed as fighters". Other pilots' opinions are mentioned by René Martel: "the Sopwith is an excellent sports plane. It is not a warplane."

It was a light plane fitted with strange air brakes at the wing roots which did actually slow it down when landing; it had a total mass of 2 035 lb as a single-seat bomber, which gave it four hours' flying time. It could carry 220 lb or 110 lb as a two-seater, or four 264-lb Gros bombs. It flew at 100 mph, a speed it held at 13 120 ft which it reached almost as quickly as a fighter. The French however remarked that their mounts were inferior to those (the same type) that the English were using. 4 500 examples were built in France and the type, which should have been withdrawn from the fighting units, still equipped 60% of the Army Corps escadrilles at the beginning of 1918. The so-called bomber version was assigned to GB4. Thus on 22 June 1916, ten planes from this group escorted by four fighters, dropped 48 264-lb Gros shells and two 110-lb shells on military buildings in Mülheim. In all more than 4 000 Sopwiths of both versions (1A2 and 1B2) were built in France.

Sopwith 1A2.

Sopwith 1A2.

Technical Specifications
Wingspan: 33 ft 6 in
Total Length: 26 ft 2 in
Height: 10 ft 3 in
Wing surface: 344.320 ft²
Maximum take off weight: 2 193 lb (1A2 two-seat reconnaissance version)
Weight (Empty): 1 302 lb

Below.
Relatively few French air force Sopwith 1A2s were camouflaged, like this one from an unknown unit.

during the First World War

Sopwith

Sopwith 1A2 from Escadrille AR 205 in 1917. France was the biggest user of Sopwith 1 1/2 Strutters which it built under licence in several versions: reconnaissance (1A2) or two-seat bomber (1B2) and single-seat bomber (1B1). AR 205 was mainly equipped with Dorand AR 1s, as its name indicates and only received two examples of this two-seat reconnaissance plane.

Sopwith 1A2 n°6165 from Escadrille BR 221 on the Italian Front, end of 1917. Escadrille 221 which served in Italy for a few months at the end of 1917 used two insignia during its existence, including this strange doll's head.

Sopwith 1A2 n°2992 from Escadrille BR 227. This machine belonged to Capitaine de Richemont in 1917. The "Gaul's profile", an emblem drawn by Lieutenant-Observer Fabre, became the escadrille's insignia and was in fact the exact portrait of Capitaine Roux, the unit's first CO, in 1917-18. After July 1917, Escadrille 106 also used this insignia.

Sopwith 1A2 from Escadrille N 62. This plane can be seen on two photos where it has run into an Adrian hut; the crew managed to get out unscathed from this spectacular mishap. The heart pierced by an arrow painted behind the fighting cockerel was a personal insignia.

Sopwith 1A2 belonging to Lieutenant Bladinières, an observer from Escadrille N62, a fighter unit equipped with Nieuports. In 1916-17 it had two Sopwith two-seaters for long-range observation. At the time the Sopwith 1A2 was the fastest reconnaissance plane in the Air Force. The Spad XI replaced it in N 62 later.

Sopwith 1A2 n°309 from Escadrille SOP 111 in February 1917.
This unit was equipped with Sopwith 1 ½ Strutters from 1916 onwards which were replaced in October 1917 by Breguet 14s.

140

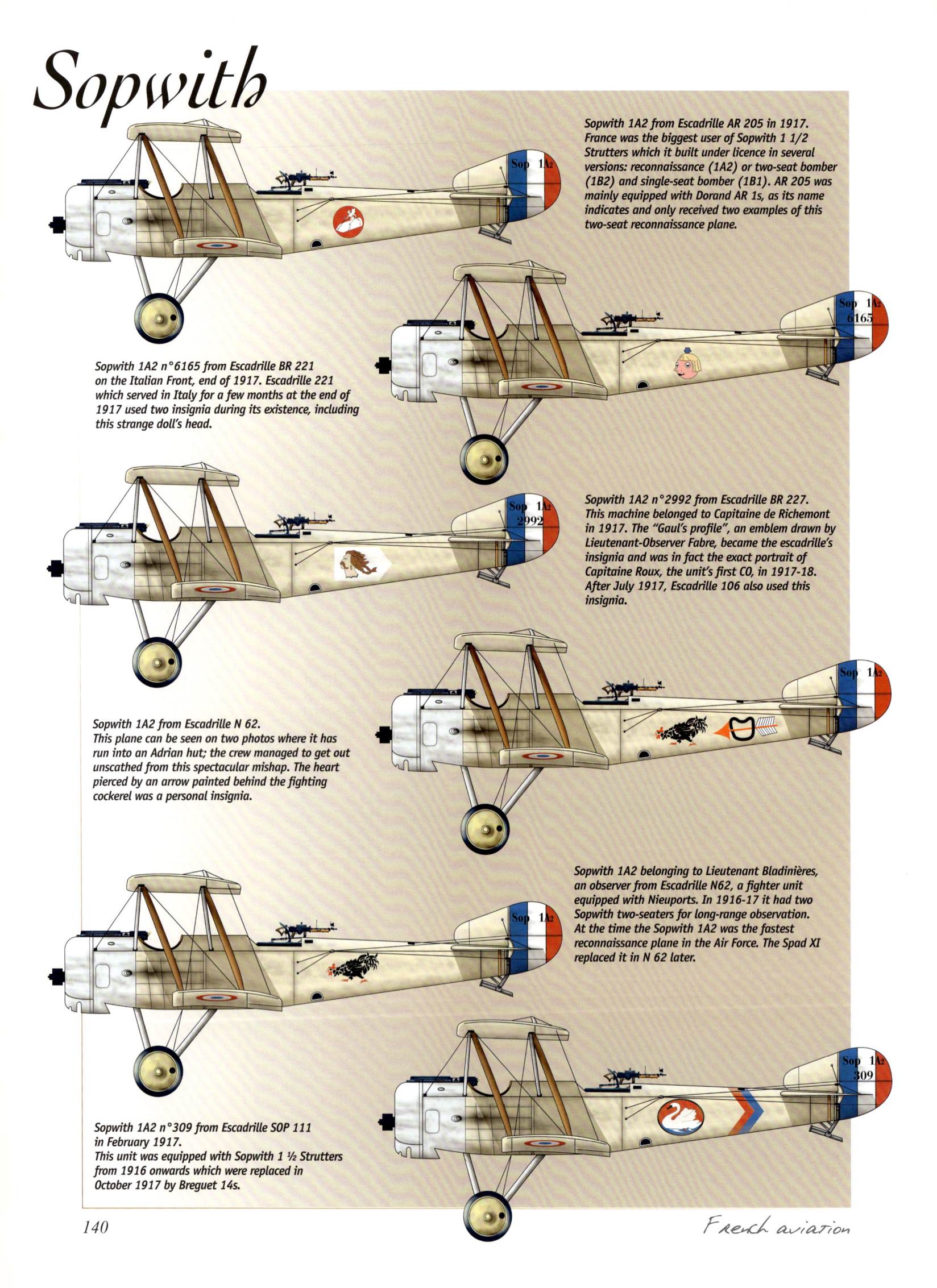

French aviation

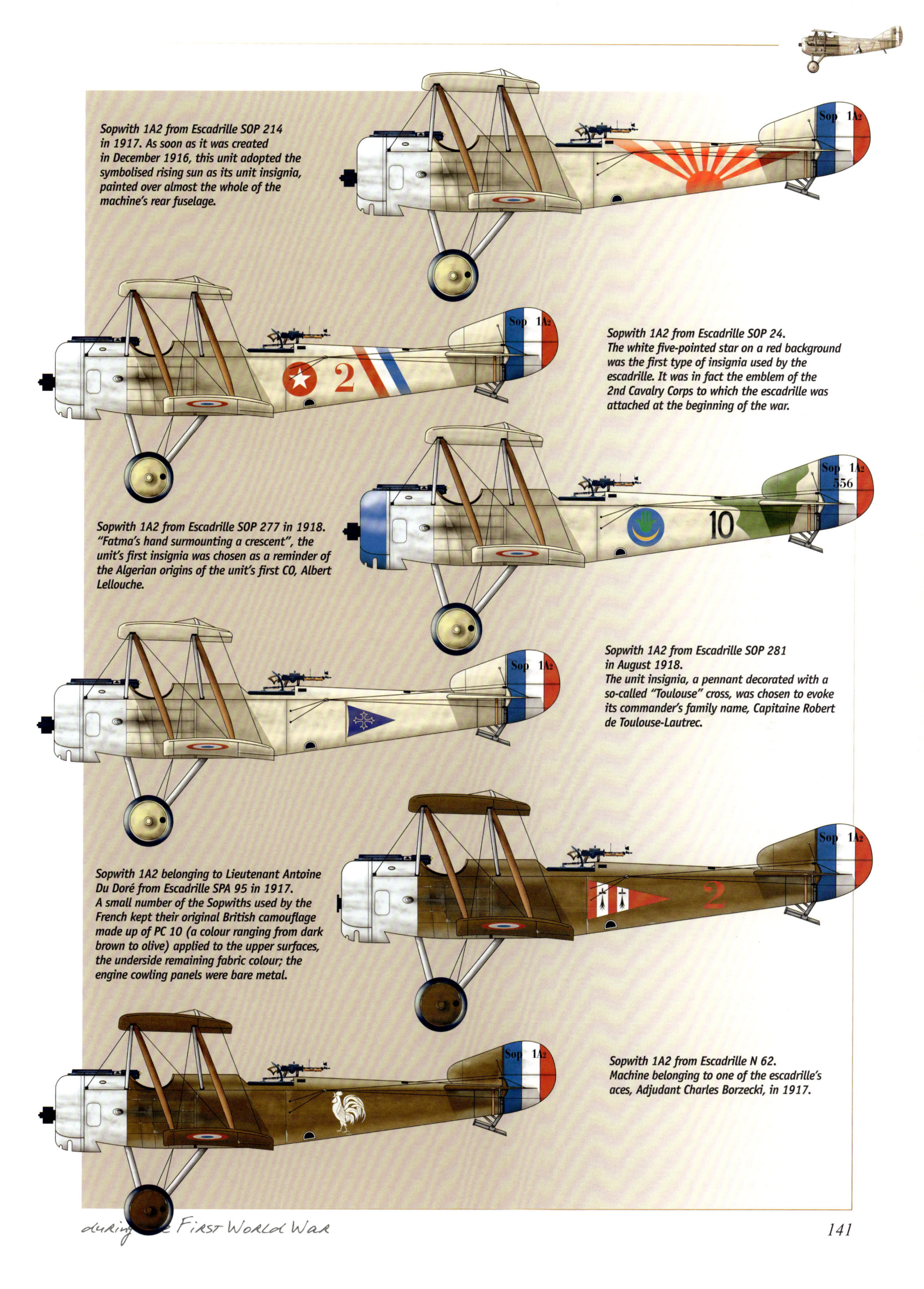

Sopwith 1A2 from Escadrille SOP 214 in 1917. As soon as it was created in December 1916, this unit adopted the symbolised rising sun as its unit insignia, painted over almost the whole of the machine's rear fuselage.

Sopwith 1A2 from Escadrille SOP 24. The white five-pointed star on a red background was the first type of insignia used by the escadrille. It was in fact the emblem of the 2nd Cavalry Corps to which the escadrille was attached at the beginning of the war.

Sopwith 1A2 from Escadrille SOP 277 in 1918. "Fatma's hand surmounting a crescent", the unit's first insignia was chosen as a reminder of the Algerian origins of the unit's first CO, Albert Lellouche.

Sopwith 1A2 from Escadrille SOP 281 in August 1918. The unit insignia, a pennant decorated with a so-called "Toulouse" cross, was chosen to evoke its commander's family name, Capitaine Robert de Toulouse-Lautrec.

Sopwith 1A2 belonging to Lieutenant Antoine Du Doré from Escadrille SPA 95 in 1917. A small number of the Sopwiths used by the French kept their original British camouflage made up of PC 10 (a colour ranging from dark brown to olive) applied to the upper surfaces, the underside remaining fabric colour; the engine cowling panels were bare metal.

Sopwith 1A2 from Escadrille N 62. Machine belonging to one of the escadrille's aces, Adjudant Charles Borzecki, in 1917.

during the First World War

141

Spad

Above.
Nungesser on the right, next to his Spad VII.

Opposite.
Reconnaissance Spad XI N° 6231.

Below.
Spad VII from SPA 3 in flight.

Below.
Spad VII N° 314 flown by Adjudant Dorme bearing the inscription "Père Dorme IV", "the stork flying with its wings on the down stroke" and the Croix de Lorraine on the back of the fuselage, of SPA 3
(SHD Air)

Faced with the very obvious qualities the Spad VII demonstrated, it was decided to build it and its variants en masse. So not only the Blériot factory in Levallois-Perret and the one built in Suresnes at the end of 1915, but also the sub-contractors Bernard, Borel, Crémont, Kellner et Fils, Levasseur, Edmond de Marçay, Nieuport, Régy, the Société d'Etudes Aéronautiques, the SCAF, the SCEM, and Roger Sommer, were all made to contribute. Building the engines involved a host of subcontractors too, including De Dion-Bouton, Fives-Lille, Delaunay-Belleville, Peugeot, Chénard et Walker, Voisin and many others whose production rates were barely fast enough to keep up with final production demands.

Type VII

It was in answer to an official specification for a fighter with a 150-hp Hispano engine, announced for the beginning of the spring of 1916, that the design team had worked on this type. The more aerodynamically researched airframe derived from the Model A and the initial design plans dated from 1 March 1916. This robust, very compact single-seat biplane, powered by a 140-hp then 150-hp Hispano engine made its first flight in April 1916 and revealed its characteristics, exceptional for the period as far as speed and rate of climb were concerned, without sacrificing anything to manoeuvrability.

Even though the trials had not finished yet, an order for 268 examples was placed on 10 May 1916, to be delivered at the beginning of the following summer. When it arrived in the units it caused such a stir that the pilots did anything to get hold of one in spite of the teething problems affecting the first fifty or so examples. Its radiator was indeed a source of concern due in fact to the viscosity of the lubricant. These defects were finally only ironed out on 6 March 1917 after Alfred Caquot had carried out systematic trials.

Technical Specifications
Wingspan: 25 ft 8 in
Total Length: 20 ft 4 in
Height: 6 ft 11 ½ in
Wing surface: 193.680 ft²
Maximum take off weight: 1 650 lb
Payload: 275 lb
Max. Speed: 123 mph at ground level, 115 mph at 6 560 ft, 112 mph at 9 840 ft and 107 mph at 13 120 ft
Rate of climb: 6 560 ft in 6 min 40 sec, 9 840 ft in 11 min 20 sec, 13 120 ft in 18 min
Flight Time: 2 ½ hrs

It was planned originally to have 1 276 Spad VIIs built in the period from 1 April 1917 to 31 March 1918, but only 1 220 were built. On 1 October 1918, 324 Spad VIIs were still on the front.
"Conclusive trials carried out by Lieutenant Guynemer on a 150-hp Spad pushed to its limits gave the expected results; the machine gained speed, 137 mph, and above all, it climbed very powerfully which gives it a clear advantage over the latest model of Albatros, a little single-seat 220-hp biplane with an easy climb to 21 320 ft."
Tests were carried out adapting an engine of the same type but whose power had been boosted to 180 hp by increasing the compression from 4.7 to 5.3 which in turn increased the speed to 130 mph at 6 560 ft and 124 mph at 13 210 ft, reaching the latter height in 13 minutes, with a service ceiling of 21 320 ft. A version with a Hispano engine rated at 200 hp reached a speed of 125 mph at 6 560 ft reached in not more than 11 ½ minutes.

Above, left
On 24 May 1917, the Spad VII belonging to the Maréchal des Logis Sardier The insignia of SPA 77 (a yellow Jerusalem Cross on a blue triangular pennant) has been painted on each half of the upper wing.
(SHD Air)

Above.
A line up of Spad VIIs from SPA 23 on the airfield at Souilly (Meuse) in July 1917. All the fighters bear a red stripe on the fuselage and the wing, as well as a personal insignia.
(SHD Air)

Below.
Spad VII N° 1371 from SPA 65. During the Great War, the unit's insignia was a "Griffon jumping on a red, white and blue tricolour stripe", painted here on the whole of the rear fuselage. (SHD Air)

Spad VII

Spad VII n° 1133 from SPA 153.
The escadrille's insignia (the Egyptian falcon carrying a magic ring in its claws), was chosen by this plane's pilot, Lieutenant Jean Gigodot, the escadrille's CO after 1 July 1917, and a distinguished Egyptologist.

Spad VII n° 1379 from SPA 65. Pilot: Adjudant Marcel Henriot.
Although this escadrille had been attached to the famous Cigognes (storks) group it adopted a black chimera as its insignia, subsequently painted on a double or triple oblique stripe.

Spad VII n° 1389 from SPA 62.
The pilot of this plane, Capitaine François Coli, a former Navy officer in the Merchant Navy and a distinguished navigator, disappeared with the ace, Charles Nungesser when they tried to cross the Atlantic on 8 May 1927. The fighting cockerel was the escadrille's second type of insignia, whereas the tricolour fuselage stripe was characteristic of SPA 62.

Spad VII n° 3493 from SPA 57.
The "seagull in flight, three quarter rear view" was the third insignia used by this escadrille. This was originally Lieutenant Chaput's personal insignia, which was adopted shortly after he died in action.

Spad VII n° 5822 from SPA 12 in 1918.
The white and blue pennant (subsequently with the figure "12" added), the colours of the Virgin Mary, was suggested by the unit's godmother, Marie de Bernis, the escadrille's CO's wife.

Spad VII n° 7912 from SPA 95.
The black and yellow oriflamme with a martinet in flight in its centre was the fourth and last insignia the escadrille used. The martinet was chosen because it was both an agile bird and its name was associated with punishment, the pilots in SPA 95 wanting to "Whip the Hun! Likewise, the yellow and black were used because they were the buccaneers' colours.

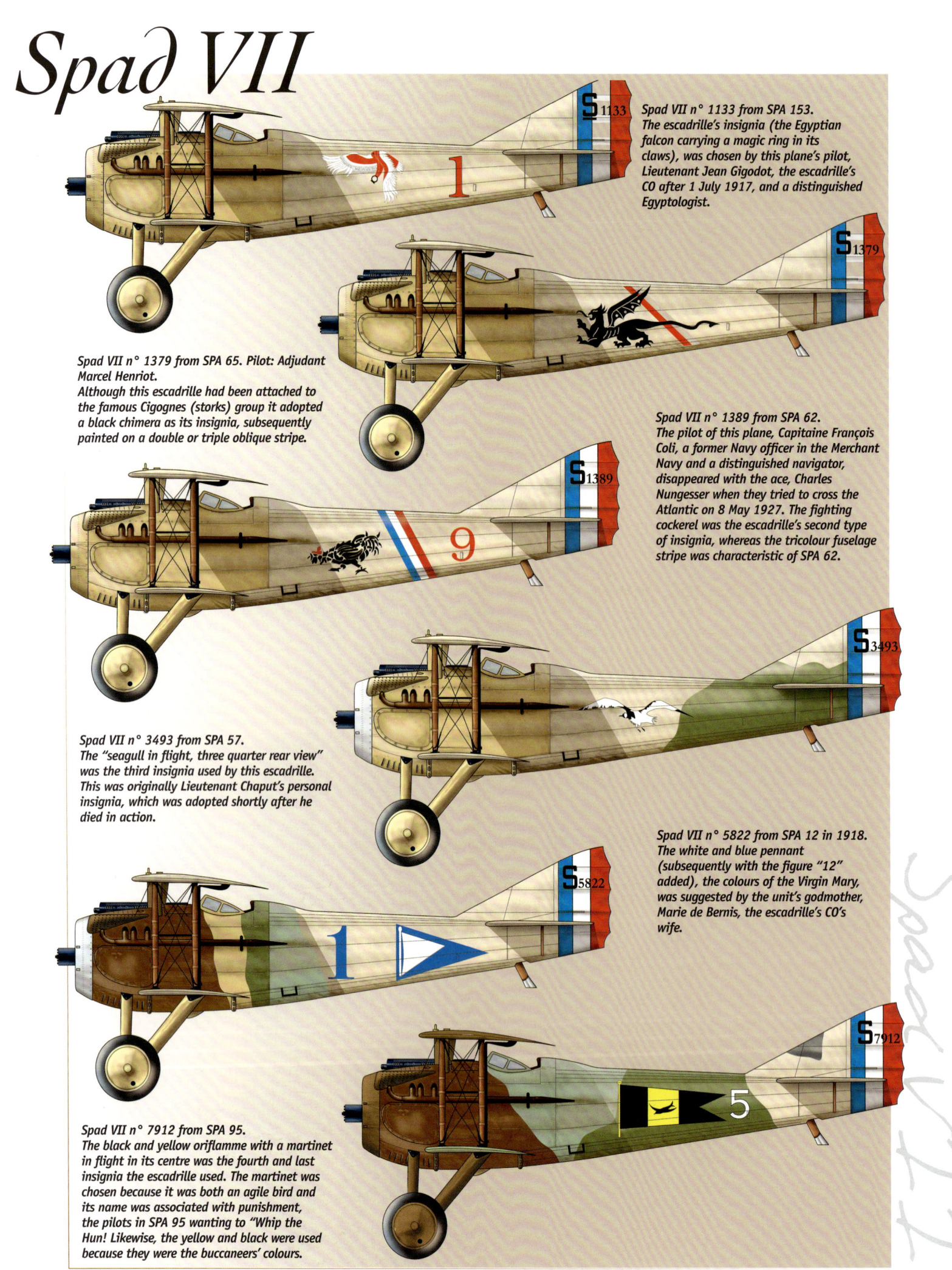

144 French aviation

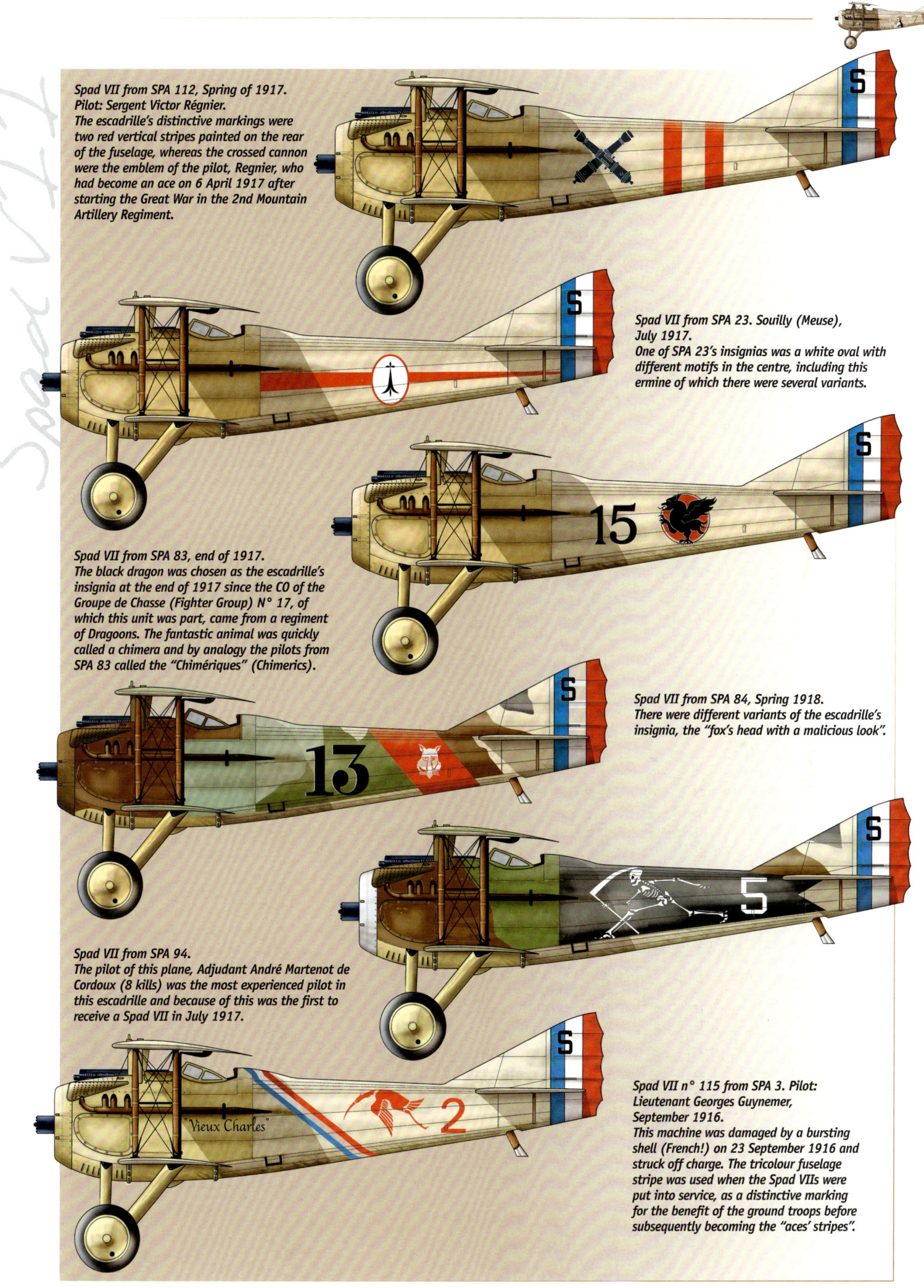

Spad VII from SPA 112, Spring of 1917.
Pilot: Sergent Victor Régnier.
The escadrille's distinctive markings were two red vertical stripes painted on the rear of the fuselage, whereas the crossed cannon were the emblem of the pilot, Regnier, who had become an ace on 6 April 1917 after starting the Great War in the 2nd Mountain Artillery Regiment.

Spad VII from SPA 23. Souilly (Meuse), July 1917.
One of SPA 23's insignias was a white oval with different motifs in the centre, including this ermine of which there were several variants.

Spad VII from SPA 83, end of 1917.
The black dragon was chosen as the escadrille's insignia at the end of 1917 since the CO of the Groupe de Chasse (Fighter Group) N° 17, of which this unit was part, came from a regiment of Dragoons. The fantastic animal was quickly called a chimera and by analogy the pilots from SPA 83 called the "Chimériques" (Chimerics).

Spad VII from SPA 84, Spring 1918.
There were different variants of the escadrille's insignia, the "fox's head with a malicious look".

Spad VII from SPA 94.
The pilot of this plane, Adjudant André Martenot de Cordoux (8 kills) was the most experienced pilot in this escadrille and because of this was the first to receive a Spad VII in July 1917.

Spad VII n° 115 from SPA 3. Pilot: Lieutenant Georges Guynemer, September 1916.
This machine was damaged by a bursting shell (French!) on 23 September 1916 and struck off charge. The tricolour fuselage stripe was used when the Spad VIIs were put into service, as a distinctive marking for the benefit of the ground troops before subsequently becoming the "aces' stripes".

Opposite.
Having become SPA 12's CO in January 1918, Capitaine Arnaud de Turenne kept the insignia of N 48 (a cock's head singing in a white circle edged with blue) on his Spad VII, in which he had scored six of his fifteen successes in aerial combat. (SHD Air)

Below, right.
Lieutenant René Fonck in front of one of the two Spad XIIIs (coded "VII") in SPA 103 that he flew. (SHD Air)

Above.
Camouflaged Spad VII from an unknown unit. The inscription "photo" on the fuselage side shows that the plane has been fitted out for photographic reconnaissance and carried a camera. (SDASM)

Below.
The Spad VIIs in SPA 124 with in the foreground, the personal mount belonging to Capitaine André d'Humières, followed by that belonging to Sous-lieutenant Marcel Robert (N°3). (SHD Air)

Type IX

This was the version of the Type VII armed with a 37-mm canon firing through the propeller hub, originally one of Guynemer's ideas. The problem of vibrations caused by the firing put a stop to the experiment, which nonetheless continued on another model. On 1 October 1918, there were still eight "Spad-canons" at the front.

Type XI

This was a reconnaissance two-seater with a 200-hp Hispano engine, equipped with a cowling-mounted machine gun and a machine gun in the rear cockpit. It had a payload of was 561 lb and had 2 ¾ hours' flying time. It flew at 105 mph at 13 120 ft reached in 17 minutes 50 seconds. Its reputation wasn't very good among the crews because they found it too heavy and its landing speed was too high. There was a variant, the "Type XVI", in June 1918, powered by a 250-hp Lorraine-Dietrich engine, in two-seat fighter or reconnaissance versions, armed with two synchronised cowling mounted machine guns and a new double turret for the observer, without being particularly better than its predecessor. In all 657 Spad XIs and XVIs were built. On 1 October 1918, 139 Spad XIs and 85 Spad XVIs were still in front-line units.

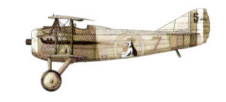

Type XII-Ca

This plane was armed with two synchronised machine guns, whilst its supercharged engine rated at 200 hp had a hollow reduction gear through which passed a 37-mm canon barrel and whose breech, when the gun was fired, rubbed the pilot's legs. Guynemer called it "Pétadou"; this plane flew at 125 mph at sea level and thanks to a supercharger whose use was restricted to only a few of the aces, at 131 mph at 13 120 ft.

Technical Specifications
Wingspan: 26 ft 10 in
Total Length: 20 ft 8 in
Height: 7 ft 6 in
Wing surface: 215.200 ft²
Maximum take off weight: 1 936 lb
Max. Speed: 128.12 mph
Service ceiling: 19 680 ft

Type XIII

The prototype of this version flew on 4 April 1917, and was still being built while the Spad VII was being produced. Delays concerning the armament and the engine delayed deliveries since, as at 1 April 1918, there were still 372 Spad VIIs in service compared with 290 Spad XIIIs with their two synchronised Vickers machine guns and 200-hp engine.
In all 8 472 were built, some with a 220-hp Hispano engine giving it a maximum speed of 131 mph at sea level and 140 mph at 6 560 ft, with a 22 960 ft service ceiling

Technical Specifications
Wingspan: 26 ft 10 in
Total Length: 21 ft 4 in
Height: 8 ft 2 ½ in
Maximum take off weight: 1 892 lb
Max. Speed: 125 mph at 13 120 ft
Flight Time: 2 hrs
On 1 October there were 764 Spad XIIIs on the front.

Type XVII

An improved version of the Type XIII intended as a fighter and for photo reconnaissance (with two cameras), powered by a Hispano engine rated at 300 hp giving it a speed of 150 mph.

Above.
Spad XIII from SPA 65, an escadrille which had the famous Charles Nungesser in its ranks and which was credited with 108 kills at the end of the war. The unit insignia, "a jumping griffon" was painted over a large part of the fuselage. *(SHD Air)*

Above.
Spad XIII N° S 1893 flown by Jacques Rocques from SPA 48 in April-May 1918. The pilot was of Swiss and Venezuelan extraction and was one of the air force's aces with five kills and two probables. *(SHD Air)*

Opposite.
Lieutenant Nungesser approaching Spad XIII N° 1039 equipped with a camera gun installed on the upper wing. Apart from his personal insignia, the ace's plane was easily recognisable by its white triangles painted on the top of the fuselage. *(SHD Air)*

Above.
Capitaine Georges Guynemer at the controls of his Spad XIII (N° 5504) at Bonneuil on 20 August 1917, the day when he made his 53rd kill with this fighter. *(SHD Air)*

Spad XIII

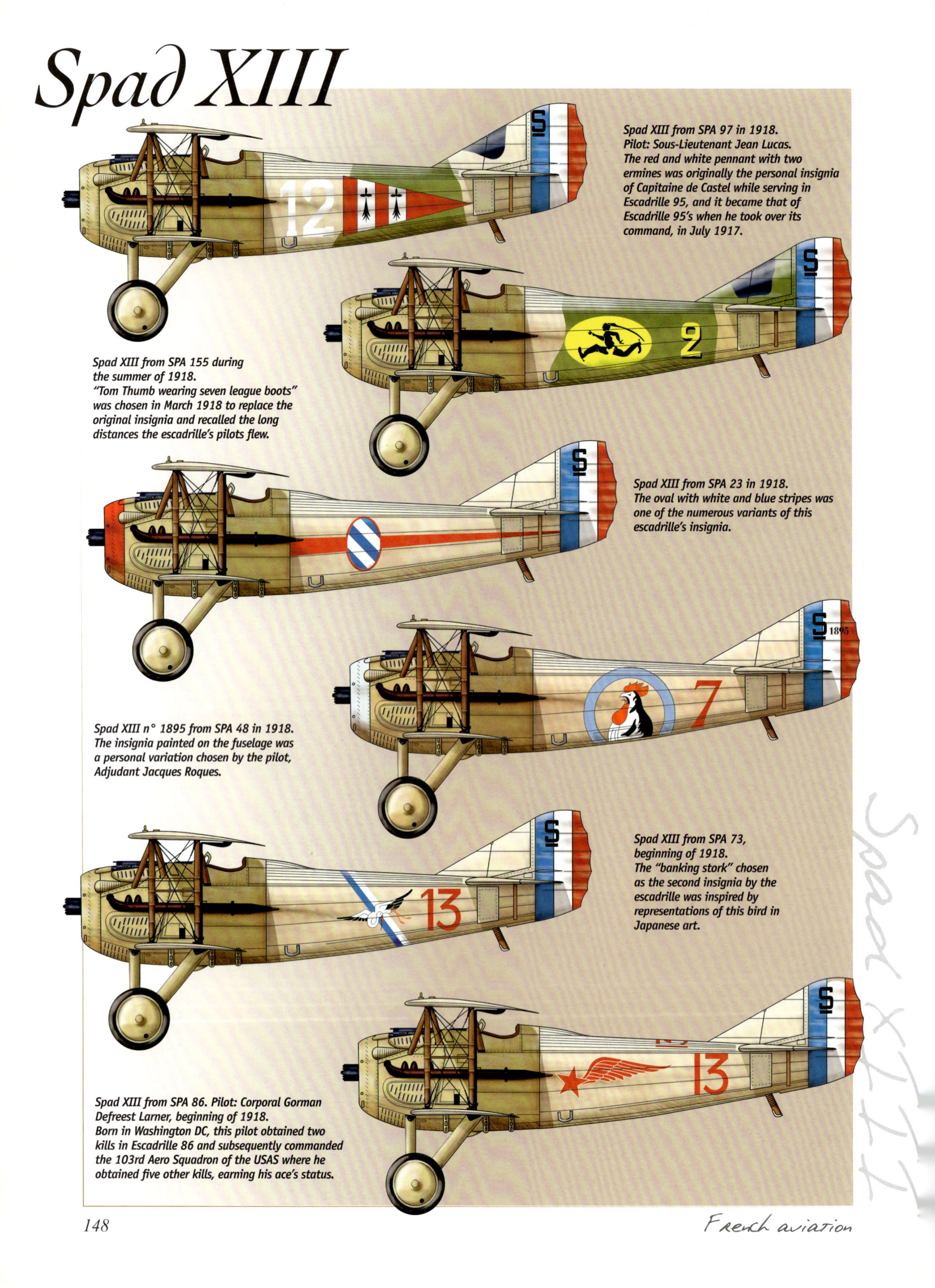

*Spad XIII from SPA 97 in 1918.
Pilot: Sous-Lieutenant Jean Lucas.
The red and white pennant with two ermines was originally the personal insignia of Capitaine de Castel while serving in Escadrille 95, and it became that of Escadrille 95's when he took over its command, in July 1917.*

*Spad XIII from SPA 155 during the summer of 1918.
"Tom Thumb wearing seven league boots" was chosen in March 1918 to replace the original insignia and recalled the long distances the escadrille's pilots flew.*

*Spad XIII from SPA 23 in 1918.
The oval with white and blue stripes was one of the numerous variants of this escadrille's insignia.*

*Spad XIII n° 1895 from SPA 48 in 1918.
The insignia painted on the fuselage was a personal variation chosen by the pilot, Adjudant Jacques Roques.*

*Spad XIII from SPA 73, beginning of 1918.
The "banking stork" chosen as the second insignia by the escadrille was inspired by representations of this bird in Japanese art.*

*Spad XIII from SPA 86. Pilot: Corporal Gorman Defreest Larner, beginning of 1918.
Born in Washington DC, this pilot obtained two kills in Escadrille 86 and subsequently commanded the 103rd Aero Squadron of the USAS where he obtained five other kills, earning his ace's status.*

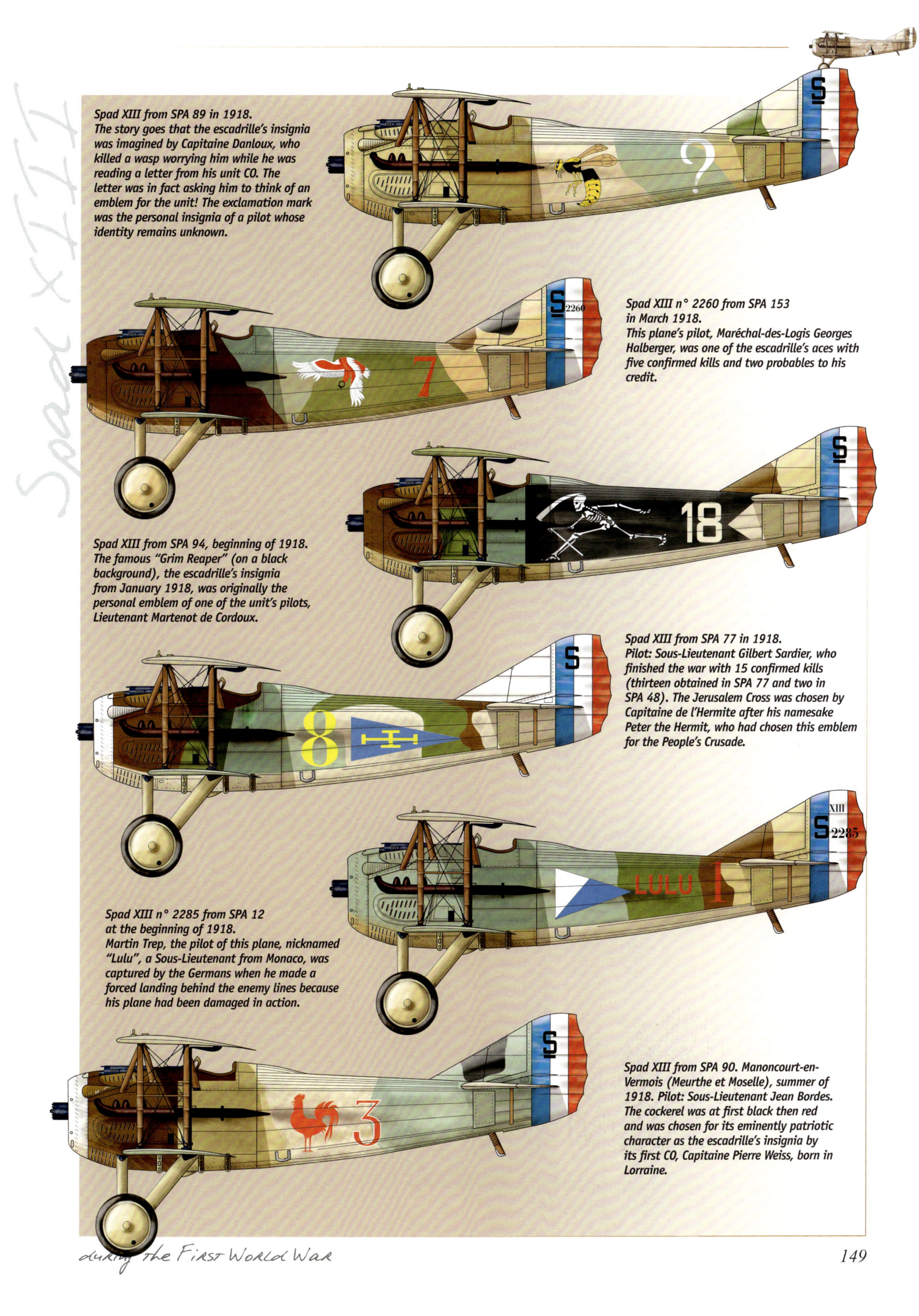

Spad XIII from SPA 89 in 1918.
The story goes that the escadrille's insignia was imagined by Capitaine Danloux, who killed a wasp worrying him while he was reading a letter from his unit CO. The letter was in fact asking him to think of an emblem for the unit! The exclamation mark was the personal insignia of a pilot whose identity remains unknown.

Spad XIII n° 2260 from SPA 153 in March 1918.
This plane's pilot, Maréchal-des-Logis Georges Halberger, was one of the escadrille's aces with five confirmed kills and two probables to his credit.

Spad XIII from SPA 94, beginning of 1918.
The famous "Grim Reaper" (on a black background), the escadrille's insignia from January 1918, was originally the personal emblem of one of the unit's pilots, Lieutenant Martenot de Cordoux.

Spad XIII from SPA 77 in 1918.
Pilot: Sous-Lieutenant Gilbert Sardier, who finished the war with 15 confirmed kills (thirteen obtained in SPA 77 and two in SPA 48). The Jerusalem Cross was chosen by Capitaine de l'Hermite after his namesake Peter the Hermit, who had chosen this emblem for the People's Crusade.

Spad XIII n° 2285 from SPA 12 at the beginning of 1918.
Martin Trep, the pilot of this plane, nicknamed "Lulu", a Sous-Lieutenant from Monaco, was captured by the Germans when he made a forced landing behind the enemy lines because his plane had been damaged in action.

Spad XIII from SPA 90. Manoncourt-en-Vermois (Meurthe et Moselle), summer of 1918. Pilot: Sous-Lieutenant Jean Bordes.
The cockerel was at first black then red and was chosen for its eminently patriotic character as the escadrille's insignia by its first CO, Capitaine Pierre Weiss, born in Lorraine.

Voisin bombers

Top.
Voisin 8 BN 2 (LAP) from VB 109.

Above.
Voisin 8 BN2 (LAP).

Above, right.
Voisin 8 BN 2 (LAP) from VB 101. The escadrille insignia was a blue star, referring to the star Vega whose blue light is very visible during night flights. (Photos Maurice Decouvrière)

Voisin Type 8 (also called LAP)

The engine was the plane's weak point and various trials with engines designed by Fiat, Panhard, etc., eventually led to the 220-hp Peugeot engine being selected. The increase in power led to an increase in the lift area which went from 645.600 sq ft to 677.880 sq ft. The fuel originally housed in nacelles was now placed between the two wings, in two faired tanks to avoid increased drag. The crews complained about a loss of handling however. Its theoretical payload was 792 lb which allowed for 3 hours' flying time at a speed of 74 mph at an altitude of 6 560 ft, reached in 17 minutes. The standard offensive load was twelve 120-mm shells and four 155-mm shells stacked under the machine, in layers and dropped using a cable attached in a lever operated by the bombardier.

Some of them (LBPs) were also equipped with a 47-mm canon in the front for use against ground targets.

The Peugeot engine however had a defective greasing system and the fuel supply and ignition were not fully operational, and in spite of correct servicing and frequent maintenance, it did not last much longer than 15 to 20 flying hours, which did nothing to reassure the crews.

Voisin type 10 (or LAR)

The 300 hp Renault engine installed on Breguet XIV giving any satisfaction, Voisin decides to mount it on a new version which appears at the end of 1917. Landing searchlights are fixed in front of the nacelle. The payload is reduced to 750 lbs, giving 3 hours of flight at the speed of 78 mph at an altitude of 6,500ft. The climb to 2,000m is made within 15 minutes.

For the protection of the groups, some aircraft (LBR) are armed with a 37-mm cannon manned by the observer. The bombardment squadrons are reequipped with this model from the end of 1917. Escadrille V 116 has fourteen of these aircraft in 1918. V 133, recently created on 1st August 1918, received seventeen of these planes numbered 2799, 2875, 2943, 2948, 2952, 3002, 3013, 3029, 3033, 3102, 3103, 3109, 3141, 3157, 3167 and 3186, giving a good idea of the importance of this series of single-engined Voisins. This model can be converted in air ambulance.

French aviation

Miscellaneous planes

Opposite.
The defensive armament of the Salmson-Moineau N° 149 made up of twin Lewis machine guns on a ring mounting.

Type 71

This big biplane equipped with four 220-hp Hispano engines placed equidistantly on either side (the so-called "square") was displayed at Buc in November 1917. The official programme for a night bomber required a 2 486 lb payload and fuel for five hours of flying at 94 mph.

Technical Specifications
Wingspan: 86 ft 3 in
Total Length: 45 ft 11 in
Height: 19 ft 8 in
Wing surface: 1 506.400 ft²
Maximum take off weight: 14 366 lb
Payload: 5 126 lb of which 2 640 lb of fuel
Flight Time: 6 hrs 40 min, or 5 hours on only two engines on the homeward leg

Moineau

René Moineau, a pioneer pilot and regulator with Breguet, was working in 1914 at the test centre at Chalais Meudon. At the request of the Army, after having prepared the Breguet-Michelin, he designed a big biplane to replace the Maurice Farmans.
The Type A9 2H was a three-seat single-engined biplane built by Salmson. Moineau studied an original solution where the 160-hp Samson A9 Canton-Unné engine was installed across the fuselage to drive two propellers (the 2H of the designation). 200 examples were built but it was not a success with the crews who used it in 1916. The following escadrilles were equipped with Salmson-Moineau: N° 29 in the summer of 1916, then during 1917, N° 2, 19, 41, 57, 63, 71, 72, 106, 229 and 289 for a short period before being replaced by Letords, Sopwiths, Dorands and others.

Morane Type AF

This single-seat biplane fighter (Mos 28) with a 150-hp single-valve Gnome engine was put in for the fighter competition and made its first flight on 23 June 1917. It had good flying qualities but its engine was at the end of its development potential and had a bad reputation. Furthermore it was decided to concentrate on producing the Spad XIII.

Below.
Salmson Moineau SM2.
(SHD Air)

Technical Specifications
Wingspan: 25 ft 6 in
Total Length: 16 ft 10 in
Height: 7 ft 8 in
Wing surface: 164.735 ft²
Maximum take off weight: 1 427 lb
Max. Speed: 130 mph at 13 120 ft
Rate of climb: 9 840 ft in 8 min 10 sec, 16 400 ft in 20 min 30 sec

Above.
Close-up of a Salmson-Moineau SM 1 engine. The propellers were placed on inter-wing struts and activated by means of a ball joint and angle drive.
(SHD Air)

during the First World War

Above.
Salmson Moineau SM 1.
(SDASM)

Schmitt Type 6

Built by the Paul Schmitt factories in Levallois (near Paris), this biplane appeared in 1917. Its fuselage was fabric-covered over a steel tube structure. The upper wing's incidence was adjustable within ten degrees with a wheel used by the pilot to adjust the plane's attitude in relation to its load and speed by keeping the fuselage constantly level. Its powerplant was a Salmson radial or a Renault Vee engine with the same rating, with enough fuel for five hours' flying time with a payload of 825 lb at 178 mph at 6 560 ft, reached in 19 minutes. Production was delayed so that the first machines reached the front at the beginning of 1917, too late to be really operational.

Type 7

This bomber was produced in small numbers, finished in the summer of 1917. It was a biplane whose wings were held in place by six pairs of struts pivoting 12° around a horizontal axis. It was powered by a 265-hp Renault. It had a large wingspan and was not really liked by its crews. The observer was armed with two machine guns in a turret and the pilot operated a machine gun fitted to the upper wing spar and the plane could carry 330 lb of ordnance. The undercarriage was fragile and was reinforced by a bogey placed well in front of the main undercarriage units to prevent nose-overs. The Type 7 equipped GB 3 from 1917, replacing the Sopwiths as follows: Escadrille 125 in February, 126 and 127 in April and 128 in May. It had great difficulty holding its position in a formation because of its large wingspan, and this and its inadequate performances, meant it was quickly withdrawn from the front line and replaced by the Voisin Peugeot in Escadrille 125 and by the Breguet XIV in the others in November 1917.

Technical Specifications
Wingspan: 57 ft 10 in
Total Length: 31 ft 6 in
Height: 11 ft 9 in
Maximum take off weight: 4 840 lb
Max. Speed: 84.37 mph at 6 560 ft
Service ceiling: 5 hrs

Below and opposite.
Paul Schmitt Type 7 n°22.

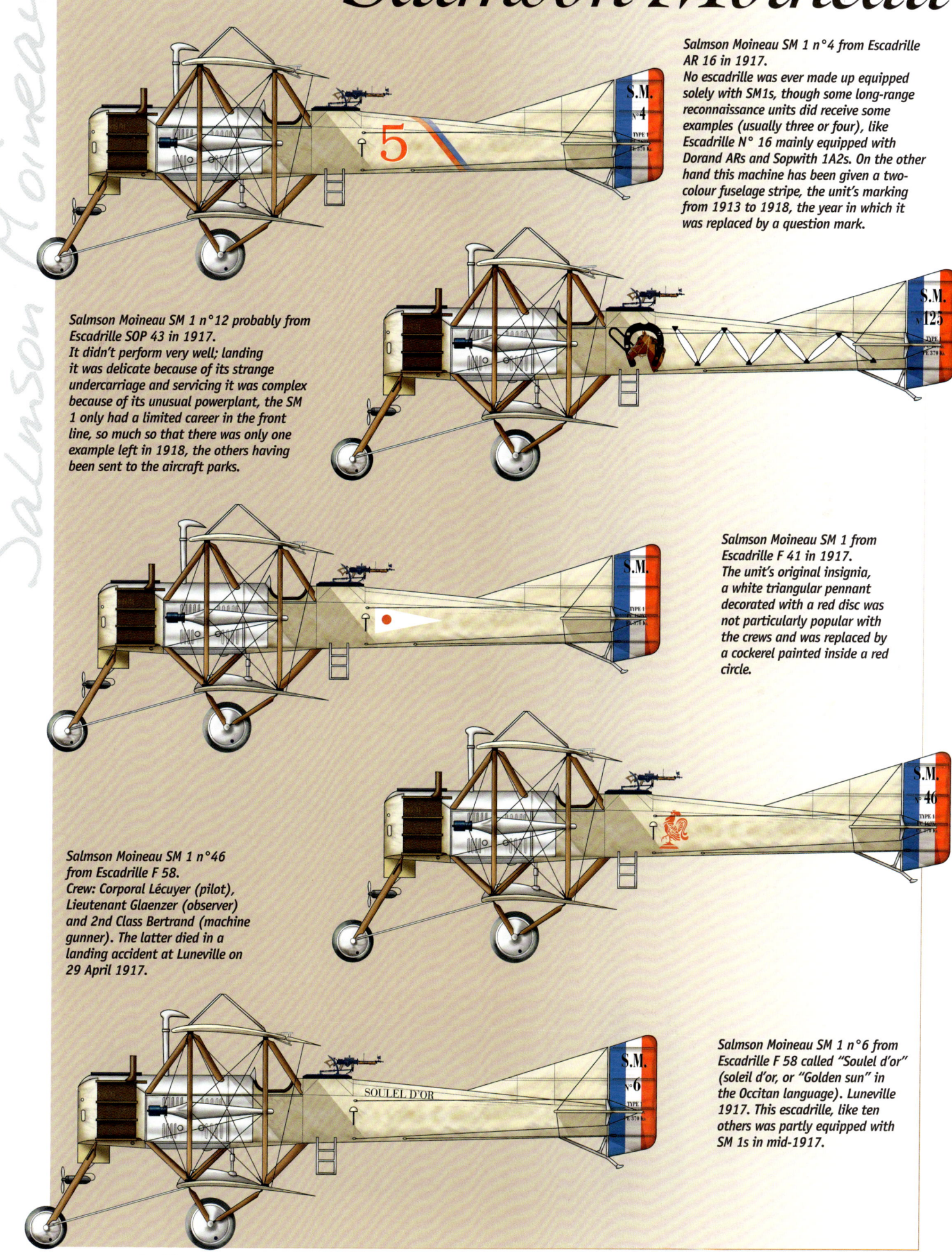

Salmson Moineau

Salmson Moineau SM 1 n°4 from Escadrille AR 16 in 1917.
No escadrille was ever made up equipped solely with SM1s, though some long-range reconnaissance units did receive some examples (usually three or four), like Escadrille N° 16 mainly equipped with Dorand ARs and Sopwith 1A2s. On the other hand this machine has been given a two-colour fuselage stripe, the unit's marking from 1913 to 1918, the year in which it was replaced by a question mark.

Salmson Moineau SM 1 n°12 probably from Escadrille SOP 43 in 1917.
It didn't perform very well; landing it was delicate because of its strange undercarriage and servicing it was complex because of its unusual powerplant, the SM 1 only had a limited career in the front line, so much so that there was only one example left in 1918, the others having been sent to the aircraft parks.

Salmson Moineau SM 1 from Escadrille F 41 in 1917.
The unit's original insignia, a white triangular pennant decorated with a red disc was not particularly popular with the crews and was replaced by a cockerel painted inside a red circle.

Salmson Moineau SM 1 n°46 from Escadrille F 58.
Crew: Corporal Lécuyer (pilot), Lieutenant Glaenzer (observer) and 2nd Class Bertrand (machine gunner). The latter died in a landing accident at Luneville on 29 April 1917.

Salmson Moineau SM 1 n°6 from Escadrille F 58 called "Soulel d'or" (soleil d'or, or "Golden sun" in the Occitan language). Luneville 1917. This escadrille, like ten others was partly equipped with SM 1s in mid-1917.

during the First World War

Crossed destinies of Planes and Men

Above.
A pilots' dormitory at the Etampes flying school.

Opposite.
A French military pilot's metal brevet.

Below.
A brassard adorned with the military pilot's insignia, worn on the uniform's left hand sleeve.

"There are no riches without men". The old adage is well-known and can easily apply to the French air force during the Great War for, apart from the planes with increasingly improved performances, there were also all those who built them, made them work and of course piloted them. Among the latter there were the aces, a term coined during this war, but there were also all the others, the anonymous ones, those who never had the opportunity to have the slightest bit of fame, some who even lost their lives before obtaining their wings while they were still training. These few pages are dedicated to all those anonymous airmen whose role was so important. The reader will able to appreciate what daily life was like for French airmen during the Great War.

Crossed destinies

Atmosphere

Above.
Escadrille C 43 mechanics beside a nine cylinder Le Rhône rotary engine.

Opposite.
Members of Escadrille C 43 in front of the radio barracks (at the time called the "TSF", téléphonie sans fil – wireless telegraphy).

during the First World War

Above.
In March 1916, Sous-lieutenant Patrick O'Quinn was forced to land his Caudron G.4 on the airfield at Oiry (Marne) after getting lost in the mist during a mission over Verdun.

Maurice Tabuteau photographed aboard his Morane Saulnier Type N monoplane just after landing on the airfield at Vinets (Aube) in January 1916. This aircraft pioneer (Aéro-Club de France licence N° 128) was appointed chief-pilot for the RGA (Réserve Générale de l'Aviation) after the mobilisation and was part of Escadrille N 12 from September 1915 to the beginning of 1916 before being made Sous-lieutenant in April of the same year.

Opposite.
A Delahaye 43 photo lorry on the airfield at Rosnay (Marne) in March 1916.

Below.
Sopwith 16s lined-up on the airfield at Tours and used for training observers in the US Air Service. Tours, renamed "Tours AFB" (Tours Air Force Base) was the USAS's 2nd Aviation Instruction Center from November 1917 to April 1919.
(SDASM)

during the First World War

157

Atmosphere

Opposite.
C 47's accommodation – tents and barracks.

Below.
The inside of a dormitory at the Etampes flying school.

Above, right.
Airmen from Escadrille C 43. Note the wide variety of uniforms they are wearing, depending on their original corps (infantry, cavalry, etc.), since there was no specific uniform at the time.

Opposite.
Officers and NCOs posing near one of the school's Blériots.

Opposite.
Opened officially in 1912, the Avord flying school became the Ecole d'Application de l'Aéronautique Militaire shortly after the beginning of the war, in October 1914. It was ideally located in the centre of France, in the Cher department, and continued expanding until the end of the conflict, ending up in the summer of 1918 by having 170 instructors, more than 2 000 mechanics, 1 000 pupils, 1 300 planes and more than 70 vehicles (cars, aircraft tractors, trucks and motorbikes) some of which can be seen here near the concrete garages built in 1917.

French aviation

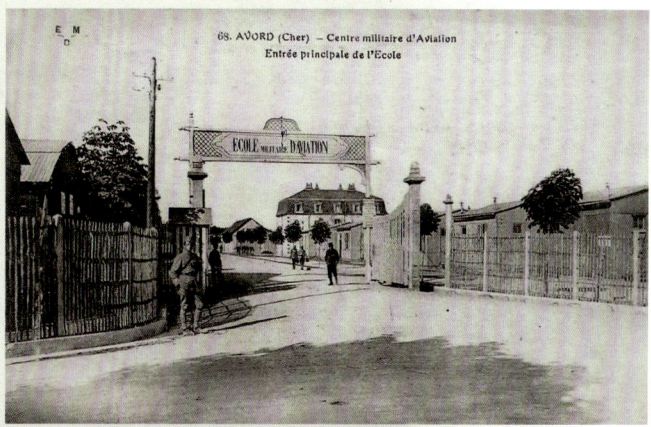

Above, left.
The Avord training camp equipped itself with specific sports facilities like the tennis courts shown here.

Above.
The entrance to the Avord flying school. At the end of the war, the centre was the biggest in France and in the whole world; it had six training groups equipped with night-time Voisins, Caudrons, Sopwiths, G.4s and Letords and the school's total surface area spread over more than 1000 hectares.

Above.
The barracks on the Longvic military airfield, near Dijon, inaugurated officially in the spring of 1914 and the base for the 1st Aviation Group.

Opposite.
Taking over the pilot training school set up by Louis Blériot on the airfield at La Ville Sauvage, the Military Flying School at Etampes-Mondésir was officially opened in 1915 and taught several thousands of pilots during the conflict.

during the First World War

The French Aces

René Paul FONCK (27 March 1894-18 June 1953) was the French and Allied World War One ace of aces with **75 confirmed kills**, to which must be added between 52 and 69 unconfirmed ones. He began the war in the Engineers and managed to get himself transferred to the air force in 1915, starting his pilot's career in C 47, an observation unit. His final tally which was rather impressive as were the number of decorations he was awarded (including the Croix de Guerre and 28 palms!) earned him the honour of carrying the Air Force standard during the victory parade on 14 July 1919. He was promoted to Inspector of the Fighters with rank of Colonel in 1940. His closeness to Pétain and his unofficial activities in the Vichy Government earned him a brief spell in prison at the end of the war, before he was finally freed, no charges being held against him.

Georges Marie Ludovic Jules GUYNEMER (24 December 1894-11 September 1917) was declared unfit for military service at the moment war was declared because he was too fragile. This son of a former Saint-Cyr (the French Sandhurst) officer managed to get in to the air force as part of the auxiliary service, as a mechanic. With a special derogation he became a pupil pilot in January 1915 and though his beginnings were far from encouraging, he owed his continued career to Jules Védrines who became his instructor. Obtaining his military licence in April 1915, Guynemer had a dazzling career in Escadrille N° 3, obtaining his first kill three months after obtaining his "wings". He was shot down seven times in action and became the most emblematic French pilot of the Great War, obtaining **54** (53 according to some sources) **confirmed kills**, four of which were shared, and 29 probables. He went off on a reconnaissance mission on 11 September 1917 and never returned; he was officially listed as missing a few days later, but neither his remains nor the wreck of his plane were ever found.

Charles Eugène Jules Marie NUNGESSER (15 March 1892-8 May 1927) returned from South America where he had gone through several jobs, so he could join the Hussars when war was declared. This true adventurer went over to the air force in 1915 and joined a bomber unit in which he never hesitated to chase German planes. He became a fighter pilot and, seriously wounded in February 1916, returned to action despite the doctors' advice and obtained the impressive tally of 43 confirmed kills, including several Drachens. After doing several post-war air shows, he disappeared with his navigator François Coli during a transatlantic non-stop crossing between Paris and New York on 8 May 1927, his plane having probably crashed into the sea following an engine breakdown near Saint-Pierre and Miquelon.

The Aces

Georges Félix MADON *(28 July 1892-11 November 1924) obtained* **41 confirmed kills** *and a further 64 probables without ever being wounded in four years' combat. Already an experienced pilot at the beginning of the war, he commanded SPA 38 equipped with Spad XIIIs and trained several pilots who in turn earned their ace's status.*

Michel Joseph Calixte Marie COIFFARD, *(16 July 1892-28 October 1918) obtained* **34 confirmed kills,** *most of them against German observation balloons (26 Drachen) and shared with another pilot. He got his last kill a few moments before being wounded during a dogfight with German fighters, and had to crash land behind allied lines. He was seriously wounded and died on the way to hospital.*

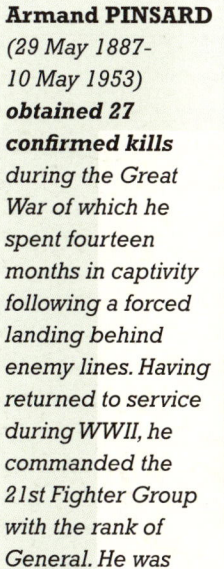

Armand PINSARD *(29 May 1887-10 May 1953)* **obtained 27 confirmed kills** *during the Great War of which he spent fourteen months in captivity following a forced landing behind enemy lines. Having returned to service during WWII, he commanded the 21st Fighter Group with the rank of General. He was sentenced at the end of the war for his activities with the Vichy collaborationist government. Pinsard saved Jean Renoir (at the time an observer) during the war and was the model for the character Lieutenant Maréchal, played by Jean Gabin in his famous film "la Grande Illusion".*

Maurice Jean Paul BOYAU *(8 May 1888—16 September 1918). This former Rugby international started the war in a cavalry regiment and only obtained his pilot's licence in February 1916. Assigned to N 77, he made* **35 confirmed kills***, most of them German observation balloons and disappeared in aerial combat near Mars-la-Tour a few weeks before the end of the conflict.*

Jean Pierre Léon BOURJADE *(25 May 1889—22 October 1924). A missionary before the war, Bourjade started the war as an artilleryman before joining the 125th Bomber Brigade in 1915 and scored* **28 confirmed kills** *in the end, of which 27 were observation balloons. He was ordained in 1921 and died of illness in Papua while he was on a mission.*

René Pierre Marie DORME *(1894—25 May 1917). The holder of* **23 kills***, Dorme (nicknamed "le Père", "l'Inimitable" or "l'Increvable" – "un-killable") was one of the "Cigognes" group's aces, with Guynemer. He died in action (during which he most likely obtained another kill), being forced to land in the trenches in circumstances which are still not clear today.*

during the First World War

Gabriel Fernand Charles GUÉRIN (25 July 1892-1 August 1918) spent the first part of the war in the infantry, winning the Croix de Guerre with two citations. Licenced in October 1916 he commanded SPA 88 in July 1918 and obtained **23 confirmed kills**. He lost his life in an accident, at the controls of a Spad VII on the airfield at Mont-l'Evêque.

Alfred Marie Joseph HEURTEAUX (20 May 1893-30 December 1985). Appointed CO of the "Cigognes" Escadrille (N 3/SPA 3) in November 1916, Herteaux ended the war with a score of **21 confirmed kills** and a further 13 probables. He was Inspector of Fighters at the beginning of the Second World War when he joined the Resistance and was imprisoned in 1941.

Marcel Émile (Claude) HAEGELEN (13 September 1896-24 May 1950). After beginning the war in the 27th Infantry Regiment, Haegelen joined the air force in July 1915 and obtained his pilot's licence the next year in January. He ended the war with **23 confirmed kills** (among which several-balloons) and three probables.

Pierre MARINOVITCH (1 August 1898-2 September 1919). Born in Paris of a Serbian father and a Polish mother, Marinovitch signed up in the Army in February 1916 at only 17 and served first in a Dragoon regiment before becoming a pupil pilot. Licenced in November 1916, he was credited with **22 kills**, plus three probables. The youngest ace was killed in an accident in Belgium during an acrobatics display in presence of King Albert I.

Albert Louis DEULLIN (24 August 1890—29 May 1923). After starting the war as a dragoon, Deullin obtained his pilot's licence in June 1915 and took over command of SPA 73 in February 1917. He was wounded three times and finished the war with a tally of **20 confirmed kills.** Chief-pilot in the Franco-Rumanian airline company after the war, he carried out several expeditions. He was killed trying out a prototype on Villacoublay airfield.

The Aces

Jacques Louis EHRLICH *(5 October 1893-10 August 1953).* Mobilised when he was already in the infantry, Ehrlich managed to get transferred into the air force only in December 1916 and received his pilot's licence the next year. Seriously wounded, he obtained **19 kills** between 30 June and 18 September 1918, all save one against balloons (three on 15 September). On 18 September 1918, shortly after having obtained his last success, he was forced to land behind enemy lines, his Spad having been hit by enemy gunfire and he finished the war as a prisoner.

Bernard Henri Marie Léonard BARNY DE ROMANET *(29 January 1894-23 September 1921).* A chasseur à cheval when the war broke out, de Romanet joined the air force in July 1915 and obtained his licence in January of the next year. At first assigned to a reconnaissance and artillery observation unit, he became a fighter pilot in SPA 37 in the spring of 1917 and ended the war with eighteen confirmed kills including one balloon. A test and competition pilot after the war, he beat several world speed records and killed himself on 23 September 1921 at Etampes while training for the Deutsch de la Meurthe Cup.

Jean Marie Luc Gilbert SARDIER *(5 May 1897-7 October 1976).* He started the war in the infantry, then he was transferred to the air force the year after and obtained his pilot's licence during the summer of 1916. Made CO of SPA 48 in July 1918, he ended the war with fifteen confirmed kills, of which five were captive balloons

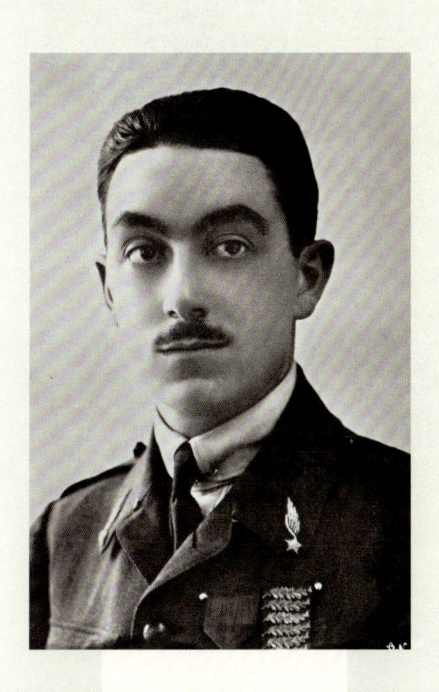

Henri Joseph Marie HAY DE SLADE *(29 May 1893—2 November 1979).* An officer cadet at Saint-Cyr before the war, de Slade joined the air force in May 1916 and was licenced as a pilot the following August. His final tally reached **19 confirmed kills** (including a Drachen) and 3 probables. He also fought in the Second World War which he ended with the rank of Colonel.

Jean CHAPUT *(17 September 1893-6 Mai 1918).* Engaged in the infantry in 1913, Chaput was transferred to the air force the following year and obtained his pilot's licence in February 1915. Wounded several times in action, he was shot down on 6 May 1918 near Montdidier while Escadrille N° 57's CO and had obtained 16 confirmed kills.

Armand Jean GALLIOT JOSEPH, the Marquis de Turenne d'Aubepeyre *(2 April 1891-10 December 1980).* A professional soldier in the cavalry in 1908, de Turenne joined the air force in 1915 and obtained his licence at the end of the year. Two years later he was SPA 12's CO and obtained several double kills, ending the war with 15 confirmed kills of which 13 were shared.

during the First World War

The "Anonymous"

***Jacques Raphaël ROQUES** (2 August 1894-24 May 1988).*
Born of a Swiss father and a Venezuelan mother; Roques joined the Foreign Legion before being assigned to the air force. He obtained his pilot's licence (N° 3495) on 26 May at Chartres and was assigned to Escadrille N 48 on the following 4 January. He finished the war with five confirmed kills earning him the status of "ace". He was naturalised French in 1919, was second in command of GC I/1 withe rank of Captain at the beginning of WWII.

Above.
Jacques Roques *in his Nieuport 17 with the small-sized escadrille insignia. All the pilot's planes had "7" as their individual number*

Above.
Nieuport 17 from N 48 before taking off on a mission over Verdun.

Opposite. Jacques Roques posing in front of his Nieuport 17 at Verdun.

Opposite.
Jacques-Raphaël Roques *wearing flying gear in his Spad XIII whose fuselage has been decorated with N 48's cockerel. Note the number of variants, depending on which machine and particularly on the skill of the respective artists who painted them.*

Opposite.
A corporal in March 1916, sergeant in April 1917 on the eve of obtaining his first confirmed kill, Roques was promoted to Adjudant at the end of the same year and ended the war with that rank of adjutant. He was decorated several times, the Belgian Croix de Guerre awarded by Albert I in person, the Military Medal and the French Croix de Guerre with three palms, and a Vermilion Star.

Opposite.
Robert Bajac *became one of Jacques-Raphaël Roques' closest friends in N 48 and shared four confirmed kills with him. Having become chief pilot with the very new company Air France, he was killed in an accident during a night-flight on 1 April 1935.*

Hubert DE BARBE DE LA BARTHE ST-LOUBERT was licenced on 31 July 1917 at Juvisy and spent part of the war as an instructor in the flying school before volunteering for the Army of the Orient and being based at Thessalonica. In 1939-40 he resumed active service as a pilot-instructor at School N° 23 with the rank of sergeant.

Above.
Instructors and pupils at the Juvisy flying school in front of a Caudron G3. In 1918, the centre also housed a Belgian pilot's school.

Opposite.
De Barbe in front of some Caudron G.3s at the Juvisy flying school.

Autographed photographs of de Barbe's former pupils.

during the First World War

Augustin Émile LECOMTE *(23 October 1895-6 February 1979). Joined up in November 1914, Lecomte fought at first in a Chasseurs à pied regiment earning a citation before he transferred to the air force in 1917, obtaining his pilot's licence N° 7525 on 19 December of the same year. Assigned to SPA 37 he scored a confirmed kill a few days before the end of hostilities. When he returned to civilian life, he continued his career in aviation, becoming a pilot for a lot of sport and industry personalities, like the famous Emile Deutsch de la Meurthe, as well as several transport companies like the Compagnie Générale Transaérienne or the Franco-Roumaine.*

Opposite.
Augustin Lecomte wearing an officer's uniform in 1939, mobilised as a pilot in the liaison aircraft section 4/109.

Above.
Augustin Lecomte and the pupils of the Etampes flying school in 1917.

Lecomte devant et dans son Spad XIII surnommé « Suzon » en septembre 1918. L'appareil, portant le numéro individuel « 8 » arbore le condor en vol de la SPA 37.

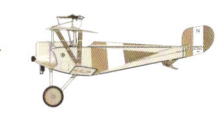

Charles OUVRARD *(11 May 1893-8 February 1916). Already serving in a cuirassier regiment, Ouvrard joined the air force and was assigned to MF 35, equipped with Farman MF 11s. He was killed in combat with his gunner, Soldier 2nd Class Eugène Bruneteau, on 8 February 1916, near Vilcey-sur-Trey (Meurthe-et-Moselle).*

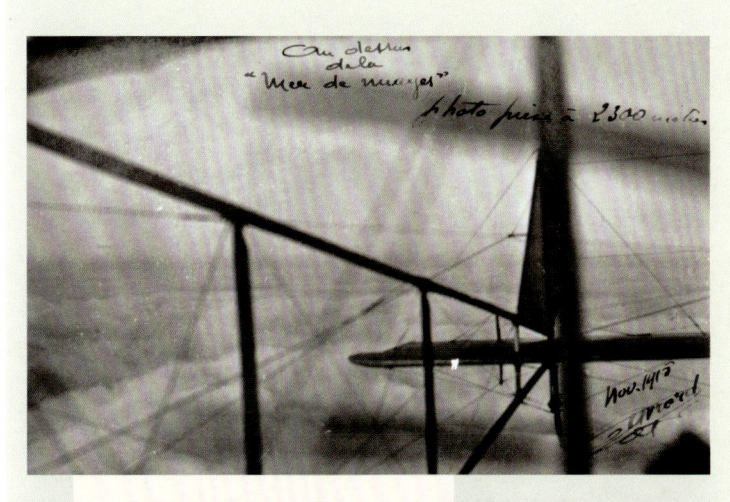

Above.
At Auve (Marne) in November 1915, Maréchal-des-logis Ouvrard posing in front of his MF 11, the front of which was decorated with a Croix de Lorraine, MF 35's insignia.

Above.
Two aerial shots (above the sea of clouds) taken by Ouvrard from his MF 11 in November 1915.

René Georges RECEVEUR *(6 November 1895- date of death unknown). After starting the war in the Engineers, Receveur was assigned as a pilot to Escadrille C 4 on 25 October 1915. His career as a pilot was particularly brief as he was listed as missing on the following 8 December. Forced to land behind the enemy lines with his observer, Sous-Lieutenant Marc Mesrine, he was captured by the Germans and remained in captivity until the end of the war.*

Paul Yves BUSSER *(1 March 1898-27 August 1953). Volunteering for a light artillery regiment in October 1915, Busser transferred to the air force and obtained his pilot's licence at Etampes on 12 June 1917. Assigned to Escadrille AR, he was seriously wounded when his Dorand AR 1 was attacked by four German planes on 3 April 1918. In spite of his wounds he managed to land his plane and save his observer which earned him the Military Medal.*

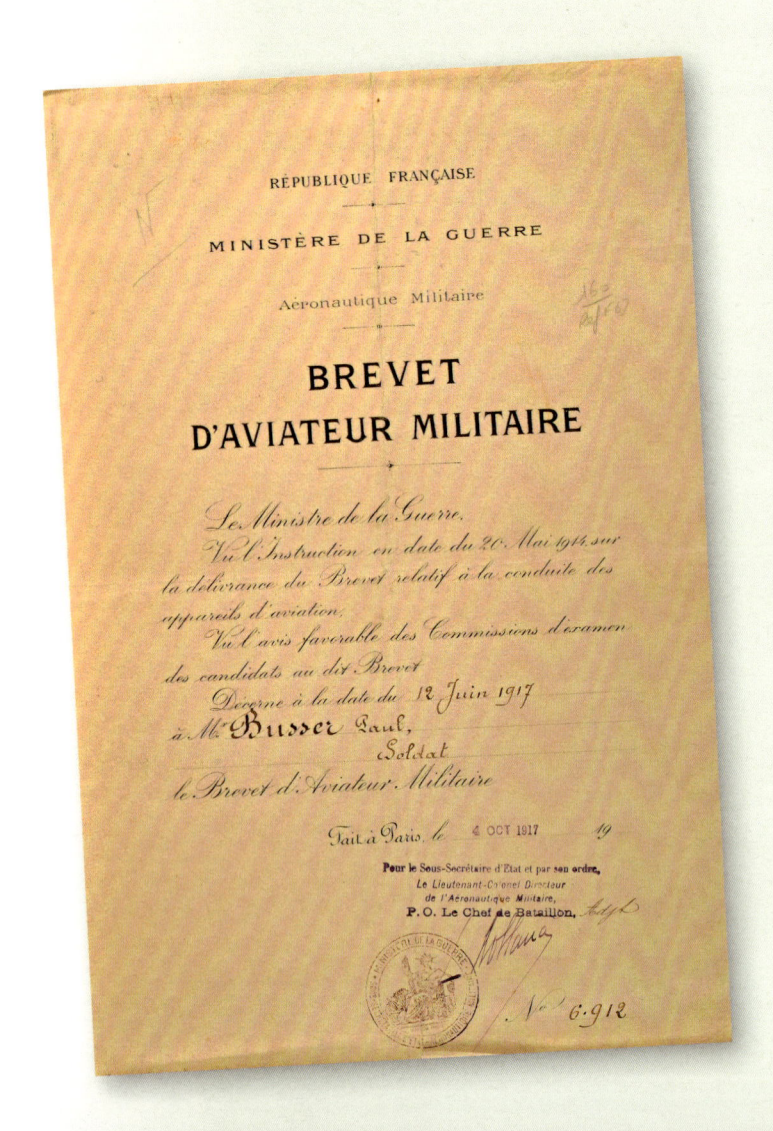

Above and below.
At the flying school at Etampes from March to June 1917, to obtain the military pilot's licence.

French aviation

Above.
Busser in front of the upper wing of a Dorand AR 1.

Opposite.
Convalescing in June 1918.

Above.
Wearing an airman's uniform with a pilot's licence.

Charles Noël DESTOPPELEIRE
(2 April 1893-23 January 1917).
Originally a soldier in the Engineers because of his studies, Destoppeleire obtained his pilot's licence at Juvisy on 21 July 1916. He never had the opportunity to fight since he was killed in an accident aboard a Nieuport 16 at Cachy (Somme) on 23 January 1917.

Jean DENIS (2 January 1893- 14 November 1970). Wounded at Verdun while serving in the 146th Infantry Regiment, Jean Denis became a military pilot on 26 April 1918, licence N°12941. Assigned to BR 120, he only took part in the last week of the conflict and the pursued all his career in civil aviation (Latécoère, Air Union, Air Orient and Air France) which he left in 1952 with only a brief interruption from September 1939 to May 1940 when he was mobilised.

Henri PHELY.
Wounded at Verdun, he became a pilot on 1 September 1918 à Châteauroux and was assigned to an escadrille equipped with Salmson 2A2s.

Above, left.
In front of Breguet 14 B2 from BR 120 in October 1918.

Above.
Jean Denis during his training period

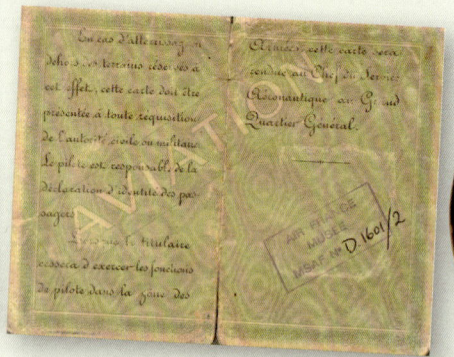

Raymond VANIER (6 August 1895 - 15 August 1965). After serving at the beginning of the Great War in the Artillery, Vanier went over to the air force and obtained his pilot's licence at the Juvisy flying school on 24 May 1917. Assigned to SPA 57 he scored four confirmed kills. After the conflict he continued his career in commercial aviation becoming a pilot for the Latécoère airlines in particular in June 1919. The head of one of the Aéropostale's stopovers, he opened up the line to Spain in the same year and was then assigned to South America in 1927 as Didier Daurat's assistant while still continuing to fly. Less well-known to the general public than Mermoz, Saint-Exupéry or Guillaumet, Vanier nonetheless played an important role in developing France's public air transport system and ended his career as the head of Air France's Postal Department.

Above and opposite.
Adjudant Vanier in front of his Spad called "Tite Maÿn".

Opposite.
Vanier posing in front of Spad VII whose fuselage sported a drawing of a running boar, the first type of insignia used by N 57/SPA 57.

170

French aviation

Charles and Marcel SIMIAN
These brothers (Marcel was born on 25 November 1883) had an almost identical military career. Originally from Algeria, they were both mobilised at the beginning of the conflict in the 3rd Zouaves and their conduct was exemplary, Marcel even earning several citations in the order of the Army. They joined the air force in August 1915 and were observers in Escadrille 55 at first, then pilots, as can be seen by the armbands they are wearing on their left arms. Captain Charles Simian was wounded on 25 June 1916 in an air accident and only resumed his service in September of the same year.

Opposite.
The pennant of MF 55, the Simian brothers' escadrille.

Index of names mentioned in the text

Aasen 9, 45
Ader 4
Albatros 6, 22, 25, 26, 27, 28, 94, 95, 105, 106, 141
Angot 47
Anzani 51, 52
Armengaud 5
Arnoux 119
Aubigny 88
Aubrun 99
Auger 47, 78
Aviatik 6, 9, 10, 21, 22, 25, 28, 29, 46
Bach 29
Baer 104
Ball 95
Balleyguier 100
Balsley Clyde 168
Barbezat 81
Barcat, pilote 168
Bardel 119
Barès 13, 14, 32, 34, 47, 74, 75, 84, 88, 95
Barne 46
Barrachini 112
Barrès 13
Barthe 36
Battle 78, 100
Baux Auguste 168
Bayle 21
Baylies 104, 112
Beauchêne 36
Beaumont 46, 81, 113
Béchereau 70, 72, 75
Bédora 168
Bellenger 11, 12, 16, 46, 76
Belok von F. 168
Bentejac 46
Bernard, 5, 140
Bernis (de) 168
Berthelot 16, 104
Besnard 33
Bessonneau 29, 98, 107
Billard 16
Birkigt 75
Bishop William 168
Bizard 111
Blaize 10
Blanc 81
Blériot 2, 3, 4, 5, 6, 7, 8, 9, 10, 11, 12, 13, 14, 18, 25, 46, 50, 51, 74, 75, 82, 140, 149, 154, 155
Blitz von 168
Bloch 47, 81
Bodin René, 168
Boillot 36, 47
Bois d'Aische (du) 168
Bon 45
Bondou 168
Bonnafont 29
Bonnard 25
Bonnefoy 81
Bordage A. 168
Borde 26
Borel 63, 140
Borzecki 81
Bosson 104
Bossoutrot 119
Boulanger 105
Bourjade 94, 104, 116, 157
Bousquet 46, 47
Bouttieaux 13
Bowmann 97
Boyau 36, 93, 104, 157
Bozon-Verduraz 97
Breguet Louis 168
Briand Aristide 168
Brindejonc des Moulinais 41, 47, 71
Brocard 25, 36, 47, 76, 81, 83, 85, 91
Brun 104
Buisson 81
Bulow von 168
Bülow von 168
Busser 102, 103, 164, 165
Cadet 32
Camplan 81
Canton Unné 78
Caproni 32, 34, 70, 71, 78, 90, 99, 101, 103, 106, 117, 124
Caquot 20, 86, 99, 118, 141
Carpentier 46
Carrus 11
Casalle 47
Castelnau 5, 6, 45
Caudron 168
Cayla 28
Cesari 9
Chabert 168
Chainat 25, 36, 40, 47, 75, 80, 81, 83, 85
Chambe 25
Chanaron, 168
Chapman 168
Chaput 31, 36, 40, 47, 80, 81, 102, 104, 142, 159
Chassaing 104
Châtelain 10
Chauvière 44
Chavannes (de) 168
Chavannes Fernand 168
Chemin 46, 90, 98, 100, 103, 106, 107
Chevillard 4
Chigurno 168
Ciccoli 47
Claude 45, 158
Clemenceau Georges 168
Clerget 52, 62, 63, 65, 66, 139
Codos 119
Cohen 8
Colibert 8
Colt 44, 52, 55
Combrond 82
Conneau Jean-Louis 168
Coppens Willy 168
Cornemont 119
Corniglion-Molinier 119
Costes 119
Coudouret 47, 81
Coutisson Armand 168
Covin 81
Cowdin 29, 47
Crémont 140
Curtiss 102
Dallas 112
Darbos 44
Darracq 120, 122
Daucourt 77
Daurat 119, 166
Davenne 104
David 25, 97, 112
Debeney 101
Decatoire 78
Delage 62
Delavaux 7
Delorme 35, 47
Demeuldre 98, 102
Denneboude 34
Deperdussin 4, 5, 6, 11, 13, 25, 47, 51, 61, 70, 71
Deramond 42
Derode 81
Desmaison 91
Deullin 36, 47, 65, 78, 81, 85, 110, 158
Deville 51, 125, 127
Diamant-Berger 168
Didier 9, 119, 166
Dion Bouton 59
Do Huu Vi 168
Dorand Jean Baptiste 168
Doret 119
Dorme 36, 47, 63, 80, 81, 83, 85, 86, 92, 140, 157
Douchy 81, 119
Dubail 6, 45
Dubonnet 78
Dubureau 4
Duchêne 5
Dufresne 12
Duperon-Niepce-Felterer 63
Dupont 104
Dutertre 29
Duval 96, 100, 106, 108
Duvau 168
Dyckoff 20
Eitel-Frédéric 42
Espanet 4
Fahler 34
Falkenstein 21
Farman 3, 4, 5, 7, 8, 9, 10, 11, 12, 13, 16, 18, 27, 29, 30, 33, 34, 37, 41, 42, 43, 44, 46, 49, 57, 58, 59, 72, 77, 82, 83, 84, 87, 93, 95, 97, 104, 111, 113, 117, 120, 129, 130, 136, 149, 163
Faure 11, 40
Fedoroff 47
Féquant 33, 45, 75, 83, 101, 106, 107, 108, 110
Ferrieux 91
Finck 7, 9
Finger 10
Flachaire 36, 47, 81
Flandin 119
Flandrin 99
Fleurieu 119
Fleury 103
Foch 3, 80, 81, 82, 83, 84, 105, 110, 111, 112, 113, 115, 116, 117
Fokker 24, 26, 32, 34, 36, 40, 44, 62, 76, 77, 94, 95, 100, 102, 105, 109, 111, 116
Fontame 104
Forquet 108
Foulot 113
Frantz 5, 9, 15, 16, 20, 21
Fresnay 63
Fronval 133
Gaillard de la Valdenne 168
Gaissert 34
Gallieni 5, 9, 12, 33, 43, 47, 74
Galliot 23, 34, 38, 39, 159
Garaix 9
Garaud 98
Garcia Calderon 24
Garin 116
Garnier 111
Garros 4, 12, 25, 26, 44, 50, 60, 61, 109
Gasse 104
Gastin 47
Gaubert 4, 10
Geffrier 87
Gérard 11, 104
Geyer 111
Gilbert 4, 12, 21, 147, 159
Girod 88
Gironde 9
Glaize 46, 110
Gnome 6, 33, 50, 52, 60, 62, 68, 70, 72, 73, 134, 149
Gondouin 8
Gondre 46
Gotha 32, 47, 83, 86, 89, 116
Gouraud 111
Goÿs 15, 21, 27, 110
Granel 12, 21
Gros-Andreau 34, 47
Grossier 98
Guerder 29
Guérin 102, 158
Guerrier 47
Guertiau 81
Guiguet 47, 81
Guillabert 88
Guillemeny 74
Guillemin 54, 88
Guynemer 25, 27, 29, 32, 35, 36, 40, 44, 46, 47, 62, 63, 75, 77, 78, 79, 81, 82, 83, 85, 86, 88, 89, 97, 109, 141, 143, 144, 145, 156, 157
Haegelen 90, 106, 158
Hall 168
Halphen 101
Hamaide 26
Handley 103, 107
Hanriot 29, 101
Happe 17, 40, 59
Harvey-Kelly 16
Hasdenteufel 104
Hay de Slade 98, 104, 159
Hébrard 104
Heller, 168
Hentschen 168
Herbelin 98
Heu 46
Heurtaux 36, 47, 63, 80, 81, 83, 85, 86, 119
Hill 168
Hindelson 9, 21
Hindenburg 91, 102, 113, 116
Hirshauer 3, 6
Hispano-Suiza 64, 141, 149
Hostein 26
Hotchkiss 11, 44, 50, 55, 63, 69, 77
Houssays 102
Houssemant 25
Hue 25
Hutier 101, 102
Hypolite 40
Isotta-Fraschini 69, 124
Jacottet 26
Jacquet 97
Jacquin 95
Jaillier 47
Janoir 140
Joffre 9, 10, 12, 13, 16, 24, 27, 32, 80, 83, 84
Johannes 46
Johnson 169
Julliot 104
Junkers 94
Kaisenberg 169
Kandulski 22, 23
Keller 169
Kérilis 169
Kluk 12
Konprinz 16, 102
Laage de Meux 89
Lachmann 81
Lacour-Grandmaison 81
Lafaille 46
Lafont 95
Langle 32
Langlois 7
Languedoc 81
Lanrezac 9, 11, 45
La Tour 83
Laulhé 78
Laurens 43, 106
Laurent-Eynac 169
Le Barazer 40
Lebrun 33
Leclercq 169
Lecointe 7

Le Coq de Kerlan 169
Lecreux 102
Lemaitre 169
Le Mettairie 11
Lemoine 29
Lenfant 46
Lenoir 32, 35, 36, 47, 78, 80, 81
Lepic 10
Le Prieur 40, 44, 59, 63, 92
Le Ray 102
Le Révérend 37, 83, 91, 101
Le Rhône 11, 51, 60, 61, 62, 64, 65, 68, 72, 125, 127, 132, 133, 153
Lesseps 23, 34, 100
Letannoux 26
Letord 14, 43, 49, 77, 89, 90, 94, 97, 102, 105, 114, 125, 126, 129, 131, 149, 155
Levasseur 140
Lewis 44, 47, 52, 55, 63, 64, 65, 73, 80, 125, 126, 135, 139, 149
L'Hermitte 169
Liorè et Olivier 169
Lorraine 5, 7, 9, 13, 21, 29, 30, 59, 83, 87, 89, 92, 99, 111, 117, 123, 129, 130, 131, 140, 144, 163
Losques 26, 29
Loste 35, 81
Lucca 43
Ludendorff 100, 101, 103, 108, 111, 113, 116
Luftbery 169
MacConnel 169
Machiavel 1
Madon 81, 103, 104, 112, 134, 157
Mailfert 44, 72
Maillard 23
Maillet 36
Maillols 29
Malavialle 47
Malherbe 46
Mallarmé 78
Mandinaud 42
Maneyrol 4, 29, 119
Mangin 91, 108, 110, 112
Mannock 112
Marçay 140
Marchal Anselme 169
Mariage 97, 108
Marin-Barrier 169
Marinovitch 104, 158
Marmier 104
Martel 139
Martin 35, 86, 115, 147
Martine 9
Marvingt 33
Masson 169
Mathieu 103
Matton 81
Maunoury 10, 81
Mauser 77

Mayen 99
Mazel 91
Meiffre 108
Ménard 46, 100, 101, 106, 107, 108, 110
Ménaud 105
Mendès 8
Mesguich 26
Mezergue 81
Michelin 20, 29, 32, 34, 43, 45, 56, 77, 90, 122, 123, 149
Millioud 105
Minier, 111
Moineau 78, 117, 129, 149, 150, 151
Moissinac 104
Molla 32
Monancourt 169
Morane 4, 5, 11, 12, 13, 16, 17, 18, 20, 25, 26, 27, 29, 31, 33, 34, 36, 44, 46, 60, 61, 72, 80, 84, 132, 133, 149
Morane-Saulnier 5, 11, 13, 16, 18, 27, 34, 44, 60, 61, 84
Mortane 4
Mouchard 21, 23
Moulines 34, 76, 102
Muiron 11
Naudin 106
Navarre 25, 27, 31, 32, 36, 37, 38, 40, 47, 63, 79, 85
Nieuport 4, 14, 19, 20, 22, 23, 25, 26, 29, 32, 33, 34, 36, 37, 38, 39, 40, 41, 43, 44, 46, 47, 61, 62, 63, 64, 65, 66, 67, 68, 75, 77, 78, 80, 81, 83, 89, 90, 91, 92, 93, 96, 106, 134, 140, 148, 155, 160, 165
Niox 33
Nivelle 84, 90, 91, 95
Noguès 40, 119
Nungesser 23, 27, 32, 33, 36, 37, 40, 41, 47, 63, 65, 80, 81, 85, 86, 89, 91, 98, 99, 102, 105, 112, 140, 142, 145, 156
Nuville 104
Ortoli 47
Pacot 105
Padieu 34
Painlevé 98
Panhard 44, 148
Paolacci 27
Parent 99
Parsons 104
Pary 169
Peck 102
Pégoud 22, 23, 46
Pelletier 8, 11, 25, 36, 40, 47, 119
Pendaries 81, 92
Pène 104
Penigaud 108
Peretti 47

Perrin de Brichambault 8
Pétain 32, 36, 95, 96, 98, 106, 156
Peugeot 82, 84, 140, 148, 150
Peuty 88, 90, 91, 95
Pezon 104
Picard 36
Pillon 104
Pinsard 16, 75, 157
Pivolo 8, 11, 25
Poincaré 6, 47
Ponton d'Amécourt 11
Poréaux 46
Potter 116
Poulet 52
Pourpe 4, 12, 17
Preshing 169
Prez de la Morlaix 111
Prince 25, 29, 77, 89
Prudhommeau 9
Puechredon 21
Puget 106
Pujo 83
Pulpe 47
Putnam 112
Quénault 15
Quillien 47
Quiquandon 8
Rabardel 113
Ragot 8
Raibaud 33
Raymond 11, 26, 44, 78, 81, 104, 109, 166
Régnier 33, 81, 88, 143
Régy 140
Renault 4, 6, 13, 27, 29, 30, 33, 56, 57, 58, 59, 69, 78, 84, 87, 99, 110, 113, 115, 120, 121, 122, 125, 129, 148, 150
Rep 21
Réservat 47
Revol-Tissot 47, 81
Ribot 98
Richard 7, 27, 76
Richthofen 95, 97, 100, 105
Risso 169
Rivalleau 103
Rives 111
Robert 25, 26, 55, 70, 73, 77, 83, 84, 91, 144, 160
Robert René 169
Robin 97
Rochefort 35, 47, 80, 81
Rockwell 169
Rodde 47
Roeckel 97, 122
Roger 9, 23, 97, 140
Roisin 23
Ropartz 105
Roper 46, 96
Roques 3, 4, 39, 47, 74, 84, 146, 160
Rousseaux 81
Royer-Massenet 47
Rumpler 21, 22, 78, 79, 81, 97

Rumsey 169
Sabatier 110
Saint-Chamond 98
Saint-Sauveur 169
Saizieu 9
Salmson 30, 68, 69, 78, 84, 102, 108, 115, 116, 117, 127, 129, 135, 136, 137, 138, 149, 150, 151, 166
Sanglier 46
Sardier 81, 147, 159
Saulnier 5, 11, 13, 16, 17, 18, 27, 31, 34, 44, 46, 60, 61, 72, 84, 109
Sauvage 35, 81, 155
Sauval 46
Savary 11, 63
Sayaret 47, 81
Schalbar 104
Schmitt 9, 13, 20, 78, 90, 91, 120, 149, 150
Schneider 36, 91, 98
Serviès 13
Sevin 78, 81, 100, 104, 106, 109
Siegfried 113, 115
Slessor 74
Soliman 91
Sommer 140
Sopwith 49, 77, 84, 89, 90, 97, 99, 112, 114, 115, 122, 123, 139, 149, 150, 151, 155
Soubiran 169
Soulier 81
Spad 43, 46, 63, 66, 72, 73, 75, 76, 80, 81, 82, 84, 86, 88, 89, 90, 93, 94, 96, 99, 104, 106, 107, 109, 110, 111, 114, 116, 117, 132, 134, 140, 141, 142, 143, 144, 145, 146, 147, 149, 157, 159, 160, 162, 166
Stiblick 169
Tailer 101
Tarascon 81, 85
Taube 6, 8, 9, 12, 13, 14, 15, 16, 20, 22, 27, 50, 97
Tenant de la Tour 81
Thaw 29, 63, 79, 89, 104
Thénault 82
Thieffry 101
Thiérry 104
Thomas 39, 102
Thoret 119
Thouroude 26, 29
Tognard 75
Touraine 29
Touvet 11
Trémeau 105
Trenchard 95
Tricornot de Rose 33, 36, 46, 47
Truffier 104
Tsar 94
Turenne 38, 39, 81, 102, 144, 159

Vachet 119
Vallin 34
Vandières 108
Vaubourgeix 45
Védrines 12, 15, 25, 26, 27, 50, 125, 156
Vergnete 169
Vialatoux 30
Viallet 29, 47, 81
Vibert 32
Vickers 40, 47, 63, 65, 72, 92, 135, 139, 145
Viguier 46, 82, 84, 87
Villa 29
Villomé 106
Vincent 97
Violet-Marty 81
Vitalis 35, 47, 81, 86
Voisin 5, 6, 7, 11, 12, 13, 14, 15, 18, 21, 23, 25, 27, 28, 29, 32, 33, 34, 43, 44, 45, 46, 49, 56, 68, 69, 75, 78, 82, 84, 90, 97, 103, 106, 107, 110, 115, 117, 128, 130, 140, 148, 150, 155
Voyer 13
Vuillemin 11, 28, 34, 38, 47, 76, 91, 119
Warneford 27
Watteau 11
Weiller 111
Weniger Wilhelm 169
Weygand 111
Willis 169
Winckler Georges 169
Wisemann 169
Wright 3
Yence 11, 29
Zarapoff 23

Bibliography

1-General works

Anon. «*Dans le ciel de Pau, Blériot et les écoles françaises*», Cairn, 2009, 214 pp., Ill.,
Apostolo Giorgio « *Caproni nella prima guerra Mondiale* », Europress, 1969, 250 pp., Ill.,
Beaupré Nicolas «*1914-1945, Les grandes guerres*», Belin, 2012, 1150 pp., Ill.,
Bornecque Cne & de Valforie «*Les Ailes dans la bataille*», Hachette, 1920, 250 pp., Ill.,
Chavagnes (de) René «*Le groupe des Cigognes*», de Guynemer à Fonck, Chiron, 1920, 220 pp., Ill.,
Gray Peter & Thetford Owen «*German aircraft of the 1st World War*», Putnam, 1962, 600 pp., Ill.,
Chant Christopher «*Austro-Hungarian Aces of WW1*», Osprey, 2002, 96 pp., Ill.,
Etévé Albert «*La victoire des cocardes*», Robert Laffont, 1970, 322 pp., Ill.,
Jackson Robert «*Fighters pilots of WW 1*», Arthur Baker, 152 pp.,
Jauneaud Marcel, commandant «*L'aviation militaire et la guerre aérienne*», Flammarion, 1923, 260pp.
«*L'évolution de l'aéronautique*», Flammarion, 1923, 300 pp., Ill.,
«*L'aviation militaire et la guerre aérienne*», Flammarion, 1923, 265 pp., Ill.,
Jeanjean Marcel «*Sous les cocardes*», Serma, 1964, 50 pp., Ill.,
Jullian Marcel «*La grande bataille dans les airs*», Presses de la Cité, 1967, 313 pp; Ill.,
Livock G.E. «*RO the ends of the air*», HMSO, 1973, 205 pp., Ill.,
Lucca D. colonel «*Création et débuts du groupe des escadrilles de protection du Camp retranché de Paris*», Les Arts graphiques, 65 pp., Ill.,
Martel René «*L'aviation française de bombardement*», Paul Hartmann, 1939, 416 pp; Ill;
Massenet de Marancour, Cdt «*La chasse en avion*», Sansot, 1921, 112 pp.,
Munday Albert M. «*The eyes of the Army and Navy*», Harper, 1918, 245 pp., Ill.,
Munson Kenneth «*British Aircraft*», Ian Allan, 60 pp; Ill.,
Nicolaou Stéphane «*Aviateurs dans la Grande guerre*», Addim, 1998, 136 pp., Ill.,
Pierrefeu (de) Jean «*GQG secteur 1 (tomes I et II)*», Édition Française Illustrée, 1920, 277 et 249 pp.,
S.H.A.A. «*Les escadrilles de l'Aéronautique militaire française*», 2011, 608 pp., Ill.,
Shores Chistopher «*British and Empire Aces f WW 1*», Osprey, 2001, 96 pp., Ill.,
Thetford O. G. «*Aircraft of the 1914-1918 war*», Harborough, 1954, 127 pp., Ill.,
Wallace Melville «*La vie d'un pilote de chasse en 1914-1918*», Flammarion, 1978, 61 pp Ill.,
Willian Lt Cl & Bishop A. «*Winged Warfare*», Bailey brothers, 1975, 275 pp., Ill.,

2-War narratives, memoirs (even romanticised ones)

André C.H.A. «*Au-dessus des batailles*», Fayard, 1917, 315 pp.,
Arnoux (d') Jacques «*Paroles d'un revenant*», Plon, 1925, 260 pp., Ill.,
Battesti François «*Les Cigognes de Brocard au combat*», La Pensée universelle, 1975, 220 pp.,
Biddle Charles J. «*Major Fighting airman: the way of the eagles*», Ace Books, 1968, 290 pp., Ill.,
Bléry Paul «*Aviateurs*», Louis Querelle, 1933, 237 pp.,
Boisnard Jacques «*Histoire de l'Aviation en Anjou*», L'Apart, 2012, 285 pp., Ill.,
Boulanger Jacques «*En escadrille*», Renaissance du livre, 1918, 255 pp.,
Bowman Gerald «*War in the air*», Pan books, 1956, 200 pp., Ill.,
Branche Joseph «*Ballons d'observation 1914-1918*», Sorepi Domergue, 1977, 210 pp., Ill.,
Chack Paul «*La route des Indes sauvée par la France*», Les éditions de France, 1941, 151 pp., Ill., «*Survivants prodigieux*», Les éditions de France, 1941, 148 pp., Ill.,
Chambe René «*Le temps des carabines*», Flammarion, 1955, 232 pp., «*Dans l'enfer du ciel*», Baudinière, 1933, 317 pp.,
Cossart Jean «*Les hallucinations du Lt Darnoux*», Berger Levrault, 1936, 291 pp.,
Debofle Pierre « *Br 29, Souvenirs d'escadrille d'André Duvau, sergent mitrailleur*», SHAA, 1976, 75 pp., Ill.,
Desgrandschamps Georges «*Impressions d'un bombardier*», Vivien, 1931, 64 pp. Ill. (de Marmier René)
Fouchardière (de la) Georges & Laubreaux Alain «*Aventures cocasses de Boulot aviateur,*» Albin Michel, 1931, 250 pp.,
Frégeolière (de la) Renaud «*A tire d'ailes*», Plon, 1916, 315 pp., «*Croisières aériennes*», Nlles éditions latines, 1933, 195 pp.,
Gann Ernest K. «*In company of eagles*», Four square, 1967, 224 pp.,
Good-Lee Arthur «*Fly Past,*» Jarrolds, 1974, 222 pp., Ill.,
Gouvieux Marc «*Haut les ailes*», Pierre Lafitte, 1914, 315 pp.,
Grinnell-Milne Duncan «*Wind in the Wires*», Panther, 1933, 210 pp.,
Johnson J.E. «*Le combat aérien (Full Circle)*», Plon, 1966, 320 pp., Ill.,
Labric Roger «*Un de l'aviation*», Editions cosmopolites, 1932 250pp. «*On se bat dans l'air*», 217 pp.,
«*Les champs bleus*», Imprimerie française de l'édition, 1919, 255 pp.,
Lambert Bill «*Combat report*» Corgi, 1973, 210 pp., ILL.,
Laneuville Jean «*Les aventures d'un chevalier du manche*», Editions Jeunesse magazine, 1937, 70 pp., illustrations de Marcel Jeanjean.
Lewis Cecil «*Farewell to wings*», Temple press, 1964, Ill.,
Lirock G.E. «*To the ends of the Air*», HMSO, 1973,205 pp., Ill.,
McKee Alexander «*The friendless sky, Mayflower, 1962, 190 pp.,*»
Mailfert André «*Les aigles*», Figuière, 1929, 265 pp.,
Milan René «*Trois étapes*», Plon, 1917, 303 pp.,
« *Les matelots aériens*», Plon, 1919, 285 pp.,
Melon Pierre (voir Molineux Paul) même tire, Néa-argo, 1930, 218 pp.,
Molineux Paul «*Le sang des Aigles*», Nouvelles éditions Argo, 1931, 220 pp.,
Mortane Jacques «*Leur dernier vol,*» Baudinière, 1932, 250 pp.,
«*Évasions d'aviateurs*», 1929, 320 pp.,
«*Missions spéciales*», 1929, 320 pp.,
«*Traqués par l'ennemi*», 1929, 315 pp.,
«*A travers les filets de l'ennemi*», 1929, 270 pp.,
«*Douaniers en mission*», 1933, 251 pp.,
«*Au poteau*», 1933, 252 pp;
«*Sentinelles de l'air*», 1936, 290 pp.,
Nadeau Marcel «*Frangipane et compagnie*», Albin Michel, 250 pp.,
«*Man'zelle monoplan*» ,1920, 320 pp.,
«*Chignole*» 1917, 217 pp.,
« *En plein vol*», Hachette, 1919, 210 pp.,
Norhoff Charles & Norman James «*Falcons of France*», Monarch, 1957, 225 pp.,
Sainte Robert «*L'épi mûr*», Racine, 1999, 126 pp., Ill.,

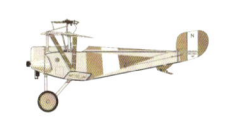

Trémeau Henri, brigadier «*J'étais pilote de chasse au-dessus des tranchées*», Editions Gilles
Parsons Edwin C. «*I flew with the Lafayette escadrille*», E.C. Seale, 1991, 335 pp., Ill.,
Platret, 2011,168 pp., Ill.,
Reynolds Quentin «*They fought for the sky*», Pan Giant, 1958, 285 pp., Ill.,
Saxon Peter «*The unfeeling sky,*» Corgi, 1968, 160 pp.,
Suarnet André «*Les rampants*», Les Etincelles, 1930, 255 pp.,
Thénault Georges LCL, «*L'escadrille Lafayette*», Hachette, 1939,128 pp., Ill.,
Vallières (des) Jean «*L'escadrilles des Anges*», Grasset, 1947, 350 pp.,
Violan Jean «*Dans l'air et dans la boue*», Editions du Masque, 254 pp.,

3-Biographies

Abraham Pierre «*Les trois frères*», Les éditeurs français réunis, 1971, 380 pp., Ill.,
Angot E. & de Lavergne R. «*Le général Vuillemin*», La Palatine, 1965, 260 pp., Ill.,
Bordeaux Henri «*La vie Héroïque de Guynemer*», Plon-Nourrit, 1918, 300 pp., Ill.,
Chambe René «*Guynemer*», Marcus, 1949, 100 pp; Ill.,
Champeaux Antoine «*Michelin et l'Aviation*», Lavauzelle, 2006, 513 pp., Ill.,
Collectif «*Marcel Haegelen*», PABB, 2010, 175 pp., Ill.,
Coppens de Houthlust Willy «*Aviateurs célèbres au temps des hélices*», Erel, 1973, 130 pp.,
«*Jours envolés*», Nouvelles éditions latines, 1932, 352 pp.,
Croidys Pierre «*Guynemer*», Maison de la bonne presse, 1939, 95 pp., Ill.,
Cussac Jean «*Un héros de France Guynemer*», s/d,
Demazière Louis «*Un grand pilote Romamet*», France-Empire, 1980, 250 pp., Ill.,
Fonck René «*Mes combats*», Flammarion, 1933, 125 pp., Ill.,
Garros Roland «*Mémoires présentées par Jacques Quellennec*», Hachette, 1966, 300 pp., Ill.,
Herlin Hans «*Ernst Udet, pilote du diable*», France-Empire, 1959, 305 pp., Ill.,
Immelman Max «*Mes vols de combat*», Vivien, 1930, 108 pp.,
Kerisel Jean «*Albert Caquot 1881-1976*», Presses Ponts et Chaussées

Kierman R. H. «*Captain Albert Ball*», Penguin, 1933, 179 pp.,
Marchal Anselme «*Après mon vol au-dessus de Berlin*», Tallandier, 1919, 345 pp.,
Mariage Pierre «*Adieu aux Ailes*», France Empire, 1967, 305 pp., Ill.,
Mortane Jacques «*Navarre, sentinelle de Verdun*», 1930, 320 pp.,
«*Deux grands chevaliers de l'aventure, M. Pourpe et R. Lufbery*», 320 pp.,
«*Carré d'As (Guynemer, Nungesser, Madon, Dorme)*», 1934, 320 pp.,
Nicolaou Stéphane «*Roland Garros, héros du siècle*», ETAI, 2000, 112 pp., Ill.,
Perrin Claude «*René Fonck*», Editions de l'officine, 2002, 320 pp., Ill.,
Poincelet Gilbert «*La vie du capitaine Guynemer*», Arthaud, 1943, 100 pp., Ill.,
Pommier Gérard & Bertrand «*Les frères Nieuport*», Les éditions de l'officine, 2004, 380 pp., Ill.,
Rickenbaker Eddie W. «*Contro il circo volante*», Longanesi, 1968, 450 pp., Ill.,
Roper Albert «*Un homme et des ailes*», Editions de l'officie, 2004, 360 pp., Ill.,
Scilocca Albertine «*Un as Corse de l'Aviation Jean Casale*», Albtana, 2008, 110 pp., Ill.,
Tabuteau Denys B. «*Maurice Tabuteau*», Lys éditions, 2000, 128 pp., Ill.,
Udet Ernst «*Ma vie et mes vols*», Flammarion, 1955, 205 pp., Ill.,
Victor Maurice «*Paul Deville*», Jeanne-Paul Deville, 1964, 78 pp., Ill.,
Viguier Armand Cdt «*Une vie avec le ciel comme horizon*», Editions des grilles d'or, 2007, 300 pp., Ill.,

4-Miscellaneous Publications

Mortane Jacques La guerre Aérienne, publication régulière
Aéro-jounal
Avions
Champs de bataille
Connaissance de l(histoire n° 24,33,
Histoire et généalogie axonaise, n°13
Le Fanatique de l'Aviation
L'Aérophile
L'Illustration
Le Miroir
Purnell's history of world war

Summary

From the Marne to the Somme	2	Breguet	120
The year 1915	20	Caproni	124
The year 1916	34	Caudron	125
Blériot aircraft	50	Farman	130
Caudron aircraft	51	Letord	131
Breguet-Michelin bombers	56	Morane	132
The Farman brothers' aircraft	57	Nieuport	134
Morane Saulnier planes (Types L, LA and P)	60	Salmson	135
		Sopwitch	139
Nieuport fighters	62	Spad	140
The Voisin Bombers	68	Voisin bombers	148
The "orphan" planes	70	Crossed destinies of planes and men	154
From the Somme to the Rhin	74		
The year 1916	74	Atmosphere	155
The year 1917	86	French aces	160
The year 1918	99	The « anonymous »	164
An assessment of First World War aviation	118	Index of names mentioned in the text	172
		Bibliography	174

Thanks

This book owes a lot to the dynamism and the attentive listening of the collection editor. Within the limits imposed by the book's format, his job was to manage all the activities whilst at the same time ensuring the illustrations were chosen and adequate. He did not spare either his time or his patience, being at all times available for all the editor-illustrators, despite a timetable crammed with other matters.

The illustrations are not always of equal quality: the passage of time has yellowed the period photos and the originals which disappeared have been replaced by reproductions which have nonetheless been chosen for their interest value and their originality.

These photos, of which some have come from collectors who have asked to remain anonymous, are mainly taken from the large collection belonging to Renaud Leblanc. They are all to be thanked, and principally Mrs. Bénédicte Cornet, Elisabeth Pesson and Marylène Vanier, Messrs Franck Simian and Philippe Warnault, without forgetting the Air France Museum.

Finally the artist-illustrator did not spare any effort in making the most accurate profiles, after comparing them with the machines now housed in the Musée de l'Air et de l'Espace at le Bourget with an attention to detail that honours him.

Vital FERRY

All right reserved. No part of this publication can be transmitted or reproduced without the written consent off all the authors and the publisher.

ISBN: 978-2-35250-370-5
Publisher's number: 35250

© 2014 Histoire & Collections

histoire & collections
SA au capital de 182 938,82 €

5, avenue de la République
75011 Paris
FRANCE

Tel: +33 (0) 1 40 21 18 20/Fax: +33 (0) 1 47 00 51 11
www.histoireetcollections.com

This boock has been designed, typed, laid-out and processed by *Histoire & Collections*. Collection directed by Dominique Breffort.

Layout, design and production
Magali Masselin

Printed by
CALIDAD GRAFICA, Spain.

December 2014